ESOPs

SAVVY STRATEGY FOR TAX MANAGEMENT, SUCCESSION, AND CONTINUITY

11359-359

Scott D. Miller, CPA, ABV, CVA

Notice to Readers

ESOPs: Savvy Strategy for Tax Management, Succession, and Continuity does not represent an official position of the American Institute of Certified Public Accountants, and it is distributed with the understanding that the author and publisher are not rendering, legal, accounting, or other professional services in the publication. This book is intended to be an overview of the topics discussed within, and the author has made every attempt to verify the completeness and accuracy of the information herein. However, neither the author nor publisher can guarantee the applicability of the information found herein. If legal advice or other expert assistance is required, the services of a competent professional should be sought.

Publisher: Amy M. Plent
Senior Managing Editor: Amy Krasnyanskaya
Acquisitions Editor: Robert Fox
Developmental Editor: David Cohen

Table of Contents

Chapter 3: Employee Stock Ownership Plan Transaction Mechanics

Chapter 4: Employee Stock Ownership Plan Transactions and C Corporations

Chapter 5: Employee Stock Ownership Plan Transactions and S Corporations

Chapter 6: Advanced Employee Stock Ownership Plan Applications

Chapter 7: Valuation Issues and Considerations

Chapter 8: Administration and Transaction Considerations

Chapter 9: Financial Considerations

Chapter 10: Litigation and Significant Cases

Chapter 11: Practical Considerations and Employee Stock Ownership Plan Resources

Introduction

Employee stocks ownership plans (ESOPs) are a very tax-efficient means of sharing owner-ship of a company with its employees. Applicable federal legislation that encourages ESOPs allows wide latitude to company owners, employees, and service providers to design and implement the plans to fulfill a wide range of interests. The tax incentives and design flex-ibility do have a cost: regulatory compliance with an exacting set of rules.

The focus of this book is to discuss the applications of ESOPs in closely held companies. The closely held company, by definition, does not have stock that is publicly traded on a recognized stock exchange. The stock is typically held by a limited number of shareholders. The purpose of the ESOP is to own stock for the benefit of the ESOP participants and their beneficiaries. This book examines the various ways an ESOP may acquire stock in a closely held company and many of the best planning practices to accomplish that goal.

The material on ESOPs is particularly timely for the following reasons:

- Approximately 78 million baby boomers are coming into retirement age during the next 10–15 years. These baby boomers often have considerable net worth captured in closely held companies, and they will have to transition that wealth to the next generation of owners. There may be more sellers than buyers as a result. The ESOP is an inside buyer that wants to have an equity stake in the company, subject to compliance with applicable regulations.
- The likelihood of sharply increased capital gain taxes on January 1, 2013, is a near certainty with the expiration of the Bush administration tax cuts of 2001 and 2003. A capital gain surtax increase is also scheduled as part of the Affordable Care Act of 2010. Due to the fact that ESOPs are so tax efficient, those tax increases magnify the attractiveness of employee ownership.
- After several years of brutal recession beginning in 2008, the economy seems poised for a revival later in 2012 and into 2013. Business owners that have deferred any strategic decisions for several years may be more willing to enter into a succession plan that may include an ESOP.

Why CPAs Need to Understand ESOPs

If a CPA aspires to be a strategic adviser to the owner of a closely held company, a wide range of business knowledge is required. One important practical area of expertise is succession planning. All business owners will have to confront business succession issues at some time. The following list includes a number of important reasons for a CPA to understand ESOPs:

- *Preservation of clients.* As a professional, it is a constant challenge to find, develop, and retain good clients. An ESOP is typically a succession vehicle for a company owner to pass all or part of the equity in the business to its employees. If the business owner simply sells the business to an outside third party, it is highly probable that the new owner has his or her own professional advisers. An ESOP is an orderly transition consisting of existing owners and the ESOP, with perhaps some combination of inside key employees. The continuity of the business is preserved, and you retain a client. It is my personal experience that the successor management team is most typically very loyal to the financial advisers who made the ESOP a reality.

- *Optimize business owners' succession negotiating strength.* In business, you do not get what you deserve; you get what you negotiate. This axiom holds true for the business owner considering succession issues. You are typically strongest in a negotiating setting when you have a number of viable options. When considering succession issues, an ESOP is an option the business owner fully controls. This option is viable under a wide range of circumstances, including the transfer of ownership to family members, the sale of the business to an outside investor, the sale of the business to managers, and so on. Having the ESOP as an option enables the business owner to negotiate the best overall deal that likely fulfills many objectives.

- *ESOP clients typically pursue higher financial reporting standards.* Many ESOPs include leverage to enable the plan to purchase employer securities. The debt, along with fiduciary responsibilities imposed on the ESOP trustee, typically results in the company having financial reporting at higher levels of assurance. It is common to have financial statements of the employer either audited or reviewed.

- *If the ESOP has over 100 plan participants, the plan requires an annual audit.* This audit of the plan is in addition to any financial reporting completed for the plan sponsor or company.

- *Knowledge of structuring ESOP transactions helps mark the CPA as a valued strategic adviser.* There is often a team of professional advisers for the ESOP company. The team of advisers becomes an opportunity to associate and network with other professionals. The business owner often has a number of options available regarding succession planning. ESOPs are one option that should be considered by most business owners because the tax incentives are so attractive. Even if the ESOP is determined to not be a match with the requirements of the business owner, the CPA adviser will be viewed as a trusted source for viable ideas.

Organization

Chapter 1, "Employee Stock Ownership Plan History and Background"—This chapter provides a brief overview of the philosophy giving rise to ESOPs and the legislative history.

ESOPs are created as a socially stated goal to encourage employee ownership in this nation. Financial incentives by Congress to encourage ESOPs have generally increased steadily over time.

Chapter 2, "Significant Events and Organization"—Significant organizations with an interest in ESOPs are examined. Those organizations include the IRS, the Department of Labor (DOL), the AICPA, the ESOP Association, and the National Center for Employee Ownership, among others. This chapter provides an overview of those organizations and how they interact with ESOPs.

Chapter 3, "Employee Stock Ownership Plan Transaction Methods"—Chapter 3 discusses basic ESOP transaction mechanics. We will examine the most common applications for ESOPs and also the various tax incentives for ESOPs. Both S corporations and C corporations may sponsor ESOPs. A number of tax regulations are unique to each type of tax election, and many regulations are common to both.

Chapter 4, "Employee Stock Ownership Plan Transactions and C Corporations"—This chapter examines a number of typical ESOP structures in C corporations, illustrated by using an example of a hypothetical company. Generally, a single hypothetical company is referenced to illustrate key ESOP concepts for the C corporation.

Chapter 5, "Employee Stock Ownership Plan Transactions and S Corporations"—This chapter examines a number of typical ESOP structures in S corporations, illustrated by using an example of a hypothetical company. Generally, the same hypothetical company in chapter 4 is referenced again to illustrate key ESOP concepts for the S corporation.

Chapter 6, "Advanced Employee Stock Ownership Applications"—This chapter discusses a number of advanced ESOP applications. Such applications include ESOPs in mergers and acquisitions and multi-investor ESOPs.

Chapter 7, "Valuation Issues and Considerations"—General administrative issues are discussed regarding the installation of the ESOP. Topics include such matters as a feasibility study, a team of ESOP advisers, strategic ESOP design considerations, stock valuation, fairness opinions, ESOP participant rights, and the repurchase obligation.

Chapter 8, "Administration and Transaction Considerations"—This chapter examines financial considerations. First, many facets of the Internal Revenue Code Section 1042 tax deferral are examined, including the purchase of qualified replacement property. We also examine a number of the most common elements of funding an ESOP using cash, stock, or debt.

Chapter 9, "Financial Considerations"—Practical ESOP installation insights are provided. ESOP resources that are generally available are identified for the professionals wishing to pursue this topic. The professional adviser is on notice that only the most current resources are appropriate to consider because Employee Retirement Income Security Act of 1974 and ESOP legislation have been recently changed. Those changes have generally made ESOP installations more attractive to business owners.

Chapter 10, "Litigation and Significant Cases"—Court decisions affecting the treatment of ESOPs are analyzed. How the IRS, the DOL, and the ESOP itself view the various cases sheds light on the key issues.

Chapter 11, "Practical Considerations and Employee Stock Ownership Plan Resources"—A successful ESOP candidate has specific qualities that are described here. Practical comparisons and insights into the distinctions between successful and unsuccessful candidates provide guidance. Resources for ESOPs are discussed, as well.

Chapter 1

Employee Stock Ownership Plan History and Background

Overview of Employee Ownership and Employee Stock Ownership Plans

There is general agreement that the one person instrumental in developing the concept of the employee stock ownership plan (ESOP) is Mr. Louis O. Kelso. Mr. Kelso was an attorney and economist who studied what he perceived to be a fundamental problem with capitalism. The problem, as he defined it, is capitalism's propensity to concentrate both capital and the benefits of capital ownership into the hands of a small minority.

According to a 1986 report by the Government Accountability Office, except for the corporate stock held in pension plans, 90 percent of equities are owned by just 10 percent of households. What is more alarming for our consumer-based economy is the fact that almost 60 percent of all stock is owned by just 1 percent of households. The majority of households do not own any equities.

Underlying Philosophy of ESOPs

Mr. Kelso notes that although the United States is a capitalistic country, we are, first, a consumer-based economy. The concentration of wealth into the hands of a few does very little to support a consumer-driven economy. The great challenge, from his perspective, is to fashion a practical approach to broaden the ownership of capital in this country without taking property from others.

One great barrier to broad equity ownership in our economy is that it most frequently takes existing capital resources to earn more capital. Virtually all financial institutions require collateral before you can borrow money, or capital. Most people are effectively shut out from amassing capital because they currently have no capital, and they cannot obtain the credit to acquire capital assets.

Our Puritan heritage suggests that the individual must work hard to save and that those savings are the wellspring of capital formation. The problem, according to Mr. Kelso, is that most people working for a salary are just barely able to purchase life's necessities. They are often unable to save and thereby build capital resources.

The way to broaden equity participation is to enhance the individual's access to credit markets for the purpose of acquiring private capital resources. Mr. Kelso was sensitive to allowing market forces to work in favor of the individual. He did not propose to socialize private capital; rather, he championed democratizing access to the credit needed to acquire private capital.

The solution to the barriers in our economy preventing broader equity participation is the ESOP. The ESOP was envisioned as a vehicle whereby employees in a company could acquire the company's stock using credit and could repay the debt from the earnings of the company. Widespread application of the ESOP principal would promote broader ownership of capital. This would be accomplished through the use of free enterprise incentives.

The full reasoning of Mr. Kelso is far more intricate and complex than this brief overview. His philosophy is more clearly outlined in several books he has written or coauthored with Mr. Mortimer J. Adler, including

- *The Capitalist Manifesto* (1958)—Kelso and Adler
- *The New Capitalists: A Proposal to Free Economic Growth from the Slavery of Savings* (1961)—Kelso and Adler
- *Democracy and Economic Power: Extending the ESOP Revolution through Binary Economics* (1990)—Kelso and Kelso

Legislative History

Mr. Kelso was particularly influential in gaining Congressional interest in his ideas for employee ownership. A critical early Congressional supporter was Senator Russell Long from Louisiana. Senator Long was the chairman of the United States Senate Committee on Finance in the early 1970s, and he witnessed firsthand some very difficult problems in capitalistic countries.

Some of those problems included the Penn Central Transportation Company bankruptcy, banks rationing credit, high interest rates, and scarce venture capital. Senator Long was one of the first political leaders to grasp the significant benefits of employee ownership, and he personally campaigned for its formal existence.

ESOPs were first specifically mentioned in the Regional Rail Reorganization Act of 1973. This bill required the feasibility study for using an ESOP in the reorganization of the Northeast rail system. The rail system was being reorganized into the government-owned Conrail, and Conrail eventually included an ESOP.

The following legislation indicates major ESOP enactments that are generally still in effect. We have omitted a number of relatively minor acts and legislation that is no longer applicable.

Employee Retirement Income Security Act of 1974

- The ESOP came into the forefront with the passage of the Employee Retirement Income Security Act of 1974 (ERISA). This law is the first specific statutory provision for the framework of ESOPs.
- ERISA included ESOPs in the definition of a qualified employee benefit plan under the Internal Revenue Code (IRC). ERISA generally standardized the rules governing pension and retirement plans, but it permitted certain exceptions to ESOPs in recognition of their special mission.
- ERISA permitted the ESOP to borrow money in the interest of acquiring employer securities, and ESOPs had to be primarily invested in employer securities. These provisions are significant because most other qualified retirement plans contain specific restrictions against the inclusion of more than 10 percent in employer securities.

Revenue Act of 1978

- This act required stock that was not publicly traded and in a leveraged ESOP to offer participating employees a put option back to the employer.
- Full pass-through voting rights on allocated shares in publicly traded securities was required. Closely held companies were required to extend voting rights to plan participants on major issues.

The Chrysler Loan Guarantee Act of 1979

- This act required Chrysler to establish an ESOP and ensure the employees a significant stake in the company by 1984. With this legislation and the Regional Rail Reorganization Act of 1973, the federal government officially encouraged employee ownership.

The Economic Recovery Tax Act of 1981

- This legislation contained two significant ESOP provisions. First, the act increased the covered payroll contribution limit from 15 percent to 25 percent in leveraged ESOPs for principal payments, and it allowed unlimited interest.
- Second, it permitted companies substantially owned by the employees to require that departing employees accept cash for the fair market value of their stock, rather than the stock.

Deficit Reduction Act of 1984

- Tremendous financial incentives were extended to ESOPs in the Deficit Reduction Act of 1984. The legislation is noteworthy because it occurred at a time when the federal government was concerned about reducing the spending deficits, and yet, ESOPs were further encouraged by extending tax-oriented incentives to them.
- Those incentives included a deferral of taxes on the gains of a selling owner to an ESOP if the ESOP owns at least 30 percent of the company, and the proceeds are reinvested in domestically qualifying securities within 12 months (this is generally referred to as the IRC Section 1042 rollover). There is also a tax deduction for cash dividends paid to ESOP participants.

Tax Reform Act of 1986

- This legislation revised many rules for qualified employee pension and retirement plans in such areas as contribution limits, employee benefit distributions, vesting, and coverage requirements.
- Several additional revisions were made to ESOPs. The significant provisions provide for the following: expansion of the deduction for dividends for the repayment of an ESOP loan, modification of the put option so that employees would be paid entirely in cash over a period not to exceed five years, imposition of new rules on the payments to ESOP participants following a break in service, and clarification of pass-through voting rights in closely held companies.
- Significantly, this legislation requires the use of an independent appraiser for the valuation of closely held securities.

Small Business Job Protection Act of 1996

- This act allows ESOPs, as well other tax-exempt trusts, to hold the stock of an S corporation, which means that for the first time, an S corporation may sponsor an ESOP beginning after January 1, 1998. Certain provisions of the act required clarification before ESOPs would likely appear in any quantities. Many of the technical issues were addressed the following year.
- The ESOP lender's interest rate exclusion applying to loans made after August 20, 1996, was repealed.

Taxpayer Relief Act of 1997

- The legislation contains expanded provisions that permit an S corporation to establish and operate an ESOP.
- An S corporation may distribute a participant's account in cash, not stock. The S Corporation sponsoring an ESOP has exemptions from ERISA-prohibited transaction rules, similar to those for a C corporation sponsoring an ESOP.
- Taxable income of an S corporation sponsoring an ESOP is prorated to the ESOP's share of ownership. The ESOP's proportionate share of income is not subject to

federal income tax, and the income may be retained in the company. Eventually, the retained income will be paid to plan participants in the future.

- In an S corporation arrangement, some of the special tax incentives for ESOPs are not available, such as the tax–deferred rollover for certain sales of stock to an ESOP (the IRC Section 1042 rollover), the deductibility of dividends paid on ESOP stock in certain circumstances, and the deductibility level of 25 percent of payroll plus interest on the ESOP loan for annual contributions to the ESOP.

The Economic Growth and Tax Relief Reconciliation Act of 2001

- The Economic Growth and Tax Relief Reconciliation Act of 2001 (EGTRRA) generally increases a broad array of benefit and contribution limits applicable to qualified plans. The increases include the cap on both the contribution limit to a qualified plan in the percentage of compensation and the actual dollar amount. Increases generally take effect beginning in 2002. Significantly, many of the increases are indexed to inflation thereafter.
- The limit on deductible contributions to a qualified plan is increased to 25 percent of qualifying payroll. This is a significant increase from prior years.
- Reasonable dividend deductions in a C corporation are permitted when the dividends are reinvested in the plan.
- Complicated compliance measures have been enacted for S corporation ESOPs. The general intent of the complex testing is to help ensure that the financial benefits of the ESOP legislation are shared by a larger percentage of the plan sponsor employees and to not have the benefits skewed to only a few key individuals. This provision of the EGTRRA is intended to eliminate perceived abusive ESOPs when the plan was installed in an S corporation with only a few employees.

Jobs and Growth Tax Relief Reconciliation Act of 2003

- Key provisions include lowering the capital gain tax rate to essentially 15 percent, and personal income tax rates were adjusted to lower amounts.

Impact on ESOPs

Since 1973, the first time ESOPs were mentioned in federal legislation, there has generally been a significant increase in the financial incentives officially extended to encourage employee ownership of their companies. Those incentives have become substantial, ranging from the deferral of taxes on a properly structured ESOP transaction in a C corporation (the IRC Section 1042 rollover) to the full deductibility of the purchase price of stock purchased by the ESOP. Most of the incentives relating to ESOPs are virtually exclusive to only this type of qualified plan.

Only a few incentives have ever been withdrawn; the most notable is the interest rate exclusion previously extended to financial institutions to encourage them to make ESOP loans. This legislation withdrawing the interest income incentive was passed in 1996. It is estimated that today over 10,000 ESOPs exist, and the greatest percentage of them are installed in closely held companies.

ESOPs have been officially created to both provide a means for employees to gain an equity investment in their employer and serve as a vehicle for retirement. ESOPs are included in ERISA as a qualified plan subject to the protections and incentives extended to all qualified retirement plans, including pensions, profit sharing plans, and 401(k) savings plans.

ESOPs Today

Increasingly, ESOPs are installed in S corporations, and many if not most of the new ESOPs have a goal of becoming a 100 percent employee-owned company. This trend is a direct result of S Corporation tax attributes generally combined with the tax incentives of ESOPs. Chapter 5, "Employee Stock Ownership Plan Transaction and S Corporation," discusses S corporation ESOPs in greater detail and illustrates the power of combining S corporation attributes with ESOP incentives.

The major tax cuts of the Bush administration, including the EGTRRA and the Jobs and Growth Tax Relief Reconciliation Act of 2003 (which lowered the capital gain tax rates and many personal income tax rates) are set to expire on January 1, 2013. Tax rates will reset to the rates in effect just before the legislation was passed. In essence, sharp tax increases appear as a near certainty in the near future. Due to the tax incentive nature of ESOPs, the higher tax rates will likely fuel an increased interest in employee ownership. Indeed, if capital gain rates increase due to a combination of the preceding Bush tax cuts' sunset provision and the impact of a capital gain surtax as part of the Patient Protection and Affordable Care Act of 2010 (nationalized healthcare), there will certainly be more interest in the C corporation-specific application of the IRC Section 1042 tax deferral provisions discussed at length in chapter 3, "Employee Stock Ownership Plan Transaction Mechanics."

Since 2007 and the beginning of what is now being referred to as the Great Recession, the nation has been incurring significant and unsustainable spending deficits. The national debt has increased by over $5 trillion is just a few years. These unsustainable deficits will have to be addressed by the federal government. Assuming there is a mixture of tax increases and spending cuts in the future, such developments bode well for ESOPs.

Certainly, a legitimate question could be asked: With all the deficit spending, are the ESOP tax incentives at risk? The correct answer is that no one knows for sure what Congress will do, given the fiscal pressure coming to bear on the budget. Because of a lengthy history of ESOPs accomplishing precisely what Congress intended, it seems unlikely that the program to encourage employee ownership will be assailed. ESOPs provide a wide range of economic and societal benefits, such as a fairer allocation of corporate profitability, converting more people into active participants in our market-based capitalistic economy, and employee owned companies financially outperforming their nonemployee owned counterparts (increasing job growth and compensation packages).

Summary

Today, it is possible to have an ESOP in both a C corporation and an S corporation. A number of significant differences between the tax incentives for C corporations and S corporations will be considered. Encouraging employee ownership and participation in a market-based capitalistic society are truly goals of our government.

Chapter 2

Significant Events and Organizations

Since their inception, a wide range of creative uses and applications of employee stock ownership plans (ESOPs) has evolved. The strong tax incentives have always been an attraction. With time, the area of ESOPs has become significantly more documented, subject to increasing levels of regulation and complexity. A number of benchmark events and organizations, from both government and industry, have a significant impact on ESOPs, and this chapter identifies those elements.

Regulations and Government Agencies

Employee Retirement Income Security Act of 1974

The passage of the Employee Retirement Income Security Act of 1974 (ERISA) marked a significant event. The retirement of working Americans until that point was typically dependent on Social Security benefits, personal savings, and pensions. Although few smaller or closely held companies sponsored pensions, they were fairly common in larger publicly held companies. A number of high-profile scandals and fraudulent activities threatened to shake the foundation of the private sector retirement system of the United States. In response to the crises, the federal government enacted wide-ranging and powerful legislation that is referred to as ERISA.

ERISA is intended to provide security and integrity to the retirement system of this country. The act protects the interests of participants in employee benefit plans by mandating a number of measures, including standards of conduct, responsibilities, and obligations of plan fiduciaries, and providing appropriate remedies when failures in those responsibilities have been breached. Significantly, ERISA provides access to the Federal Courts for relief.

ERISA classifies ESOPs as a tax qualified defined contribution employee benefit plan intended to invest primarily in the securities of the plan sponsor (the employer). As a tax qualified defined contribution plan, ESOPs enjoy many of the same benefits of similar tax qualified plans, such as profit sharing plans, 401(k) plans, and pensions.

Various Sections of ERISA

As originally passed, ERISA contains a number of sections briefly described as follows.

Title 1—Protection of Employee Benefit Rights

This is often referred to as the labor title. It provides general standards of responsibilities and conduct for plan fiduciaries, in addition to establishing such factors as the rules for structuring plans and prohibitions against certain types of transactions.

- Significantly, the establishment of plan fiduciaries introduces a mandatory level of conduct that is subject to severe penalties and high standards of conduct. The Department of Labor (DOL) has primary oversight responsibility for ERISA compliance in these areas.
- Because an ESOP must have a plan fiduciary, the DOL introduced its own regulations to ensure compliance with ERISA statutes. The DOL will be considered separately later in this chapter.

Title 2—Amendments to the Internal Revenue Code Relating to Retirement Plans

This is often referred to as the tax title. The Internal Revenue Code (IRC) was amended in certain areas as a result of the legislation. Additionally, the legislation introduced or expanded the IRC and had an impact on federal revenue collections. The IRS has primary oversight responsibility for tax collections.

ESOPs contain significant tax incentives, and the IRS is the general government gatekeeper for tax revenues and IRC compliance. The IRS will be considered separately later in this chapter.

Title 3—Jurisdiction, Administration, Enforcement; Joint Pension, Profit-Sharing, and Employee Stock Ownership Plan Task Force, Etc.

This title establishes responsibilities within ERISA for appropriate federal agencies and the remedies available. The title contains narratives coordinating the efforts between the Department of the Treasury and the DOL.

Title 4—Plan Termination Insurance

This final title is listed, although it is not significant at this time for our purposes.

IRS

The IRS has the primary oversight responsibility to enforce sections of the IRC. ESOPs fall under IRS review because many tax incentives are related and often unique to the plans.

General Audit and Compliance Areas

Because an ESOP is a tax qualified defined contribution employee benefit plan, the compliance provisions from a tax and benefits viewpoint are often complex. To gain an understanding of the perspective of the IRS, the agency periodically publishes audit guidelines for its agents.

Recent audit guidelines cover in considerable detail the areas to be examined by agents. Only a few of the more important audit topics are listed to provide an indication of the far-ranging review of ESOPs imposed by the IRS. Generally, the IRS looks at the significant amount of detail regarding ESOP transactions and verifies compliance with often complex reporting and computation issues.

We will shortly examine the DOL and its relationship with ESOPs. Like the IRS, the DOL will often be involved with ESOP audits, but its orientation is less on the mechanics of account balance computations and more on fiduciary obligations and prohibited transactions.

Overall IRS Audit Matters

- Verify timely filing of Form 5309. Verify if a determination letter was filed indicating if the ESOP is leveraged. Appendix 2A, "IRS Form 5309, *Application for Determination of Employee Stock Ownership Plan*," has a copy of Form 5309.
- Verify the ESOP includes such things as suitable language for compliance with qualified joint and survivor annuity and qualified preretirement survivor annuity requirements and diversification and distribution requirements.
- Check that the ESOP satisfies all applicable matters relating to participation, coverage, and nondiscrimination requirements.
- Check that ESOP participants properly vest in their accounts in accordance with IRC Sections 411 and 416 rules.
- Verify that IRC Section 404 payroll deduction limits have not been exceeded.
- Check to determine if dividends have been used for ESOP obligations. Verify that any dividend payments are within regulation guidelines, and determine if the dividends are reasonable.
- Verify that the ESOP provides the participants with the right to get a distribution in the form of employer securities. Verify the existence of multiple classes of securities, if any.
  - Special note: Although this is a guaranteed provision of the federal statutes, it is highly advisable that the company amend appropriate articles of incorporation and bylaws to restrict ownership to the ESOP and employees, which will have the effect of disallowing a distribution of stock to any terminated participants. It is permissible to make such a modification because the federal government recognizes that potentially creating shareholders no longer associated with the closely held company could be a highly negative development.

- The rights of actual shareholders in a closely held company are likely to be much greater than the rights of a participant in a qualified plan. Shareholder rights are typically subject to state statutes and regulations, and it is recommended such rights be reviewed by legal counsel.

- Determine that participants have a put option (a demand for the company to purchase stock for cash) back to the company for securities not readily traded on public markets. If the company requires a participant to take a note for all or a portion of the amount due, the obligation must be secured by the company. The type of security offered by the company for the unpaid note should be examined.

- Verify the ESOP holds qualifying employer securities and that the ESOP is primarily invested in such securities. Verify that such securities are not readily traded on public markets.

- Determine if the ESOP holds preferred stock, and determine if the conversion price is reasonable.

IRS Valuation and Financial Audit Issues

- Verify the timely and accurate filing of Form 5500.

- If the stock is not publicly traded, determine that the value of the stock is properly determined in a timely basis.

  - For example, the fair market value of the stock for all transactions between the ESOP and a disqualified person must be determined as of the date of the transaction. If the stock has been valued for a number of years, obtain several valuation reports to see if the stock has been consistently valued.

- Determine if the securities are not traded on public markets. If the securities are not publicly traded, determine if they are valued by an independent appraiser. There will be significant discussion on independence and appraisers when we shortly consider the role of the DOL.

- Look at the valuation report to see if the proper standard of value is indicated (fair market value and adequate consideration). Examine the valuation report for compliance with applicable valuation standards.

- Check to see that participants are entitled to vote on employer securities allocated to their accounts, as required by IRC Section 409(e).

- Check to see that the ESOP provides the proper diversification election under applicable IRC sections.

- If the ESOP is leveraged, examine documentation regarding the loan for reasonableness. Look to ensure that the loan is in compliance with the primary benefit requirement. Determine arm's-length dealing by examining such things as interest rate, collateral, prepayment penalties, and other restrictions.

- When the ESOP is leveraged, check to ensure that the stock held as collateral is being properly released from the suspense account and allocated to the accounts of the participants. Make sure that any recourse by the lender does not exceed the permissible collateral limits.

- When IRC Section 1042 is elected, determine if the ESOP owns at least 30 percent of either each class of stock or the total value of all outstanding stock of the corporation. Verify that all applicable holding periods have been observed. See if qualified replacement property was purchased in the prescribed time period. Determine that rules of attribution are in compliance.

Stock Valuation Issues in a Closely Held Company ESOP

One primary concern of the IRS when an ESOP is established in a closely held company is the valuation of the nonactively traded stock. Prior to ERISA, the IRS established considerable expertise in the valuation of stock in closely held companies through such things as gift taxes, estate taxes, certain mergers, and charitable deductions.

Standard of Value: Fair Market Value (Revenue Ruling 59-60 and Other Applicable Regulations)

- The definition of *fair market value* is the price at which the asset would change hands between a willing buyer and willing seller, neither being under any compulsion to buy or sell and both having reasonable knowledge of relevant facts and are able to enter into the transaction.
- Additional fair market value considerations are as follows:
  - Fair market value is a hypothetical standard.
  - Financial buyer is assumed, not a strategic or specific buyer.
  - Terms are assumed to be for cash.
- Valuation issues regarding ESOPs will be specifically considered in chapter 7, "Valuation Issues and Considerations."

Securities and Exchange Commission

The Securities and Exchange Commission (SEC) is oriented to the regulation of the public equity markets and certain other industries. Generally, there is not a significant overlap with SEC interests and the installation of ESOPs in closely held companies, but a couple items are worth noting:

- *Regulated industries.* The SEC does have regulatory authority in certain industries, such as commercial banks and insurance companies. The regulations typically involve two primary areas relating potentially to ESOPs. The first is capital or surplus requirements. The second is filing proceedings regarding a change in control.

  Leveraged ESOPs may be a problem with banks (for example, because the debt could negatively impact the capital requirements for the institution). The impact of Statement of Position (SOP) 93-6, *Employers' Accounting for Employee Stock Ownership Plans*, must be carefully considered before an ESOP can be installed.
- *Independence.* The SEC has looked very closely at the relationship between certain professional service providers and their publicly held clients. Significant disclosure and other changes have been initiated in this area.

- *Auditors and publicly held companies.* The SEC is concerned about the issue regarding large accounting firms auditing publicly held companies when the accounting firms also maintain substantial management consulting relationships. This concern has, in part, prompted several of the large firms to segregate or spin–off their consulting units, so they can concentrate on auditing.
- *Investment bankers, brokers, and publicly held companies.* There is also considerable concern regarding the relationship between investment bankers and brokers when both are part of the same entity underwriting and marketing stock in the same publicly held company. Changes in such relationships to ensure a higher degree of independence have been initiated.

The SEC's focus on independence has alerted the Government Accountability Office to review a wider range of interfaces between the private professional service sector and government agencies relying on such services either in whole or part. An example of one area that may come under review is a clarification of what constitutes an independent appraiser for the purposes of an ESOP-based valuation. Currently, the IRS and the DOL have their own understandings of an independent appraiser, with no common definition. Over a longer term, a more proactive stance on the part of the federal government and its myriad agencies may have an impact on the service providers to ESOPs.

DOL

The passage of ERISA brought ESOPs into the forefront of mainstream attention as a tax qualified employee benefit plan. The DOL assumed considerable oversight responsibility for ESOPs.

ERISA created the requirement for all qualified plans to have a trustee. Every plan trustee is bound by applicable fiduciary responsibilities. Fiduciary responsibilities often extend to other parties that are not trustees. Service providers to ESOPs must be mindful of the various fiduciary responsibilities that are imposed by ERISA because the plan trustee is not the only one subject to the standards of fiduciary conduct.

General Areas of Oversight

The DOL has many responsibilities regarding ERISA, but in general, two major areas are emphasized for the purposes of this book. First, the DOL is focused on compliance with fiduciary responsibilities imposed by ERISA. Second, the DOL monitors applicable activities, looking for prohibited transactions.

Many of the disputes regarding ESOPs typically entail violations of fiduciary responsibilities. For the purposes of this book, we are examining ESOPs in closely held companies. In addition to fiduciary matters, when an ESOP is installed in a closely held company, the value of the stock is also a common area that is a candidate for dispute. Most typically, litigation involves overvaluation issues of stock not publicly traded.

General Audit and Compliance Areas

In a prior section of this chapter, we briefly examined a general listing of audit and compliance areas by the IRS where there is an orientation to computational and compliance issues with the IRC. The DOL is primarily looking at fiduciary issues and prohibited transactions. The DOL may also review the areas of audit by the IRS, but such items are often less emphasized.

- Verify the timely and accurate filing of Form 5500.
- Examine relationships of parties in interest. Parties in interest represent a special category of individuals and entities that have a relationship with the ESOP. The term *parties in interest* is defined in IRC Section 4975(e)(2), and it has a similar definition in ERISA Section 3(14). ERISA refers generally to such relationships as disqualified persons. For purposes of this book, we will use the term *parties in interest*.
- This DOL examination is intended to look for such things as breaches of fiduciary responsibilities and prohibited transactions relating to parties in interest. Generally, parties in interest include the following nonexclusive listing:
  - Plan fiduciary, including, but not limited to, the following: administrator, officer, trustee, or custodian.
  - Plan legal counsel (generally not the legal counsel to the employer).
  - Employees and participants in the plan.
  - Service providers to the plan.
  - Related unions and employee organizations.
  - Sponsoring employers.
  - Direct or indirect owner of 50 percent or more of the ownership interests in the plan sponsor. Relatives of the owners, including spouse, ancestor, and lineal descendent of spouse of a lineal descendent.
  - Corporation, partnership, trust, or estate at least 50 percent owned or controlled by the previously described persons.
  - Certain organizations classified as a control group.
  - For more information, please read the article "ERISA Liability for CPAs" in the December 2000 issue of the *Journal of Accountancy*.
- Examine potential prohibited transactions between the plan and parties in interest. Prohibited transactions are typically instances when self-dealing enrichment has occurred at the expense of plan participants. Candidates for prohibited transactions may include items from the following nonexclusive list:
  - Sales, exchanges, or leasing of property.
  - Extensions of credit or lending money.
  - Transfer of plan assets.
  - Providing goods and services.
  - A number of specific ESOP exemptions within ERISA for a limited number of situations. For example, an ESOP is permitted to borrow money for the purpose of buying employer securities. Additionally, the ESOP is intended to be primarily invested in employer securities, providing relief from ERISA-mandated diversification

issues. Finally, shareholders in the company typically sell stock to the ESOP, subject to an independent appraisal in compliance with all applicable regulations.

— Examine fiduciary conduct, looking for examples of such things as self-dealing, divided loyalty, and improper commissions. Apply the prudent person standard to fiduciary conduct.

— Examine valuation reports for adherence to applicable valuation standards and guidelines. Determine if the ESOP paid more than fair market value for the employer's stock.

General ERISA Fiduciary Considerations

This section is intended to provide an overview of general fiduciary issues established by ERISA. This overview must be viewed in concert with ESOP and ERISA court cases. It is beyond the scope of this book to develop a detailed accounting of applicable court cases, but litigation in this area is an integral part of setting and establishing the parameters of appropriate behavior for ESOP fiduciaries. The experienced ESOP professionals will have a general knowledge of relevant court cases. Over time, it is a fair statement to say that the courts have generally increased the obligations and duties of fiduciaries to higher standards of conduct. ERISA Sections 401–408 contain general fiduciary rules.

Who May Serve as a Trustee

According to ERISA Section 403(a), an ESOP must have a trustee that is bound by fiduciary responsibilities to make decisions regarding the administration of the plan and protecting the interests of the plan participants.

- Fiduciary responsibilities must be seriously considered because the failure to perform the duties may expose the fiduciary to considerable personal legal liability for losses to the plan.
- The trustee must generally have exclusive authority and discretion over the management of the ESOP assets.
  - An exception to this general rule exists when the trustee is subject to the "proper" directions of another named fiduciary, and such directions are not contrary to ERISA and are in accordance with the ESOP. Per ERISA Section 403(a)(1), this trustee is referred to as a directed trustee. The most common application of this is a bank trust department serving in this limited capacity.
  - Anyone may become a trustee, including company officers or company employees. The seller of the stock to the ESOP may also be a fiduciary, but there is obviously a conflict of interest in that relationship. Many ESOP companies have a plan committee that acts as the trustee. These persons are generally referred to as "inside" trustees because they have a close affiliation with the company.
- An option for an ESOP company to consider regarding the fiduciary obligations is to have an outside independent fiduciary, such as a bank's trust department. The outside fiduciary may serve as a directed trustee or a trustee with full discretion. A directed trustee, as the name implies, is typically directed into actions by the company's board of directors regarding certain ongoing and customary business activities. The directed

trustee will still exercise due care while discharging its duties. For many closely held companies, the option of having an outside trustee is too expensive, but that expense should be compared to potential fiduciary risks.

Basic Overview of Fiduciary Duties

Generally, according to ERISA, a *fiduciary* is someone who has discretionary authority in the administration of a qualified plan and exercises discretionary control over the management of the plan or its assets. Additional interpretations regarding fiduciary responsibilities have been defined by the courts. The following is a general listing of significant fiduciary responsibilities, but it is not all-inclusive.

Acting Solely in the Interest of the Participants and Beneficiaries

The fiduciary must act for the sole and exclusive benefit of plan participants. According to ERISA Section 404(a), this is often referred to as the exclusive benefit rule or the duty of loyalty. This standard imposes a high degree of duty on the fiduciary, especially if the fiduciary is an officer, a shareholder, or a director of the company.

- When the fiduciary is someone such as a shareholder, an officer, a director, or another insider, there is the heightened possibility of a potential conflict of interest. Such individuals are commonly referred to as conflicted fiduciaries.
- Conflicts may naturally arise between an inside fiduciary and the requirement to act in the exclusive best interests of the plan participants and their beneficiaries. When conflicts do arise, generally, the fiduciary must demonstrate that the exclusive benefit standard has been met by documenting that appropriate actions were conducted.
- Courts generally will hold the conflicted fiduciary to very high standards and are intolerant of conflicts of interest. The fiduciary is barred from self-dealing for personal benefit at the expense of the plan participants.

The "Prudent Man" Obligation

According to ERISA Section 404(a), the fiduciary should discharge duties "with the care, skill, prudence, and diligence under circumstances then prevailing that a prudent man acting in a like capacity and familiar with such matter would use in the conduct of an enterprise of a like character and with like aims." This is a high standard of conduct. Good intentions are noble, but they are not likely to be an adequate defense against improper conduct if a problem arises.

- The fiduciary commonly relies on the advice and reports of other professionals in the discharge of applicable responsibilities. Such advisers commonly include ESOP legal counsel and an independent appraiser. The fiduciary should examine the professional credentials of all its advisers to ensure appropriate expertise in ERISA and ESOP procedures.
- The fiduciary must still perform his or her own independent investigation into matters and should understand the work of other advisers in sufficient detail to reach his or her own conclusion. Blind reliance on other professionals is not a "prudent

man" response. The amount of appropriate investigation required will depend on the facts and circumstances of each event.

- Ultimately, the responsibility for conduct will reside with the fiduciary.

The Exclusive Purpose Rule

Generally, under ERISA Section 404(a), the trustee is required to consider the interests of the plan participants only in their position as participants in a qualified retirement plan. The trustee may not consider other interests.

This standard of conduct for an ESOP trustee may lead to potentially difficult conflicts of conscience. According to the ERISA standards, the trustee must not take into consideration the impact of a decision on employment in the plan sponsor. The conflict arises when the spirit of the ESOP installation in a given installation was to provide and preserve employment. The conflict may become more pronounced if the ESOP company is in a small community where employment and jobs are not as plentiful as in a larger metropolitan area.

The ERISA standards are clear in this matter, but the courts may provide some modest relief from this standard, depending on the circumstances.

Following Plan Documents

Per ERISA Section 404(a), the fiduciary is expected to act only in a manner permitted by the plan documents and ERISA. Knowledge of the plan documents is integral to the duties of being a fiduciary.

The fiduciary must both read and understand the plan documents, including, at a minimum, such items as the trust agreement, the plan, and the summary plan description (typically given to participants). Some of the more visible duties imposed by the ESOP documents include

- keeping the ESOP in compliance with changing statutes.
- filing all tax reports (particularly Form 5500) in a timely manner.
- having the company stock valued at least annually, as stated in the plan documents.
- complying with applicable pass-through voting requirements.
- comparing the summary plan description with the plan documents for compliance.
- responding to purchase offers.
- other specified duties detailed in the plan documents.

Guarding Against Prohibited Transactions

The fiduciary must be aware of prohibited transactions generally but must understand specific exemptions from ERISA rules that exist specifically for ESOPs. According to ERISA Section 406(a)(1), prohibited transactions generally are transactions between the qualified benefit plan and a party in interest and include

- the sale, lease, or exchange of any property between the plan and a party in interest.
- providing goods and services between the plan and party in interest.
- transferring plan assets for the personal benefit of a party in interest.
- lending money or extending credit to the plan from a party in interest.

- prohibiting the fiduciary from dealing with the assets of the plan for personal benefit.
- prohibiting the fiduciary from acting in a transaction on behalf of a party with interests adverse to the ESOP and its participants and beneficiaries.
- the fiduciary not receiving any consideration from any party with a transaction involving plan assets. For example, under ERISA statutes, a fiduciary could not allow a shareholder to sell his or her stock to a qualified plan. ESOPs are specifically excluded from this standard because the ESOP is to be primarily invested in the employer securities.
- generally not permitting loans between a plan and party in interest. An exception is made under ERISA Section 408(b)(3) for ESOPs when the loan is for a leveraged ESOP for the primary benefit of the ESOP participants, and the loan bears a reasonable interest rate. There are a number of other qualifying aspects, but the intent is to exempt ESOPs from this issue.

Generally, a fiduciary should be on notice for heightened scrutiny between any dealings with the ESOP and parties in interest. Although certain exemptions to the general rules exist only for ESOPs, the fiduciary needs to be alert for conflicts and take appropriate steps to ensure that such actions are not consummated.

Breach of Fiduciary Duties

The penalties for the breach of fiduciary responsibilities are potentially severe. The fiduciary shall be personally liable for the losses the plan may suffer due to the breach of his or her duties.

- According to ERISA Section 409(a), the amount of financial exposure includes both the losses suffered by the plan and also any gains enjoyed by the fiduciary as a result of the use of plan assets. The fiduciary may be subject to a civil action.
- The fiduciary is subject to other equitable relief determined by the court, per ERISA Section 409(a).

If the prohibited transaction rules are violated, in addition to the remedies mentioned, excise taxes may be imposed on the transaction. The excise tax may range from 15 percent to 100 percent of the transaction, depending on the circumstances.

- Fiduciary issues may become complex in ESOP applications, and it is recommended that the ESOP fiduciary retain the services of experienced legal counsel when questions arise.

Proposed DOL Regulations Specific to ESOP Valuations

Guidance for valuing the shares of a closely held company in an ESOP came primarily from the IRS. The IRS requires that the ESOP is prohibited from paying more than the fair market value for the securities of the employer.

The IRS and the DOL generally cooperated on the valuation of ESOP securities, but the DOL issued its own *Proposed Regulation Relating to the Definition of* Adequate Consideration, as published in the *Federal Register* on May 17, 1988.[1] The proposed regulation has not yet been adopted as final, but professionals must consider it carefully in discharging their responsibilities. ESOP valuations are considered separately in chapter 7.

Prohibited Transactions

The DOL looks carefully at situations that may be classified as a prohibited transaction. Briefly discussed at the beginning of this section, prohibited transactions generally relate to instances when there is self-dealing between parties in interest and the qualified plan. Candidates for prohibited transactions may include items from the following nonexclusive list:

- Sales, exchanges, or leasing of property
- Extensions of credit or lending money
- Transfer of plan assets
- Providing goods and services

The liability to the fiduciary exits when the fiduciary either knew, or should have known, that he or she caused the plan to enter into a prohibited transaction. The fiduciary is liable for losses suffered by the plan. The "prudent man" standard of conduct is imposed on the fiduciary.

From the perspective of an ESOP, many traditional conflicts generally identified under ERISA have been provided specific waivers from liability. These waivers had to occur because the ESOP is intended to foster employee participation in our capitalistic society through ownership of company stock in a qualified retirement plan.

Major Exceptions to ERISA for the Benefit of ESOPs

- *Loans between the ESOP and a party in interest.* Loans may be permitted between the ESOP and a party in interest (such as a bank or selling shareholder), per ERISA Section 408(b)(3). Such loans are referred to as exempt loans and must meet the following guidelines:
    - The interest rate on the loan must be reasonable.
    - The loan proceeds must be used to acquire qualifying securities of the employer or to refinance another exempt loan.
    - The loan must exist for the primary benefit of the ESOP participants.
    - There is no recourse against the ESOP, and the only collateral that may be provided for the loan are qualifying employer securities purchased with the loan proceeds and contributions to repay the loans.
    - As the loan is repaid, the encumbrance against qualifying employer securities must be released.

---

[1] The Department of Labor's (DOL's) *Proposed Regulation Relating to the Definition of* Adequate Consideration was originally referred to as Title 29 U.S. *Code of Federal Regulations* (CFR) Part 2510, as published in the *Federal Register*, on May 17, 1988. An examination today of 29 CFR 2510 does not disclose the *Proposed Regulation Relating to the Definition of* Adequate Consideration because the regulation has not been finalized. The proposed regulation is considered as the view of the DOL, as referenced in employee stock ownership plan valuation reports and Employee Retirement Income Security Act of 1974 litigation.

These guidelines are instructive because many selling shareholders elect to provide the financing for an ESOP transaction. These "self-funded" ESOPs often provide significant advantages to the selling shareholder, the ESOP, and the company; however, such loans must be carefully structured to remain in full ERISA compliance.

- *Investment in employer stock not subject to diversification requirements.* The stock in a closely held company not actively traded on a public market may be purchased by the ESOP. That stock must generally have such attributes as the highest class of voting rights; the highest class of dividend rights; and, typically, the most senior features of equity offered by the plan sponsor. According to ERISA Section 402(2)(2), ESOPs enjoy an exemption from diversification requirements because the stock of the employer is a significant attribute.
  - The ESOP is intended to be primarily invested in the stock of the plan sponsor. Although there is no established percentage test, *primarily invested* is typically interpreted to mean more than half the ESOP assets are invested in company stock.
- *ESOP may purchase stock from a party in interest.* The stock must be a qualified security meeting the regulatory definition. The ESOP cannot pay more than fair market value for the stock (or the DOL standard of value of adequate consideration).
- Additionally, as stated in ERISA Section 408(c), the ESOP is not permitted to pay the seller of the security a commission.

When considering prohibited transactions, the DOL will often give considerable weight to the procedures and behavior of the conflicted parties in interest. The DOL is often very concerned with parties in interest following accepted procedures in the discharge of their fiduciary duties. It wants to know if parties in interest exercised the appropriate amount of care in preparation for the transaction.

A prohibited transaction is a very serious violation of ERISA, and penalties may be severe. Federal statutes permit the imposition of an excise tax on the prohibited transaction, in addition to any losses and damages suffered by the ESOP.

ESOP and ERISA Litigation

The ERISA legislation, in many instances and by design, is very general in its wording. In 1974, it was deemed to be important to have a national program in place to encourage retirement saving. Congress knew that having legislation as sweeping as ERISA would eventually have to be interpreted by the courts and appropriate administrative agencies regarding a broad range of implementation issues.

The interpretation of the statutes over time becomes essential to an understanding of the application of the ERISA legislation. It is beyond the scope of this book to discuss in any significant detail the major cases involving ESOPs. The cases of particular interest for CPAs typically involve breach of fiduciary duties and improper stock valuations.

Due to the special dual nature of ESOPs, they come under the direct administration of both the IRS and the DOL:

- The IRS has a direct interest due to the fact that contributions to an ESOP are tax deductible for qualified plans within certain prescribed limits. The IRS is also involved because excise taxes may be imposed in the case of a prohibited transaction.

- The DOL has a direct interest because it is the agency established by the ERISA legislation to enforce the provisions of the law and protect the retirement system of the country. One important area of concern for the DOL is the conduct of plan fiduciaries and their duties to the plan.
  - We emphasize that the power of the DOL is substantial, and the agency has a mandate to ensure that the retirement system of the country is being safeguarded.
  - When ERISA was enacted, the legislation contained comprehensive rules to provide its own remedies. It was recognized by Congress that any dispute between plan participants and a plan is typically very one-sided, particularly when the plan is backed by the full resources of the plan sponsor: the company. Congress enhanced the ability of plaintiffs in such disputes.
  - ERISA provides to the prevailing party the right to recover attorney's fees and other costs incurred in the litigation. This recovery of litigation costs is in addition to any other recovery of resources attained by the prevailing party. In effect, the legislation provides that the full resources of the plan may be committed to pay the legal costs of the attorney suing the plan.

Pronouncements and legal actions brought by the DOL with regard to ESOPs are closely watched by professionals and other interested parties because of the DOL's broad authority and the far-ranging potential penalties.

Summary

The DOL often looks at compliance issues regarding ESOPs and ERISA from a different perspective than the IRS. The DOL looks at fiduciary issues and the potential for conflicts of interest that may lead to prohibited transactions. ERISA compliance is often very technical and complex. Broadly worded or even vague legal principles must be applied to the circumstances of each transaction. Generally, the behavior and actions of parties in interest are closely monitored for compliance with the spirit of ERISA.

Professional service providers to qualified plans, including ESOPs, must be aware of the duties imposed by ERISA. The general trend in the courts is to impose increasing responsibilities on professional service providers for the advice and service supplied to qualified plans and their representatives. Failure to understand those requirements may lead to costly settlements.

Industry Organizations and Standards

The AICPA

The AICPA is involved directly with the financial reporting of certain ESOP transactions and other related accounting issues. Specifically, the AICPA issued SOP 93-6 that was originally effective for fiscal years beginning after December 15, 1993, and was extended to fiscal years beginning after December 15, 1994. SOP 93-6 requires certain financial reporting, particularly when debt is part of an ESOP-based transaction.

SOP 93-6

SOP 93-6 applies to all employers with ESOPs, both leveraged and nonleveraged. Many of the accounting issues relating to ESOP companies are complex and involve such things as dividends, additional classes of stock, and reporting the debt of a controlled group of companies. This book is oriented to the closely held company, and the reporting issues are typically less complicated.

For more information, please read the article "Employers' Accounting for Employee Stock Ownership Plans," in the February 1993 issue of the *Journal of Accountancy*.

General Provisions of SOP 93-6

- SOP 93-6 supersedes SOP 76-3, *Accounting Practices for Certain Employee Stock Ownership Plans*. Originally, SOP 76-3 was issued to guide accounting and reporting issues relevant to plan sponsors with ESOPs. One problem with the superseded SOP 76-3 is that certain significant financial facts, primarily ESOP-related debt, did not have to be reported on the plan sponsor's balance sheet; rather, the debt could be disclosed only in the footnotes.

  Since the issuance of SOP 76-3, the federal laws regulating ESOPs have changed several times. Those changes have had a direct impact on the way ESOPs operate and how they are structured. The dramatic growth in ESOPs (in excess of 10,000 plans today) and their increasing complexity created a need to revisit the accounting standard in light of this expanding environment.

- Major provisions of SOP 93-6 require that the financial reporting of the ESOP-related debt and the recognition of compensation expense (the fair value of the ESOP shares committed to be released to the plan participants in a period) remain separate entries. The ESOP-related debt is recorded on the balance sheet of the plan sponsor. This requirement holds as long as the plan sponsor has the primary responsibility of servicing the ESOP-related debt, which is typically the case. The major provisions of SOP 93-6 are as follows.

Leveraged ESOP

The most common application is the leveraged ESOP. The purchase of stock by the ESOP frequently results in the plan sponsor incurring debt, typically from a financial institution. The ESOP-related debt is recorded as a liability on the plan sponsor's balance sheet. The offsetting entry is a contraequity account: unearned ESOP shares (conceptually representing future compensation to ESOP participants of shares committed to be released).

Typical entry reporting initial ESOP transaction	
Credit ESOP-Related Debt (From Bank)	$XXX
Debit Unearned ESOP Shares	$XXX
(Contraequity Account)	

- The offsetting contraequity entry, unearned ESOP shares, is often a negative development for the financial statements of the plan sponsor. When ESOP-related debt is incurred, the reduction in recorded equity is often substantial and may even produce a negative net worth. This negative development is only temporary because the contraequity account will be reversed over time when the ESOP-related debt is repaid and compensation expense recognized.

— The mechanics of the reduction are more complex than the mere repayment of debt and are related to the recognition of compensation expense (the fair value of ESOP shares released from the suspense account).

— The repayment of plan debt reduces the ESOP-related debt account directly. The shares of stock purchased with the debt are held in an ESOP suspense account. unearned ESOP shares (conceptually the suspense account), similar to a collateral account. The suspense account is reduced as compensation expense is determined for the period. This reduction in the unearned ESOP shares account is separate from the dollar reduction of the ESOP-related debt.

— The compensation expense is determined by establishing the fair value of the stock committed to be released for the period. The determination of the fair value (the *fair value* of an ESOP share is the amount the seller could reasonably expect to receive between a willing buyer and willing seller, as defined in SOP 93-6) is most often a function of taking the average of the fair market value of the stock at the beginning and end of the period. The difference between the reduction in the ESOP-related debt and the unearned ESOP shares accounts (as a result of determining the compensation expense) is posted to paid-in capital. The unearned ESOP shares account is reduced by the actual cost to the ESOP of the shares committed to be released.

— We note that the preceding entries for reporting the ESOP transaction are for illustration purposes, and actual entries are typically more complex.

— The determination of fair market value, as defined by Revenue Ruling 59-60, must consider the book value of the business. Even though the book value of the business is often not the best indicator of fair market value, it is important to understand the reporting requirements of SOP 93-6.

Reporting ESOP-related debt assumes one of these forms:

○ Loan to the ESOP from an outside source (typically a bank) is reported as debt on the employer's balance sheet, as discussed. Interest expense is reported as a cost of the debt.

○ Internally leveraged ESOP should not report the loan on the employer's balance sheet.

Nonleveraged ESOPs may acquire stock in a number of ways, and the employer should report compensation cost equal to the contribution.

— Compensation cost should be the fair value of the shares contributed or committed.

Shares to the ESOP may be in several forms.

— Authorized but unissued
— Issued and outstanding shares
— Treasury stock

- If the employer declares dividends, the reporting of the dividends in relation to the ESOP is dependent on how the dividends are used. Dividends are typically reported as a reduction of debt, an interest expense, or compensation cost. The key point is deciding if the dividends are used to service debt or if they have been paid to plan participants. Dividends on allocated shares of stock are charged to retained earnings.
- The repurchase liability, as represented by the current value of the allocated shares, should be disclosed. The compensation cost for the period should also be disclosed.
- If earnings per share (EPS) are computed, the ESOP shares not committed for release are not considered outstanding for the purposes of the computation. Once the ESOP shares are committed, they are considered outstanding for the purposes of computing EPS.
  - We note that when the fair market value of stock of the plan sponsor is determined for ESOP valuation purposes, the price per share is typically computed based on all outstanding shares. Both allocated and unreleased shares are considered outstanding in the determination of a price per share.

Footnote Disclosure Under SOP 93-6

The general consensus of accounting authority recommends disclosure of the following information. Although this disclosure is related to dates established in SOP 93-6, most practitioners apply the reporting to shares acquired prior to 1993:

- Plan description, including the purpose, qualified status, contribution formula, and a description of the employer's securities held by the plan. Further, the number allocated, released, or committed to be released and unallocated shares should be disclosed.
- A description of the accounting policies followed for ESOP transactions.
- The amount of the compensation cost recognized during the period.
- ESOP loan description, including the terms, interest rate, and payment commitments.
- The number of allocated shares, committed-to-be-released shares, and suspense shares held by the ESOP at the balance sheet date. This disclosure should be made separately for shares accounted for under SOPs 93-6 and 76-3.
- The fair value of unearned ESOP shares at the balance sheet date at original cost for shares accounted for under SOP 76-3.
- Disclosure of the repurchase commitment on nontraded distributed shares. To the extent that shares have been put to the employer before the end of the fiscal year, the liability would have to be booked, not just footnoted. Under pre-1993 accounting authority, there was no requirement to record the projected repurchase liability, even if the amount was significant. Under SOP 93-6, repurchase liability is still not required to be recorded on the financial statements nor is any actuarial projection to be required for footnote disclosure. Instead, the footnote disclosure will require that the current value of any allocated shares be disclosed. For this purpose, *current value* means as of the most recent valuation date.

If you are providing an ESOP-based valuation, it is important that you become familiar with the reporting issues that are discussed in SOP 93-6. The conclusions in SOP 93-6 cover a wide range of topics on leveraged ESOPs, including reporting the purchase of shares by ESOPs, reporting the release of ESOP shares, the fair value of the ESOP shares, reporting dividends on ESOP shares, reporting redemptions of ESOP shares, reporting of debt and interest, computing EPS, and accounting for terminations.

SOP 93-6 also discusses nonleveraged ESOPs, pension reversion ESOPs, issues related to accounting for income taxes, and disclosures. The AICPA has also provided financial reporting guidance on other issues that have an impact on ESOP companies, although SOP 93-6 is the major pronouncement for closely held companies.

Financial Accounting Standards Board Accounting Standards Codification *480*

The Financial Accounting Standards Board (FASB) issued FASB *Accounting Standards Codification* (ASC) 480, *Distinguishing Liabilities from Equity*, in May 2003 to address significant accounting issues when there are mandatorily redeemable obligations, including stock that may be put back to the sponsor.

Other Reporting Considerations

Although most of the discussion on ESOPs is related to SOP 93-6, a number of other reporting issues may have an impact on ESOP transactions. Although it is beyond the scope of this book to discuss such matters with any detail, a number of accounting issues may have an impact on a more complete understanding of ESOP installations.

Readers may review FASB ASC 320, *Investments—Debt and Equity Securities*; FASB ASC 260, *Earnings Per Share*; and FASB ASC 805, *Business Combinations*.

The ESOP Association

The ESOP Association (EA) is the largest national, nonprofit association of companies with ESOPs and service providers with a professional commitment to ESOPs. The EA is an advocate for employee ownership and is located in Washington, D.C. The organization has many initiatives briefly summarized subsequently.

Employee Ownership Advocacy

The EA is the leading source for employee ownership. Located in Washington, D.C., its proximity to legislators has been instrumental in the passage of legislation favorable to ESOPs.

The mission of the EA is dedicated to educating its members and the American public about employee ownership and advocating the growth of employee ownership through ESOPs:

- The EA has been instrumental in numerous initiatives that have expanded tax incentives for the creation and maintenance of ESOPs. More recently, the organization played an integral role in securing the passage of favorable S corporation legislation.
- The EA sponsors the largest employee ownership conference in the nation each year in Las Vegas, NV. Another major annual conference is held each year in Washington, D.C. This event offers the opportunity for a wide range of employee-owned companies, along with their associates, professional service providers, and interested legislators, to meet and discuss the merits of employee ownership.

- The EA vision is as follows:

    We believe that employee ownership improves American competitiveness...that it increases productivity through greater employee participation in the workplace... that it strengthens our free enterprise economy and creates a broader distribution of wealth...and that it maximizes human potential by enhancing the self-worth, dignity, and well-being of our people.

    Therefore, we envision an America where employee ownership is widely recognized as a catalyst for economic prosperity...where the great majority of employees own stock in the companies where they work...and where employee ownership enables employees to share in the wealth they help to create.

    We look for our nation to become for all the world an example of prosperity with justice through employee ownership.

Networking—State Chapters, Conferences, and Meetings

The EA is dedicated to providing many opportunities for interested parties to meet and discuss the many facets of employee ownership. The following activities are representative of the many EA initiatives:

- Annual meeting in Washington, D.C. (typically the month of May each year).
- Annual two-day conference on technical issues (typically the month of November each year). Emphasis is on learning opportunities on the range of introductory to advanced ESOP-related topics. The largest technically oriented ESOP meeting in the nation.
- Local chapter meetings are supported throughout the nation. This infrastructure is intended to assist ESOP companies with an opportunity to meet with other employee owners on a cost-effective local basis. The local chapters typically hold periodic meetings to facilitate interaction between ESOP companies.
- Specialized seminars on a range of issues are periodically held, covering such topics as S corporation ESOPs, communications, employee-owner retreat, public and large employer seminars, and repurchase obligations.

Technical Support—Publications, Videos, Multimedia

The EA provides an ongoing library of employee ownership-related materials that encompass a wide range of topics. Many of the more significant pieces are specifically mentioned in chapter 11, "Practical Consideration and Employee Stock Ownership Plan Resources." A representative number of technical capabilities is listed subsequently:

- Publication of the monthly newsletter *ESOP Report*.
- Publication of the annual Membership Directory, the largest such publication listing a wide range of associates that comprise the ESOP community. This directory is noteworthy for such listings as ESOP companies by location and industry, professional service providers by specific discipline, the EA committees, and so on.

- Standing inventory of relevant materials for immediate sale, including books, periodicals, employee communication materials, video presentations, and other items.

Media and Research Services

The EA assists members with media requirements covering such things as getting media placement, working with reporters, writing press releases, assisting with internal communications, and providing insights on such items as company newsletters.

Committees and Organization

A number of committees are ongoing, including such representative areas as the Legislative and Regulatory Committee, the Valuation Committee, the Administration Committee, the Communications Committee, the Finance Committee, and the Public and Large Employer Section. Each of the local chapters is organized with officers.

Contact Information

The EA is located in the central part of Washington, D.C., and it encourages interested parties to call or visit its offices. You may contact it at the following address:

Mr. J. Michael Keeling, CAE
President

Ms. Lisa R. Betts, CAE
Vice President, Membership

The ESOP Association
1726 M Street, NW—Suite 501
Washington, D.C. 20036
(202) 293-2971
www.esopassociation.org

A special thanks is extended to the EA and its staff who have been very generous in their time and resources to help make this book possible.

National Center for Employee Ownership (NCEO)

The National Center for Employee Ownership (NCEO) was founded in 1981 to provide reliable, objective, and comprehensive information about employee ownership. It is a private nonprofit membership and information corporation. Its main emphasis is providing information on ESOPs, broadly granted employee stock options and related programs, and ownership culture.

The NCEO does not lobby. The services and information provided by the NCEO are very complimentary with those efforts of the EA.

Employee Ownership Communication

The NCEO does not lobby on behalf of employee ownership; rather, it provides the most extensive library of publications dealing with virtually every facet of employee ownership:

- NCEO publishes the *Issue Brief* series, a monthly journal that typically addresses one major topic each month in significant detail. The *Issue Brief* is well-researched, peer reviewed, and often considered an authoritative resource for the employee ownership community.
- Related to the *Issue Brief* series, the NCEO publishes a number of excellent books and publications on a wide range of issues relating to employee ownership. The source for many of the titles are features in the *Issue Brief* series.
- The NCEO publishes the periodical *Employee Ownership Report* that appears on a bimonthly basis. The *Employee Ownership Report* features a wide range of topics, such as legal cases, legislative updates, original research, and significant events.

Technical Support—Publications and Videos

The NCEO provides a standing inventory of relevant materials for immediate sale, including books, periodicals, employee communication materials, and research reports.

Networking—Conferences, Seminars, and Meetings

The NCEO is dedicated to providing many opportunities for interested parties to meet and discuss the many facets of employee ownership. The following activities are representative of the many NCEO initiatives:

- Annual meeting with a new location each year (typically the month of April). This meeting is not held in the same location, so that the widest range of NCEO members will have the chance to attend a conference when it is in a region.
- Numerous employee ownership workshops are conducted throughout the country. Broad-based mailings are sent to business owners and other interested parties, introducing them to these workshops to learn more about primarily ESOPs. Workshop topics range from introductory topics on ESOPs to more advanced issues, such as stock options.

Research and Academic Support

The NCEO has supported a number of scholarly and academic studies related to employee ownership. A number of representative works is as follows:

- *A Statistical Profile of Employee Ownership*
- *Selling Your Business to an ESOP*
- *The Decision-Maker's Guide to Equity Compensation*
- *Executive Compensation in ESOP Companies*
- *The ESOP Communications Sourcebook*
- *ESOPs and Corporate Governance*
- *Wealth and Income Consequences of Employee Ownership*, University of Washington

Contact Information

The NCEO is located in Oakland, CA, and it encourages interested parties to call or visit its offices. You may contact it at the following address:

Mr. Loren Rodgers
Executive Director
National Center for Employee Ownership
1736 Franklin Street, 8th Floor
Oakland, CA 94612-3445
(510) 208-1300
www.nceo.org

A special thanks is extended to the NCEO and its staff who have been very generous in their time and resources to help make this book possible.

Ohio Employee Ownership Center

The Ohio Employee Ownership Center (OEOC) was founded in 1987 by Dr. John Logue, professor of political science at Kent State University. The OEOC is a nonprofit outreach center of Kent State University and actively supports the development of employee ownership of business throughout the Midwest, the nation, and internationally. The OEOC's work rests on the principle that broader ownership of productive assets is a good thing for employees, communities, and our economy. The OEOC has been proactive, working directly with privately held companies with succession planning, particularly when employee ownership is involved. The impact of the OEOC is immediately realized by the fact that Ohio has one of the largest number of ESOP companies in the country.

The Cooperative Development Center at Kent State University is one of the few places that is organized, knowledgeable, and promotes employee cooperatives. Mr. Roy Messing is the contact at the OEOC regarding the Cooperative Development Center. The OEOC publication *Solidarity as a Business Model: A Multi-Stakeholder Cooperatives Manual* is particularly noteworthy and worth the read for those with an interest in the topic. Contact information for the OEOC is as follows:

Mr. William McIntyre, CPA
Director
Ohio Employee Ownership Center
113 McGilvrey Hall
Kent State University
Kent, OH 44242
(330) 672-3028
www.oeockent.org

Appendix 2A—IRS Form 5309, *Application for Determination of Employee Stock Ownership Plan*

Form **5309** (Rev. January 2012) Department of the Treasury Internal Revenue Service	**Application for Determination of Employee Stock Ownership Plan** (Under section 4975(e)(7) of the Internal Revenue Code) ▶ Attach to Form 5300.	OMB No. 1545-0284 For IRS Use Only

1   Name of plan sponsor (employer if single-employer plan)

2   Employer identification number (EIN)   **3**   Plan number

All Plans (Complete lines 4a through 4k.)

Yes   No

4a ☐ ☐   Is the plan designated as an employee stock ownership plan (ESOP) within the meaning of section 4975(e)(7)?

b ☐ ☐   Is the plan designed to invest primarily in employer securities as defined in section 409(l)?

c ☐ ☐   Is each participant or beneficiary entitled to direct the plan to vote the allocated securities as required by section 409(e)?

d ☐ ☐   Does the plan provide that each participant who is entitled to a distribution from the plan has a right to demand that the benefit be distributed in the form of employer securities?

If the answer to d is "No," please answer the following questions:

(i) ☐ ☐   If the charter or bylaws of the corporation restrict substantially all outstanding stock ownership to employees or to a 401(a) trust, does the plan provide that participants are entitled to receive distributions in cash, except that such plan may distribute employer securities subject to a requirement that such securities may be resold to the employer under a fair valuation formula? (See section 409(h)(2))

(ii) ☐ ☐   If the plan is maintained by an S corporation, does the plan provide that participants are entitled to receive distributions in cash, except that such plan may distribute employer securities subject to a requirement that such securities may be resold to the employer under a fair valuation formula? (See section 409(h)(2))

e ☐ ☐   If the plan is established and maintained by a bank which is legally prohibited from redeeming or purchasing its stock, does the plan provide that participants are entitled to receive distributions in cash? (See section 409(h)(3))

f ☐ ☐   If the trust makes a distribution in stock and the securities are not readily tradable on an established market, can the participant require the employer to repurchase the securities under a fair valuation formula within the time frames prescribed by law? (See section 409(h)(1)(B))

g ☐ ☐   If the plan holds employer securities consisting of stock in an S corporation, does the plan provide that no portion of the assets of the plan attributable to (or allocable in lieu of) such employer securities may, during a nonallocation year, accrue (or be allocated directly or indirectly under any section 401(a) plan of the employer) for the benefit of any disqualified person? (See section 409(p))

h ☐ ☐   Does the plan provide that a qualified participant may elect to diversify a portion of his or her account investment in employer securities, as described in section 401(a)(28)(B)?

If the answer to h is "No," please answer the following question:

(i) ☐ ☐   Does the plan provide that an applicable individual may elect to diversify a portion of his or her account investment in employer securities as described in section 401(a)(35)?

i ☐ ☐   With respect to activities that are carried on by the plan, are all valuations of employer securities acquired after December 31, 1986, which are not readily tradable on an established securities market, made by an independent appraiser? (See section 401(a)(28)(C))

For Paperwork Reduction Act Notice, see instructions.   Cat. No. 11835F   Form **5309** (Rev. 1-2012)

Yes   No

j ☐ ☐ Does the plan provide that a participant may begin receiving a distribution of his or her account that is attributable to employer securities after the participant has separated from service upon reaching normal retirement age, or after death, disability, or other separation from service, within the time frames specified in section 409(o)?

k ☐ ☐ If the plan is maintained by a C corporation, does the plan provide that the assets of the plan attributable to (or allocable in lieu of) employer securities acquired by the plan in a sale to which section 1042 applies cannot accrue (or be allocated directly or indirectly under any section 401(a) plan of the employer) for the benefit of persons specified in section 409(n) during the nonallocation period?

Plans Applying Under Section 4975(d)(3) and Regulations Section 54.4975-7 (Leveraged ESOPs) (Complete lines 5a through 5g.)

5a ☐ ☐ Does the plan provide that the exempt loan proceeds must be used within a reasonable time to acquire qualifying employer securities, repay such loan, or repay a prior loan as required under Regulations section 54.4975-7(b)(4)?

b ☐ ☐ Does the plan provide for the establishment and maintenance of a suspense account as required under Regulations section 54.4975-11(c)?

c ☐ ☐ Does the plan provide that the collateral must be limited to qualifying employer securities purchased with such exempt loan or qualifying employer securities used as collateral on a prior exempt loan repaid with the proceeds of the current exempt loan as required under Regulations section 54.4975-7(b)(5)?

d ☐ ☐ Does the plan provide that no person entitled to payment under an exempt loan shall have any right to assets of the ESOP other than collateral given for such loan, contributions (other than contributions of employer securities) made to repay such exempt loan, and earnings attributable to such collateral and the investment of such contributions as required under Regulations section 54.4975-7(b)(5)?

e ☐ ☐ Does the plan provide that payments made with respect to an exempt loan by the ESOP during the year must not exceed an amount equal to the sum of contributions and earnings received during or prior to such year less such payments in prior years as required under Regulations section 54.4975-7(b)(5)?

f ☐ ☐ Do plan terms provide that qualifying employer securities will be forfeited only after other assets as required under Regulations section 54.4975-11(d)(4)?

g ☐ ☐ Does the plan provide that the protections and rights provided to participants and beneficiaries with respect to employer securities are nonterminable as required in Regulations section 54.4975-11(a)(3)(i) and (ii)?

Under penalties of perjury, I declare that I have examined this application, including accompanying statements and schedules, and to the best of my knowledge and belief, it is true, correct, and complete.

SIGN HERE ▶ _____   **Date ▶** _____

Type or print name

Type or print title

Form **5309** (Rev. 1-2012)

What's New

The IRS has created a page on IRS.gov for information about Form 5309 and its instructions, at *www.irs.gov/form5309*. Information about any recent developments affecting Form 5309 will be posted on that page.

General Information

Section references are to the Internal Revenue Code unless otherwise noted.

Use this form to apply for a determination letter for an employee stock ownership plan (ESOP) that meets the requirements of section 4975(e)(7). Attach Form 5309 to Form 5300, Application for Determination for Employee Benefit Plan.

The plan you establish must be designed to invest primarily in employer securities. For a definition of employer securities and how it applies to your plan, see section 409(l) or section 4975(e)(8). Also see Regulations section 54.4975-11 for the formal plan requirements of an ESOP.

More information. For more information about the latest developments on Form 5309 and its instructions, go to *www.irs.gov/ form5309.*

General Instructions

A Change To Note

The questions with regard to tax credit ESOPs have been deleted. If your plan involves such a plan, please state so in the cover letter and refer to Regulations section 1.46-8(d) for the formal requirements of a tax credit ESOP. The question relating to type of plan has been deleted from the form.

Who May File

1. Any corporate employer who has established an ESOP intended to meet the requirements under section 4975(e)(7).

2. Any corporate employer who amends an ESOP under section 4975(e)(7).

An S corporation-sponsored ESOP must provide that no prohibited allocation of employer stock may be made to a disqualified person for a nonallocation year. This applies to all plan years beginning on or after January 1, 2005. This applies to plan years ending after March 14, 2001, if:

1. The ESOP was established after March 14, 2001, or

2. The ESOP was established on or before March 14, 2001, if the employer maintaining the ESOP had not made an S-corporation election in effect on such date.

How To Complete the Application

• If a number is requested, a number must be entered.

• If an item provides a box to check, written responses are not acceptable.

• The application has formatted fields that will limit the number of characters entered per field.

• All data input will need to be entered in Courier 10 point font.

• Alpha characters should be entered in all capital letters.

• Enter spaces between any words. Spaces do not count as characters.

What To File

To receive a determination on whether a plan, initially or as a result of a plan amendment, meets the requirements of section 4975(e)(7), submit Form 5309, Form 5300, and a copy of all documents and statements required by those forms. Attach the completed Form 5309 to Form 5300.

Signature

Form 5309 must be signed by the principal officer authorized to sign.

Note. Stamped signatures are not acceptable; see Rev. Proc. 2012-4, 2012-1 I.R.B. 125, at *www.irs.gov/ pub/irs-irbs/irb12-01.pdf.*

Paperwork Reduction Act Notice. We ask for the information on this form to determine whether you meet the legal requirements for the plan approval you request. Your filing of this information is only required if you wish the IRS to determine if your plan qualifies under section 4975(e)(7).

You are not required to provide the information requested on a form that is subject to the Paperwork Reduction Act unless the form displays a valid OMB control number. Books or records relating to a form or its instructions must be retained as long as their contents may become material in the administration of any Internal Revenue law. Generally, tax returns and return information are confidential, as required by section 6103.

The time needed to complete and file this form will vary depending on individual circumstances. The estimated average time is:

Recordkeeping . . 6 hr., 13 min.

Learning about the law or the form . . 2 hr., 10 min.

Preparing and sending the form to the IRS . . . . . 2 hr., 22 min.

If you have comments concerning the accuracy of these time estimates or suggestions for making this form simpler, we would be happy to hear from you. You can write to the Internal Revenue Service, Tax Products Coordinating Committee, SE:W:CAR:MP:T:M:S, 1111 Constitution Ave. NW, IR-6526, Washington, DC 20224.

Chapter 3

Employee Stock Ownership Plan Transaction Mechanics

This chapter will introduce the most common features of employee stock ownership plan (ESOP) installations relevant to this book. An understanding of these mechanics is helpful in gaining a fuller appreciation of the issues relating to ESOP valuations.

Note: Beginning for fiscal years commencing on or after January 1, 1998, S corporations may have an ESOP. This significantly increases the options for companies that are considering an ESOP. When appropriate, distinctions between S and C corporations are noted. Unless there is a specific reference, it is generally the case that the comments apply to both corporate elections.

Traditional Uses of an ESOP

There are a number of time-honored applications of ESOPs for closely held companies. Due to the significant tax incentives associated with ESOPs, many of the most common applications involve optimizing the tax incentives that exist. Several traditional uses of an ESOP are subsequently listed.

Provide Liquidity and Diversification for Shareholders

Typically, older shareholders wishing to retire may sell all or a portion of their stock to the ESOP. Selling stock to the ESOP is often a preferred option, rather than selling to a third party that may not continue operating the company in the historical manner or same geographical area.

The ESOP may also be used to provide liquidity for other shareholders, typically minority owners. These minority shareholders are often inactive members of a family who acquired the stock through gifts or estates. The ESOP provides a means of converting stock in an illiquid closely held company to another more liquid investment.

Provide a Means of Capital Formation

A plan sponsor may contribute stock to an ESOP and thereby take a deduction for the fair market value of the stock contributed to the plan. This tax deduction provides an expense without a corresponding cash outlay.

The tax savings of this "paper" transaction stay in the company and become part of the equity of the company. The tax savings are typically computed as the ESOP contribution multiplied by the marginal tax rate of the company. When marginal tax rates are approximately 40 percent (combined federal and state), the tax savings are significant, as expressed in the following example:

ESOP contribution (fair market value of contributed stock, compensation expense)	$100,000
Marginal tax rate estimated at 40%	× 0.40
Tax savings—increase in equity	$40,000

Finance Corporate Acquisitions

An ESOP may be creatively used to acquire another company with pretax dollars. The company may also use the ESOP to acquire such things as equipment and facilities using pretax dollars.

An Incentive to Increase Employee Productivity and Retain Personnel

Studies have demonstrated that employees are more productive when they understand they have a direct vested interest in the success of the company. Providing an ESOP and communicating the benefits of employee ownership are typically a winning combination that increases the sales and profitability of the employer.

- As the markets become more competitive, employers often understand that it is increasingly difficult to retain the best employees. Employers install ESOPs with the purpose of providing a vested interest among the employees in the financial outcome of the company.

- When associates are respected and treated as owners, many companies discover that turnover significantly decreases. This is particularly important when employees possess a high level of skills.
- One creative CPA firm, Saltz, Shamis & Goldfarb, adopted an ESOP for all its professional associates. Providing an equity interest in the firm was extended to all members on the professional staff, not just a limited number of partners. For more information, please read the article "A Piece of the Action" in the August 1996 issue of the *Journal of Accountancy*.

Provide a Succession Plan

The ESOP is used as part of an overall succession plan to pass control of a company to the next generation of managers and employees. If the ESOP uses debt to acquire the stock in the company, both the interest on the loan and the debt principal are deductible for tax purposes. This tax saving, deducting debt principal, is often significant. It means that the company may pass to the next generation of owners using pretax dollars, not after tax dollars.

Provide Liquidity in Divorce Situations

The traditional use for an ESOP is an exit vehicle for a shareholder typically facing such things as either retirement or a significant lessening of involvement in the business. This application may be invoked during a divorce when one of the major assets in the family is a closely held business. Divorce situations involving closely held companies often become highly complicated and very emotional.

The consideration of an ESOP under such circumstances may be a viable alternative for the parties to consider. An equity interest in the business is sold to an ESOP tax free, and liquidity is raised for settlement purposes. If debt is incurred to purchase the stock, the debt will be repaid with pretax dollars because the contributions to the ESOP within payroll limits are deductible.

If an ESOP is installed, the employees of the company gain an equity interest in the business. Under such potential circumstances, it is hoped that the potential ESOP is still installed with the spirit of providing the employees with a benefit that will ultimately be beneficial for all parties.

Provide Negotiating Leverage for Any Proposed Transaction

Typically, if business owners are considering transition options, they will be in a stronger negotiating position if options exist. An ESOP is not necessarily the best option for many potential applications for any number of good reasons. However, knowledge of a potential ESOP will frequently enhance negotiating positions. The consideration of an ESOP is almost always an option that is controlled by the controlling shareholder(s) of a company.

If an ESOP is to be considered under such circumstances, it is important to underscore that the standard of value for a potential ESOP transaction is fair market value (as defined by the IRS) and adequate consideration (as defined by the Department of Labor).

Summary

The statutes related to the creation of ESOPs provide for a wide range of flexible options for employers. Once the goals are determined, and they are compatible with the requirements of an ESOP, it is very likely that an ESOP may be designed and installed to achieve those goals. The preceding examples only indicate the most common ESOP applications. A skilled professional experienced in the design of ESOPs will be knowledgeable on a far wider range of applications.

Alternatives to an ESOP

The overall strength of an ESOP is often related to shareholders understanding what options exist. Typically, an ESOP is an integral part of a shareholder transition strategy. The transition is from the current shareholder(s) to a successor team.

Sell or Transition the Business to Family Members

This is often the wish of owners in a closely held business. If family members exist to assume the ownership of the business, this is often the preferred option. In many cases, there are complications in that the family member candidates are not direct lineal descendants, such as a son or daughter.

Family members may assume a broader context, including such individuals as son-in-law, daughter-in-law, brother, sister, cousin, grandchildren, and so on. As the relationship becomes more distant, the issues typically become more complex. Family transition plans with close relatives often involve such time-honored tax strategies as gifting, selling, or passing equity interests under more conservative economic and financial assumptions. When there is some distance in the relationship, an arm's-length relationship may evolve. Under such circumstances, passing an equity interest without the tax incentives of an ESOP becomes far more costly after taxes have been considered.

Sell to Management or Key Employees

This option often has strong emotional appeal to shareholders. Typically, a limited number of key employees have disproportionately contributed to the success of the business. Such contributions, loyalty, and commitment may be rewarded with the opportunity to acquire a portion or all of the business. In many instances, such candidates do not typically have the personal resources to acquire the equity interest in the business. If the key employees require financial assistance, the relatively unfavorable tax climate for passing the equity interest from the shareholders to the success team must be considered.

Sell or Merge With a Third Party — Financial Buyer

This is often an exceeding difficult task. Financial buyers may have investment dollars they are willing to extend for an opportunity, but they typically have very high financial expectations for the investments they make. Most closely held companies fall short of such financial expectations; therefore, this is a limited option. Unfavorable taxes also hurt this as an option.

Financial buyers often have a very limited time period of interest and expected ownership, typically only from three to five years. In such instances, the business will be sold again, accompanied by significant debt.

Sell or Merge With a Third Party—Strategic or Investment Buyer

This is more common, but such transactions are still very difficult to complete. The significant problem for most company owners is revealing too much confidential information to competitors. Competitors are most typically the potential investors with the requisite knowledge and financial resources to purchase the company. The most common fear is that the competitor will gain the confidential insights into the target company, and the deal will fail to be completed. Such confidential knowledge could easily be turned against the shareholder, even if there is a confidentiality agreement. There is also the very real risk of key employees learning that the company is being shopped. Confidentiality is always a challenge to maintain, but when a competitor is involved, the challenge is that more daunting.

Sell Stock Through an Initial Public Offering

Yes, this is an option, but the journey and requirements are so onerous that it is not a viable consideration for virtually most closely held companies. The public markets have very high expectations for initial public offerings (IPOs). Such considerations as disclosure requirements, audited financial statements, projections, and professional fees are very expensive, intrusive, and negative. Most investors do not look favorably upon an IPO as an exit strategy for current shareholders. Typically, in an IPO, not more than 30 percent of the offering may be shares owned by existing shareholders. Public markets prefer to find companies that need the financial strength of such markets to grow the business and take advantage of market opportunities.

Liquidate the Business

This option in not very common due to very unfavorable tax consequences in most instances. On occasion, this option may be the best alternative. The circumstances under such a scenario are often extreme because most companies are worth far more as a going concern. One instance of liquidation being the best choice is when the underlying assets of the business have considerable value not really related to the core business. An example is a marginal business with a long stretch of prime waterfront property owned by the company. The land may be far more valuable than the operating company, and liquidation may be the best option.

Summary

The transition journey for shareholders in a closely held company is a harrowing and an emotional experience. For many owners, it is a career-defining event. There are a myriad of options and alternatives to consider. The sheer number of considerations is often enough to discourage business owners to the point where literally nothing is completed. There are some exceptional opportunities for professional advisers to provide highly valuable services to business owners regarding transition options.

Integral to virtually all the options are the tax consequences of any decision. Knowing the tax consequences of the various options, in part, helps business owners successfully chart a transition strategy.

Basic Features of ESOPs

Operating Considerations of an ESOP

The following items in this category are intended to highlight a number of important factors surrounding the installation of an ESOP. The orientation is general and not an exhaustive listing of all considerations because such a goal is beyond the scope of this work.

ESOPs are Qualified Defined Contribution Employee Benefit Plans

An ESOP is a tax qualified defined contribution employee benefit plan intended to be primarily invested in the securities of the employer. An ESOP must meet the requirements of Internal Revenue Code (IRC) Sections 401(a) and 4975(e)(7). The employer is also referred to as the plan sponsor. An ESOP is tax qualified, which means that certain rules have been adopted by the plan that are intended to protect the interests of the plan participants. In return for the adoption of protective rules, the ESOP receives certain tax benefits.

ESOPs are Intended to be Primarily Invested Company Securities

Clearly, the intent of an ESOP, according to the Employee Retirement Income Security Act of 1974 (ERISA), is to be a vehicle that provides an equity interest to employees in the securities of their employer. There is no precise definition of what is meant by the term *primarily invested*, but the general understanding is that an ESOP will have more than 50 percent of its assets invested in the stock of the employer. Often, an ESOP in a closely held company is substantially invested in the securities of the company.

From a practical standpoint, most ESOPs in closely held companies invest in the common stock of the employer, although an ESOP may own preferred stock that is convertible into common stock. There are circumstances when having convertible preferred stock is beneficial because of the dividends. The ESOP may only hold the class of stock with the highest voting, dividend, and liquidation rights. Unlike other qualified employee benefit plans, only an ESOP may borrow money from the company, shareholders, or other disqualified persons to acquire company stock.

- ERISA added the provision that the ESOP is a stock bonus plan intended to be invested in the securities of the employer. The stock bonus plan is similar to other qualified profit sharing plans, with the additional provision that distributions may be in the stock of the employer. ERISA permits both leveraged and nonleveraged ESOPs, indicating the anticipation that the percentage of employer stock in the ESOP may range from a nominal amount to 100 percent. Prior to 2002, some ESOPs added a money purchase plan in order to increase deduction limits. Recently expanded contribution limits no longer make this strategy necessary.

- ESOPs, like all individual retirement account plans, are exempted from the rule that generally prohibits a qualified plan from owning more than 10 percent of the fair market value of the assets in the plan in employer securities (see ERISA Section 407b]).
- Employer securities are defined in IRC Section 409(1). In this book, we are concerned with the employer securities that are not publicly traded on an established market. The stock in a closely held company that is sold to an ESOP must have voting and dividend rights that are equal to or exceed that of the common stock of the plan sponsor having the greatest voting and dividend rights.

A Legal Entity, the Employee Stock Ownership Trust, Must be Created

We carefully make the distinction between the employee stock ownership trust (ESOT) and the ESOP. The ESOT is the legal entity that will eventually own stock for the beneficial interest of the plan participants, and it governs the trustee. The ESOP is the document that provides instructions to the ESOP administrator on managing the assets for the benefit of the plan participants, although ERISA states that the plan is to be treated as an entity. To establish an ESOP, the employer must first create an ESOT, according to ERISA Section 403(a).

The ESOT is funded for a closely held company typically by any one of several methods to acquire company stock.

Common Funding Methods for an ESOP

Once the legal entity is created, assets are initially contributed to the ESOP at some point. The ESOP is intended to be primarily invested in the stock of the plan sponsor, so most assets are eventually intended to be employer stock. The assets may originate from a number of sources, with the most typical subsequently listed:

- *Cash.* Cash may be contributed to the ESOP by the company to purchase stock. A common strategy with ESOP installations is to contribute cash (or a "prefund") to the ESOP for a period of time prior to selling stock. Prefunding in this manner enables the ESOP to purchase stock with a reduced reliance on debt. If shareholders are debt resistant, this is an excellent strategy. The company will receive a tax deduction for the cash it contributes to the ESOP.
- *Contribute company stock.* Stock may be directly contributed to the ESOP. The company will receive a tax deduction for the fair market value of the stock contributed. Companies will consider this strategy because a tax deduction is gained for the stock contributed, but there is no outflow of cash. Instead, cash will be conserved due to the tax deduction for a noncash expense. The disadvantage is dilution to existing shareholders because more stock is outstanding and the future repurchase obligation.

- *Incur debt.* The ESOP is authorized to borrow money for the purpose of purchasing employer stock. An ESOP is specifically exempted from the general ERISA rules barring a qualified retirement plan from borrowing money to purchase stock of the employer. The ESOP may borrow the money, but it may only provide the stock it is buying and earnings on the stock as collateral for the bank debt to the extent it is not allocated.

- *Employees rarely purchase stock directly.* As a general rule, in closely held companies, the ESOP is an employer-provided benefit. Employees are typically not permitted to purchase stock in the ESOP (unlike some public companies that encourage stock purchases in qualified retirement plans). The reason for the prohibition is that closely held companies wish to avoid securities laws and the applicable onerous disclosure requirements if the employees became investors and purchased the stock directly. If the employees purchased stock, they become actual shareholders. The legal rights of shareholders are likely to be greatly expanded beyond the rights of ESOP participants (when legal rights of the participants, not the ESOP, are deliberately restricted).

- *Sources of employer stock for the ESOP.* Stock in the ESOP will come from one of three traditional sources, and each source has its own merits. Most commonly, stock is sold to the ESOP from a shareholder. No new shares of stock are created, and there is no dilution regarding outstanding shares. If newly issued stock or treasury stock is issued, the number of shares outstanding increases, and there is dilution. The three sources are as follows:
  - Newly issued stock
  - Treasury stock
  - Outstanding stock (typically owned by an individual)

Stock Ownership

The ESOT actually owns the shares for the benefit of the plan participants. The trustee buys, sells, and holds shares for the plan participants. The plan participants do not actually own the stock as ESOP members.

Upon leaving the ESOP, federal statutes allow the ESOP participant the option of taking either cash or stock as settlement of the account balance. The ESOP participant may put his stock back to the company, and the company has to purchase the stock. The company may either direct the trustee to purchase the stock back into the ESOP or redeem the stock to its treasury.

Generally, closely held companies do not want any former ESOP participants with company stock because the potential rights of minority shareholders may invite unintended and potentially very negative consequences.

Prior to the ESOP installation, most companies amend the articles of incorporation or bylaws to restrict stock ownership in the company to employees and the ESOP. This effectively eliminates the option granted to ESOP participants to gain company stock directly. The practical application is that the company will be able to call the stock in an ESOP account and remit the balance in cash. Also, S corporations may prevent stock from being owned directly by former employees, even without a restriction in the articles of incorporation or bylaws.

Voting Rights

The voting rights of the stock in the ESOP are generally exercised by the plan trustee acting as a fiduciary. Certain major corporate actions, such as the sale of the company, require a pass-through vote to the plan participants. Plan participants may direct the trustee on how to vote shares of stock allocated to their account, and the trustee generally votes unallocated shares of stock in the plan. IRC Section 409(1) states that the stock owned by the ESOP must have the greatest voting and dividend rights. Many times, the company's board of directors will direct the voting by the trustee.

Multiple Qualified Benefit Plans

ESOP companies often have multiple benefit plans. The most common situation is that the company has separate stand-alone plans, such as an ESOP and a 401(k) plan. The plans are separate, but the plans in total are subject to overall payroll limits for both company and employee contributions. The ESOP is primarily invested in the company stock (not well diversified), and the 401(k) plan often provides a wide range of diversification options. The combination of the two provides employees with a more comprehensive retirement program.

- An ESOP may actually be legally combined with another qualified benefit plan. One common example is an ESOP combined with a 401(k) plan (often referred to as a KSOP). Although this is technically possible, most applications are with publicly held companies or very large closely held companies.
- Potential combinations require the careful review of experienced legal counsel. There may be significant personal liabilities and penalties to the plan fiduciary if a combination subsequently proves to be a financial disaster.

Tax Incentives Related to ESOPs

This section will consider the tax environment relating to ESOPs in both C corporations and S corporations). It is emphasized that there are a number of different tax considerations, and they do not equally apply to C and S corporations. The major tax issues will be discussed in this section. Illustrations of the tax statutes will be provided in chapters 4, "Employee Stock Ownership Plan Transactions and C Corporations," and 5, "Employee Stock Ownership Plan Transactions and S Corporations."

ESOP legislation often makes the distinction between a plan sponsor that is either a C corporation or an S corporation. As the following sections illustrate, a number of tax-related issues must be carefully monitored for applicability to a client, depending on the corporate tax election. This section briefly lists a limited number of major corporate attributes that may have an impact in the installation of an ESOP.

Major C Corporation Attributes

- Potential multiple classes of stock provide enhanced planning flexibility. Different classes of stock with varying dividend preferences and voting rights may be available to meet the requirements of the company.
- Unlimited number of shareholders.
- No limitations on the types of shareholders permitted. There is no chance of voiding a tax election as in the case of an S corporation.
- Potential use of dividends on allocated and unallocated ESOP-owned stock for ESOP acquisition debt.
- Corporation pays income taxes. This is potentially a significant disadvantage if the company is subsequently sold, often resulting in double taxation to selling shareholders in asset sales.

Major S Corporation Attributes

- Limited to a single class of stock (only voting rights may vary). All shareholders, correspondingly, are treated similarly with regard to such things as S corporation dividends.
- Total shareholders limited to 100 (ESOP counts as a single shareholder, and a husband and wife count as a single shareholder).
- Many restrictions on the types of shareholders. Care must be taken to avoid inadvertent termination of an S election. A trust for an employee qualified benefit plan may be a shareholder (such as an ESOP) but not an IRA. Momentary ownership by an IRA, however, may be acceptable under certain circumstances.
- The company may make distributions (dividends), but only distributions on unallocated stock may be used to repay ESOP-related debt.
- Corporation pays no income taxes, income passed through to shareholders. Having the income tax liability passed through to the shareholders may be very positive in the case of a company with a high percentage of its stock in an ESOP because an ESOP is a qualified plan and exempt from income taxes. Some exceptions are to be noted regarding S corporation taxes, including built-in gain tax; last in, first out reserve recapture; and a tax on excessive passive income.

Contributions to an ESOP Are Tax Deductible Within Statutory Limits

Participants in an ESOP acquire an equity interest in the plan sponsor with tax-deductible contributions. This is a significant tax incentive, particularly when the ESOP borrows funds to purchase stock from a selling shareholder. Debt principal payments are typically not deductible for federal income tax purposes. Debt principal payments for virtually all transactions except ESOPs must be made with after-tax funds.

ESOP-Related Debt Principal Becomes Tax Deductible

Assuming the ESOP borrows funds to purchase stock, the company makes a contribution to the ESOP in an amount to amortize the debt principal and pay the interest expense within statutory limits. This has the practical effect of making the ESOP-related debt principal and interest tax deductible.

Tax Deductible Contributions to the ESOP in a C Corporation

Periodic contributions to an ESOP are tax deductible within established limits set by statute. Those contributions may be made in either cash or stock, subject, for example, to certain specified payroll limitations, such as those that may apply to contributions allocated to the accounts of highly compensated employees under certain circumstances. Generally, the ESOP contribution and allocation limits are found in IRC Sections 404 and 415.

- *All qualifying contributions to the ESOP are tax deductible.* If the ESOP uses the contributions for the repayment of ESOP-related debt, then the employer has, in effect, made the debt principal a tax deduction. Debt is repaid with pretax dollars, a significant saving considering the effective tax rate.
- *Twenty-five percent contribution limit.* For years after 2001, the maximum deductible contribution is 25 percent of IRC Section 404 qualifying annual payroll, subject to a number of limitations. Based on the Economic Growth and Tax Relief Reconciliation Act of 2001 (EGTRRA), the 25 percent limit will not apply to a participant's deferral contributions to a 401(k) plan, for purposes of IRC Section 404, but will apply for IRC Section 415. The EGTRRA increases the IRC Section 401(a)(17) cap on compensation that may be included for all qualified plan purposes to $250,000 in 2012 and indexes the cap in $5,000 increments. The total annual addition limit (which includes such things as forfeitures) is the lesser of 100 percent of qualifying pay or $50,000 in 2012, and this amount will be indexed in increments of $1,000, according to IRC Section 415(c)(1).
  - This amount may be used for prefunding the ESOP or repaying ESOP-related debt.
  - This contribution limit does not include interest expense on ESOP-related obligations. This is a significant advantage for leveraged ESOPs because the entire ESOP-related interest expense is deductible without regard to the 25 percent contribution limit.

Example 3-1   Sample Computation for a C Corporation

Qualifying payroll	$2,000,000
Payroll contribution limit 25% (0.25 x $2,000,000)	$500,000
ESOP-related note (with 5-year amortization)	$2,500,000
Interest rate 8% (interest expense first year 0.08 x $2,500,000)	$200,000
Total deduction for the company first year	
Debt amortization (just happens to be 25% of payroll)	$500,000
Interest expense	<u>200,000</u>
Total deduction	$700,000
Actual employee share of contribution ($700,000/$2,000,000)	35%

In this case, the actual economic benefit to the employees is the value of the stock allocated as a result of the contribution. In total, the contribution percentage is 35 percent of qualifying payroll. In a subsequent chapter, the use of dividends illustrates that an even higher percentage of economic benefit may be possible. As the debt is repaid, the economic benefit, expressed as a percentage, will decline significantly.

- *Allocation limit increased.* There is a difference between the contribution amount and the allocation amount (which includes participant forfeitures). Under the EGTRRA, allocation amounts have been significantly expanded for all qualified retirement plans, including ESOPs. The limits for allocation amounts as of 2012 are the lesser of $50,000 or 100 percent of the participant's salary. The dollar amount will be indexed to inflation in the future in $1,000 increments, per IRC Section 415(c)(1). For an ESOP that is leveraged, the higher allocation limits are a tremendous benefit in long-term planning.
  - Prior to the EGTRRA the rules regarding ESOP contributions to a C corporation were more complex. Briefly, the payroll contribution limit was 15 percent of qualifying payroll with an unleveraged ESOP. If the ESOP borrowed money (becoming leveraged), the qualifying payroll percentage jumped to 25 percent plus interest. Planning could become complex if a company wanted the 25 percent payroll limit during a prefunding phase because the ESOP could be combined with a money purchase pension plan, thereby increasing the limit to 25 percent.
- *401(k) contributions by employee do not count against ESOP contribution limits.* Under the EGTRRA, 401(k) employee deferral contributions are not counted against the ESOP contribution limits under IRC Section 404, but they do count against IRC Section 415 limitations. This is a significant benefit because it permits leveraged ESOPs to

offer employees the benefit of the employee ownership (a nondiversified investment) and another retirement plan with diversified investment options.

- *Excess contributions.* If the employer contributes more than what may be deducted, it is subject to a 10 percent excise tax on the excess amount, per IRC Section 4972.
- *Excess allocations.* If the employer contributes more than what may be allocated to plan participants' accounts, the plan may be subject to disqualification.

Tax Deductible Contributions to the ESOP in an S Corporation

Periodic contributions to an ESOP are tax deductible within established limits set by statutes. Those contributions may be made in either cash or stock. Such contribution levels are subject to certain specified payroll limitations. Many contribution issues are the same as with C corporations, but there are a number of key distinctions, especially the treatment of interest expense on an ESOP loan.

- *All qualifying contributions to the ESOP are tax deductible.* If the ESOP uses the contributions for the repayment of ESOP-related debt, then the employer has, in effect, made the debt principal a tax deduction. Debt is repaid with pretax dollars, a significant saving considering the effective tax rate.
- *Twenty-five percent contribution limit.* The maximum deductible contribution is 25 percent of IRC Section 404 qualifying annual payroll, subject to a number of limitations. Based on the EGTRRA, the 25 percent limit of IRC Section 404 will not apply to a participant's deferral contributions to a 401(k) plan, although it will apply for IRC Section 415. The EGTRRA increases the IRC Section 401(a)(17) cap on compensation that may be included for all qualified plan purposes to $250,000 in 2012 and indexes the cap in $5,000 increments. The total annual addition limit under IRC Section 415 (which includes such things as forfeitures) is the lesser of 100 percent of qualifying pay or $50,000 in 2012, and this amount will be indexed in increments of $1,000, according to IRC Section 415(c)(1).
  - This amount may be used for prefunding the ESOP or repaying ESOP-related debt. This contribution limit includes interest expense on ESOP-related obligations.
  - A key distinction between C and S corporations for ESOP purposes is the treatment of interest costs associated with ESOP-related debt. C corporations are permitted to deduct all interest on ESOP debt, and none of the interest is counted toward the 25 percent contribution limit. An S corporation must include ESOP interest costs toward its 25 percent contribution percentage. In highly leveraged S corporation ESOPs, the practical impact of this rule is that it will take longer for the ESOP to complete the payment for its stock purchase using qualified payroll limits.

Example 3-2   Sample Computation for an S Corporation

Similar facts as the previous C corporation example, except the S corporation is limited to 25 percent of payroll contribution for debt principal and interest. Correspondingly, it will take longer for the ESOP-related debt to be repaid with deductible contributions. We have assumed an approximate debt amortization of 8.3 years, which keeps total contributions within the payroll limits.

Qualifying payroll	$2,000,000
Payroll contribution limit 25% (0.25 x $2,000,000)	$500,000
ESOP-related note (with 8.3-year amortization)	$2,500,000
Interest rate 8% (interest expense first year 0.08 x $2,500,000)	$200,000
Total deduction for the company first year	
Debt amortization (2,500,000/8.3 years approximately)	$300,000
Interest expense	200,000
Total deduction	$500,000
Actual employee share of contribution ($500,000/$2,000,000)	25%

In this simplified case, the actual economic benefit to the employees is the value of the stock allocated as a result of the contribution. In total, the contribution percentage is 25 percent of qualifying payroll. It will take the S corporation approximately 8.3 years to repay the debt versus the C corporation repaying the debt in 5 years.

- *Allocation limit increased.* There is a difference between the contribution amount and the allocation amount (which includes participant forfeitures). Under the EGTRRA, allocation amounts have been significantly expanded for all qualified retirement plans, including ESOPs. The limits for allocation amounts as of 2012 are the lesser of $50,000 or 100 percent of the participant's salary. The dollar amount will be indexed to inflation in the future in $1,000 increments, per IRC Section 415(c)(1). For an ESOP that is leveraged, the higher allocation limits are a tremendous benefit in long-term planning.
  - Prior to the EGTRRA, the rules regarding ESOP contributions to an S corporation were more complex. Briefly, the payroll contribution limit was 15 percent of qualifying payroll with either an unleveraged or a leveraged ESOP. Planning could become complex if a company wanted the 25 percent payroll limit. The ESOP could be combined with a money purchase pension plan, thereby increasing the limit to 25 percent. As noted, interest expense on the ESOP note was counted against the payroll contribution percentage.
- *Excess contributions.* If the employer contributes more than what may be deducted or if the contribution exceeds the IRC Section 415 limits, the employer is subject to a 10 percent excise tax on the excess amount, the same as a C corporation, per IRC Section 4972.

- *Excess allocations*. If the employer contributes more than what may be allocated to plan participants' accounts, the plan may be subject to disqualification, the same as a C corporation.

S Corporation Antiabuse ESOP Provisions in the EGTRRA

Congress reacted to a number of abuses with S corporation ESOPs that exploited certain unintended windfall economic advantages. Generally, the message Congress is sending is that S corporation ESOPs are encouraged with favorable tax incentives, as long as the employee ownership is broad-based and not concentrated into the hands of a few. The resulting legislation does prevent the continuation of the abuses, and it imposes on the ESOP community a series of complex compliance rules. Since the passage of the EGTRRA, the IRS has issued further regulations refining the broad provisions of the original legislation. Final IRS regulations were issued on December 20, 2006, generally effective for plan years beginning on or after January 1, 2006. This section briefly discusses a few overriding considerations. The EGTRRA legislation is well-intentioned, and it effectively eliminates the abuses Congress was targeting. This is very complex legislation, and it requires careful review before an S corporation ESOP transaction.

- The EGTRRA is intended to eliminate the use of an ESOP in an S corporation that is meant to benefit only a small number of highly compensated employees. The law defines a *disqualified person*, under IRC Section 409(p)(4), as someone who owns 10 percent or more of all the deemed-owned shares (defined shortly) of a corporation or who is a family member who owns 20 percent or more of the deemed-owned shares. The definition of a *disqualified person* goes on to include any family member of an individual who is a disqualified person under the 20 percent family rule just mentioned. *Family* is defined broadly to include such individuals as a spouse of the individual, an ancestor or a lineal descendant of the individual, a brother or sister of the individual or individual's spouse, and any lineal descendant of the brother or sister. The notion of family is expansive, and it is always best to ask professional advice on possible rules of attribution.
- Under IRC Section 409(p)(4), a disqualified person is someone who has deemed-ownership of 10 percent or more of the allocated shares in the ESOP, prorated portion of shares in the ESOP loan suspense account (mock allocation), and synthetic equity. Stock owned directly by a candidate outside the ESOP is not considered in the computation of deemed-owned shares in the 10 percent test to determine a disqualified person.
- Deemed-owned shares that encompass stock in the ESOP are easily understood. The far more complex concept is the idea of synthetic equity. The IRS has issued guidelines regarding its understanding of what constitutes synthetic equity for purposes of the disqualified person test. In summary, synthetic equity includes such items as stock options, warrants, restricted stock, deferred issuance stock rights, stock appreciation rights, nonqualified deferred compensation, and a right to acquire interests in a related entity. Nonqualified deferred compensation is a broad-based concept that includes such things as any remuneration for which a deduction would be permitted under IRC Section 404(a)(5), split dollar insurance, and any other remuneration under a

plan deferring receipt of compensation beyond two and one-half months after the end of a year in which the services were rendered (may include bonuses). Clearly, the concept of synthetic equity is very extensive. This is not a comprehensive list of items constituting synthetic equity, and it is recommended that professional advice be obtained in cases when this may apply.

- Once disqualified persons are identified, the second part of the antiabuse testing is to determine if a nonallocation year has occurred. If at any time during a year, disqualified persons own at least 50 percent of the stock in an S corporation, including synthetic equity, a nonallocation year has been established. The complexity of the law is apparent in that the second part of the test (determining a nonallocation year) considers both deemed-owned shares—shares directly owned by the disqualified individual—and synthetic equity.

- If there is a set of circumstances in which a nonallocation year occurs, the penalties are severe. Generally, the rules state that no portion of the assets of the plan attributable to (or allocated to) the company stock may accrue for the benefit of any disqualified person in a nonallocation year. The penalty applies to the value of any prohibited allocation (including prior allocations) that is considered distributed to the disqualified person. A 50 percent excise tax is imposed on the amount of the prohibited allocation (including prior allocations); a 50 percent excise tax is imposed on the synthetic equity of the disqualified persons; and, if a prohibited allocation occurs, the plan loses its ESOP status and could lose its qualified plan status, and the corporation's S election would terminate. The penalties are intended to be onerous. The clear message is that a nonallocation year must be avoided at all costs.

- Companies sponsoring ESOPs may take steps to prevent a nonallocation year, but such steps must satisfy all legal and qualification requirements, including the nondiscrimination requirement of IRC Section 401(a)(4). Any method undertaken to avoid a nonallocation year must be completed before the nonallocation year occurs. The plan sponsor must prevent the nonallocation year, not correct it.

The rules are very complex, and it is beyond the scope of this book to consider them fully. If an ESOP is proposed for an S corporation, it is mandatory, in this author's opinion, to engage a professional thoroughly familiar with the antiabuse regulations.

Contributions to an ESOP Based on Dividends (C Corporation)

Dividends from a C corporation are generally not deductible for federal income tax purposes. One exception to this rule is that dividends paid on ESOP stock may be deductible, according to IRC Section 404(k). The EGTRRA recently expanded the considerations for dividend deductions. C corporations are able to deduct dividends paid on ESOP stock in two primary ways:

- *Applying dividends directly to loan principal.* The first method of dividend deduction is to apply the dividends directly to the ESOP loan repayment. This is the most common application.

- *Paying dividends to ESOP participants.* The second method of dividend deduction is to pay the dividend directly to the ESOP participants. Plan participants (and their beneficiaries) now have the option, under the EGTRRA, of taking dividends paid to them and investing in additional qualifying employer securities. Although this is an option, it is likely to be used only by larger and financially sophisticated companies with registered securities.
  - Participants are now making an investment in the company by applying dividends received to the purchase of stock. This activity makes them investors, and it will subject the company to certain investment disclosure statutes. This is a step that many closely held companies will likely avoid.
- *Dividends must be reasonable.* Dividend deductions are not subject to C corporation payroll contribution limits. The dividend payments must be reasonable, per IRC Section 404(k). Because the dividends are not subject to payroll contribution limits, this effectively allows C corporations a great deal of flexibility in meeting ESOP debt obligations.
  - In a C corporation, a separate class of stock is established for the ESOP. Typically, this class of stock is a convertible preferred stock that pays a stated dividend amount. The dividend is used to repay ESOP debt during the leveraged period. Once the ESOP debt is retired, there is often no need to have the deductible dividend feature. At this point, the convertible preferred stock is exchanged for common stock at a predetermined exchange rate.

Example 3-3   Sample Computation for a C Corporation

This example is similar to the prior computation illustrating payroll limits. In this case, the employer has sold the ESOP a convertible preferred stock with a 6 percent dividend. The ESOP note equals the face value of the convertible preferred stock: $2.5 million.

Qualifying payroll	$2,000,000
Payroll contribution limit 25% (0.25 x $2,000,000)	$500,000
ESOP-related note (with 5-year amortization)	$2,500,000
Interest rate 8% (interest expense first year 0.08 x $2,500,000)	$200,000
Dividend on 6% convertible preferred stock (0.06 x $2,500,000)	$150,000
Total deduction for the company first year	
Debt amortization (just happens to be 25% of payroll)	$500,000
Interest expense	200,000
Dividend on convertible preferred stock	<u>150,000</u>
Total deduction	$850,000
Actual employee share of contribution ($850,000/$2,000,000)	42.5%

In this case, the actual economic benefit to the employees the first year is the value of the stock allocated as a result of the contribution and the dividend on the preferred stock. In total, the employee benefit percentage is 42.5 percent of qualifying payroll.

- A critical tax planning issue is that the dividends are not deductible from income when computing the alternative minimum tax.
- S corporations may not deduct dividend payments, but they may make distributions to the shareholders. The distributions will be considered shortly.

Contributions to an ESOP Based on Distributions (S Corporation)

The S corporation does not pay dividends in a traditional sense of dividends paid by C corporations. Income from the company is pro rata taxed directly to the shareholders individually based on the percentage of stock owned. It is common for the S corporation to make cash distributions to shareholders in an amount adequate for the shareholders to pay their personal income taxes. The distribution percentage is typically at the highest end of the personal income tax rate percentage. There is a single class of stock requirement for S corporations; therefore, the percentage distribution must be the same for all shareholders.

- The S corporation deductible ESOP payroll contribution limits are the same as those of a C corporation, except that interest payments do not count for C corporations when the one-third test is satisfied. Assuming the S corporation has multiple shareholders comprising both individuals and the ESOP, the individuals will require some percentage cash distribution to meet federal personal income tax obligations.
- The cash distribution from the S corporation will be made to all shareholders. The ESOP counts as a single shareholder for purposes of determining the number of qualifying shareholders for S corporations (currently 100 shareholders are permitted). Every shareholder will receive the distribution, including the ESOP.
- There is a difference between a payroll-based contribution and a distribution. The contribution is allocated to the ESOP account balances according to qualifying payroll. The distribution is allocated to all shareholders generally according to the amount of stock they own.
  - In the case of the ESOP, the collective S corporation distribution made to the plan may be used to repay ESOP-related debt. This is a significant benefit because it effectively overcomes the payroll contribution limits previously discussed. If the distribution made to the ESOP is greater than the amount of debt to be repaid, then the excess cash will be allocated to the ESOP participants according to the stock allocated to their account (both vested and unvested). The rules regulating the allocation of the S corporation distribution are complex and may involve elements whereby amounts are allocated to compensation and stock already allocated to the individual's account.
- The cash distribution allocated to individual ESOP account balances will remain in the individual account balance.

Example 3-4   Comparing a 40 Percent ESOP in a C and an S Corporation

	C Corporation	S Corporation
Pretax income before ESOP contribution	$1,200,000	$1,200,000
Less: ESOP contribution	200,000	200,000
Pretax income	$1,000,000	$1,000,000
Federal income taxes (@35%)	350,000	
Net income to retained earnings	$650,000	
Distribution to all shareholders (38%)		380,000
Retained by company		$620,000
Taxes paid to federal government (38% x 60% x $1,000,000)		$228,000
Funds retained by ESOP (38% x 40% x $1,000,000)		152,000
Distributed to shareholders		$380,000

In this case, the effective tax rate between the C corporation and S corporation shareholders is slightly different (35 percent versus 38 percent). The C corporation will pay $350,000 in federal income taxes. The S corporation will have fewer dollars retained in the company, but its shareholders will pay only $228,000 in federal income taxes. The ESOP will be paid $152,000 that represents funds that may be used, in part, for future repurchase obligations or ESOP debt repayment.

The distribution to the ESOP will be made according to the stock in each participant's account, not the participant's qualifying payroll.

Example 3-5   Comparing a 100 percent ESOP in a C and an S Corporation

	C Corporation	S Corporation
Pretax income before ESOP payment	$1,200,000	$1,200,000
Less: ESOP contribution	200,000	200,000
Pretax income	$1,000,000	$1,000,000
Federal income taxes (@35%)	350,000	
Net income to retained earnings	$650,000	
Distribution to all shareholders—None		0
Retained by company		$1,000,000

In this case, the effective tax rate between the C corporation and S corporation shareholder is striking. The C corporation has an effective federal income tax rate of 35 percent, but the S corporation with the 100 percent ESOP has no corporate federal income tax obligation. The S corporation has no tax obligation, and the sole shareholder is a qualified benefit plan with no income tax obligation. When participants leave the ESOP, their ESOP distribution is similar to any other distribution from a qualified benefit plan and will eventually be subject to ordinary individual income taxes or, in some cases, long-term capital gain.

The S corporation in this example clearly has an advantage over the federal income tax-paying C corporation. Generally, the higher the percentage of stock in the ESOP, the more attractive the S corporation election.

Computations regarding payroll limits and individual allocations may become very complex, and an employer is recommended to use the services of an experienced plan administration company.

IRC Section 1042 Tax-Free Rollover (C Corporation)

One ESOP-related tax advantage is extended only to a C corporation, subject to certain conditions. A qualifying sale to the C corporation ESOP will earn significant tax benefits for a selling shareholder. Offsetting the benefits in part, a number of restrictions apply to the transactions.

IRC Section 1042 Tax-Free Rollover on the Sale of Stock By a C Corporation

An investor in the closely held C corporation selling stock to an ESOP may qualify for a tax-free rollover of the proceeds into qualified replacement property (QRP).

ESOP May Only Buy Qualified Employer Securities

Employer securities qualifying for the IRC Section 1042 provisions must meet several criteria, including

- stock must be an *employer security*, as defined in IRC Section 409(1).
- stock must be issued by a domestic corporation.
- the corporation (and each controlled group member) must not have any outstanding readily traded publicly held stock.
- the stock cannot be acquired by the selling shareholder from any of the following: a qualified retirement plan, a stock option from the company, or any other right to acquire stock granted by the company.
- the stock must have been held by the selling shareholder for at least three years prior to the IRC Section 1042 transaction.

Thirty Percent Test

The sale of the company stock will qualify for the tax-free rollover (the IRC Section 1042 tax-free rollover election) if the ESOP owns at least 30 percent of the fully diluted outstanding stock or 30 percent of the overall value of the company after the sale. The taxable gain received from the sale by the shareholder subject to the IRC Section 1042 limits is deferred from capital gains taxes if the shareholder reinvests the proceeds in QRP within a period of 3 months prior to the sale and 12 months after the sale to the ESOP.

Two or more shareholders may combine their stock to meet the 30 percent threshold to qualify the entire transaction for the IRC Section 1042 rollover.

Example 3-6   Selling Stock to the ESOP With IRC Section 1042 With One Shareholder

The company has a single shareholder owning 100 percent of the stock. To qualify for the IRC Section 1042 tax-free rollover, the shareholder must sell at least 30 percent of the outstanding stock in a single transaction. The following schedule illustrates the minimum number of shares to be sold to the ESOP:

Shareholder A   1,000 shares x 30% = 300 shares to the ESOP.

Example 3-7   Selling Stock to the ESOP With IRC Section 1042 With Multiple Shareholders

Same as the previous example, only the company has 5 equal shareholders. To qualify for the IRC Section 1042 tax-free rollover, the shareholders each agree to pro rata sell enough stock to reach 30 percent. The following schedule illustrates this transaction:

Shareholders	Shares of Stock	Sale to ESOP	Balance
Shareholder A	200 (20%)	60	140 (14%)
Shareholder B	200 (20%)	60	140 (14%)
Shareholder C	200 (20%)	60	140 (14%)
Shareholder D	200 (20%)	60	140 (14%)
Shareholder E	200 (20%)	60	140 (14%)
ESOP	0	—	300 (30%)
Total	1,000	300	1,000

In this case, each shareholder sold the same amount of stock. In fact, each shareholder may decide to sell any amount of stock, as long as the total is at least 30 percent of the outstanding shares, in the single transaction.

QRP

The QRP must be purchased within the specified period of time: 3 months before and 12 months after the transaction date. IRC Section 1042(c)(4) and various Private Letter Rulings have expanded the understanding of what does and does not qualify as QRP.

QRP includes

- securities of domestic (U.S.) operating corporations, both public and private, in which 50 percent or more of the assets must be used in the active conduct of a trade or business.
- individual company securities, including such investments as stocks, bonds, notes, and debentures.
- brother and sister companies.

The corporation issuing the QRP may not have passive investment income in excess of 25 percent of gross receipts in the preceding taxable year in which the purchase occurs.

QRP does not include

- mutual funds.
- real estate.
- subsidiary of the plan sponsor.
- government securities and municipal bonds.
- foreign securities.
- partnerships and limited liability companies.

It is important to note that the tax-free rollover election extends only to the QRP. If the QRP is sold prior to the property going into the estate of the owner, a taxable event will likely occur.

Active or Passive Investment of the QRP

The tax-free rollover is extended only to the QRP. If the QRP is sold, the selling shareholder will then pay taxes on the transaction. The gain will typically be the difference between the basis of the employer stock and the transaction price of the QRP (if higher than the basis of the QRP). The basis of the QRP is the purchase price reduced by the amount of gain that would have been recognized if IRC Section 1042 did not apply.

- *Passive investment of the QRP.* Many selling shareholders are of retirement age and wish to exercise the IRC Section 1042 rollover by purchasing QRP with a long-term view of investment. The intent is typically to hold the QRP for many years to defer taxes. If the QRP is held until death, under current statutes, the QRP will become part of the selling shareholder's estate and will be subject to estate taxes after a step-up in basis. The step-up in basis effectively permanently defers all capital gain or income taxes on the sale to the ESOP.
- *Active investment of the QRP—ESOP notes.* One such financial product suited to IRC Section 1042 rollovers when active investment of the proceeds is desired is generally referred to as an ESOP note.
  - The ESOP notes are generally long-term corporate bonds. Common attributes of these long-term bonds typically include a maturity date ranging from 40–60 years, combined with long-term call protection ranging from 20–30 years. The ESOP notes typically pay a variable interest rate, so the investor is somewhat protected from interest fluctuation risk.
  - The ESOP note serves as the QRP. The ESOP note may be used as security for an account with a brokerage firm that will advance (lend) in cash a percentage of the face amount of the ESOP note to the selling shareholder. What the shareholder opens, in essence, is a margin account with the broker. The shareholder may, in turn, invest the cash in virtually any investment because the restrictions of the QRP only apply to the ESOP note. The cash advance percentage may range from 75 percent to 90 percent of the face amount of the ESOP note, depending on the source of the funds.
  - Traditional brokerage companies may be more restricted on the percentage amount they may advance on a margin account. Specialty financial institutions may be able

to advance a higher percentage of funds against the margin account. Accordingly, such specialty capabilities may have other collateral aspects that permit the higher advance percentage.

- *Caution:* The total interest income on the ESOP note normally will not pay for all the interest expense on the loan from the brokerage firm. The difference may be small, but there may still be an expense that will reduce gains on the other investments. The margin account with the broker will almost certainly be subject to margin calls if the equity balance falls below certain prescribed amounts.

Before investing in any securities, it is always advisable to talk to experienced professionals. IRC Section 1042 transactions contain a number of unique qualities, and it is best to deal only with professionals who are knowledgeable about ESOP-based transactions.

QRP Transaction Documentation

All procedural paperwork must be completed in a timely manner for the IRC Section 1042 election to be successfully completed. It is important to emphasize that a voluntary election must be made to defer the taxes on the sale of stock to the ESOP.

Three basic procedural pieces of paper must be completed (appendix 3A, "Sample Documents Relating to the Internal Revenue Code Section 1042 Election," contains examples of the documents):

1. *Statement of election.* The selling shareholder must elect not to recognize the taxable gain on the sale of stock to the ESOP. This is done by completing a written statement of election that is filed with the seller's tax return for the year of sale. Once the election is made, it is irrevocable.

2. *Statement consenting to the imposition of excise tax.* The employer must provide a written and verified statement consenting to the imposition of potential additional taxes if certain events occur for the year in which the stock is purchased. A 10 percent excise tax may be imposed if any of the stock sold to the ESOP that is subject to the IRC Section 1042 election is sold or disposed within 3 years following the date of sale. Additionally, a potential 50 percent tax may be imposed if the stock in the ESOP is allocated to individuals prohibited from receiving such allocations.

3. *Statement of purchase.* Within 30 days after the purchase of QRP, the selling shareholder must complete a statement of purchase. The statement of purchase must be notarized to be valid. It will declare that the security being purchased is QRP, and it will be filed with the seller's tax return.

Subsequent Sales of Stock to the ESOP

Any subsequent sales of stock to the ESOP in any amount will also qualify for the IRC Section 1042 tax-free rollover election if the ESOP maintains its 30 percent ownership. Therefore, even a small additional sale of stock to the ESOP (for example just 5 percent of the remaining stock) will also qualify for the IRC Section 1042 rollover if the ESOP owns more than 30 percent of the outstanding shares after the transaction.

IRC Section 1042 Restrictions

If a shareholder elects to use the IRC Section 1042 rollover provision, note a number of limitations, per IRC Section 409(n):

- *Rules of nonallocation.* The shares sold to the ESOP as part of the IRC Section 1042 rollover may not be allocated to ESOP accounts of a number of specified individuals. Prohibited allocations apply to the selling shareholder; family members of the shareholder (spouse, ancestors, and siblings); lineal descendants of the selling shareholder (child, grandchild, great-grandchild, legally adopted child); and other shareholders owning more than 25 percent of the stock individually or by rules of attribution.

    IRC Section 409(n)(3)(A) provides a limited exception to the prohibited allocation rule. Allocations may be made to lineal descendants of the selling shareholder if the total amount of stock allocated does not exceed 5 percent of the amount sold by the selling shareholder. This exception does not apply to lineal descendants of any 25 percent shareholder.

- *Holding period.* The selling shareholder must have owned his or her stock in the company for at least three years prior to the sale to the ESOP. The selling shareholder cannot qualify for the IRC Section 1042 rollover if the proposed stock was acquired through exercising stock options.

- *Excise tax penalty.* If the ESOP sells shares subject to the IRC Section 1042 election within 3 years after the sale, the employer is generally subject to a 10 percent excise tax on the proceeds.

Nontaxable Income Related to ESOP Stock (S Corporation)

The S corporation is generally referred as a pass-through entity for federal income tax purposes. The taxable income (or loss) of the company is passed through (or reported on Form K-1) to the shareholders, and the shareholders will pay federal income taxes on the reported income at their personal income tax rates. Our discussion will assume an S corporation that is profitable.

Typically, the shareholders will be receiving the reported S corporation income, in addition to any other income that is earned (Form W-2) or other investment income. The income from the S corporation is often taxed at the highest marginal tax rate for the individual shareholder.

- *The ESOP has no federal income tax liability.* The ESOP is a qualified retirement plan, and it has no federal income tax liability. Income taxes are typically paid only when plan assets are distributed to retiring participants, and then, it is the participants who pay the income tax. If the ESOP is one of several shareholders in the S corporation, the other shareholders will have a federal income tax liability, not the ESOP.

- *An S corporation that is 100 percent owned by the ESOP will not pay federal income taxes.* All the stock is owned by the ESOP, a nontax paying qualified retirement plan. The long-term financial implications for the company are positively affected because of the tax environment.

Example 3-8   Comparing a C Corporation and an S Corporation (100 Percent ESOP)

This example is nearly identical to an earlier illustration in this chapter.

	C Corporation	S Corporation
Pretax income before ESOP payment	$1,200,000	$1,200,000
Less: ESOP contribution	200,000	200,000
Pretax income	$1,000,000	$1,000,000
Federal income taxes (@35%)	350,000	
Net income to retained earnings	$650,000	
Distribution to all shareholders—None		0
Retained by company		$1,000,000

In this case, the effective tax rate between the C corporation and S corporation share-holder is striking. The C corporation has an effective federal income tax rate of 35 percent, but the S corporation with the 100 percent ESOP has no corporate federal income tax obligation. The S corporation has no tax obligation, and the sole shareholder is a qualified benefit plan with no income tax obligation. When participants leave the ESOP, their ESOP distribution is similar to any other distribution from a qualified benefit plan and will eventually be subject to ordinary individual income taxes or, in some cases, long-term capital gain.

The S corporation in this example clearly has an advantage over the federal income tax-paying C corporation. The tax savings realized by the S corporation ESOP may be retained by the employer for any number of good business reasons.

Note: The tax savings are a deferral of obligations only. Eventually, the S corporation ESOP participants will leave the company, and distributions will be made. The source for cash for these distributions is the obligation of the company. However, the deferral of income taxes for possibly many years is a very attractive attribute of ESOPs in such circumstances.

Assets in ESOP Remain Untaxed Until Retirement

Assets in the ESOP increase free of income taxes until withdrawn. Most typically, the largest asset in the ESOP is the block of company stock. If the company grows and prospers, the likelihood of substantial stock valuation growth is substantial. Because the ESOP is a qualified retirement plan, such asset growth will not be taxable to the plan participants until they retire.

This benefit is true of virtually all qualified benefit plans, including the ESOP. When all the other tax-related benefits are considered, the ESOP enjoys many compelling advantages. Exhibit 3-1, "ESOP Summary Chart Comparing C Corporation and S Corporation Tax Provisions," highlights the major tax differences between the C corporation ESOP and the S corporation ESOP.

Exhibit 3-1: ESOP Summary Chart Comparing C Corporation and S Corporation Tax Provisions

	C Corporation	S Corporation
Payroll contribution deduction	Twenty-five percent eligible compensation excludes elective contributions to 401(k).	Twenty-five percent eligible compensation excludes elective contributions to 401(k).
ESOP loan interest deduction	Not counted against 25% eligible compensation.	Yes, it is counted against 25% eligible compensation.
Dividend deduction	Permitted. May be paid to participants (rare) or to repay loan directly. Must be reasonable. Deductible from taxes.	Distributions are made in same percentage to all shareholders. ESOP distribution allocated by shares in each account, but may be used in full to repay debt. Not deductible.
IRC Section 1042	Yes, tax deferral election permitted. Several restrictions apply to relatives and 25% owners.	Not available.
Classes of stock	Multiple classes available. May use a separate class of stock for ESOP to enhance dividend deduction.	Single class of stock.
Attributes of ESOP stock	Must have highest voting and dividend preference.	Must have highest voting and dividend preference.
Number and type of shareholders	Unlimited number; few shareholder restrictions.	One hundred maximum (ESOP is one).
Restrictions on type of shareholders		
Federal income taxes	Paid by company.	Paid by shareholders. ESOP as a shareholder not subject to income tax.
ESOP antiabuse provisions	Not applicable.	Substantial penalties if ESOP is determined to violate federal statutes.

Appendix 3A—Sample Documents Relating to the Internal Revenue Code Section 1042 Election

This appendix contains the following three sample documents:[1]

- Statement of election
- Statement of consent
- Statement of purchase

---

[1] The sample documents in this appendix are adapted with permission from those that appear in chapter 6, "The Section 1042 Rollover," of Keith Apton et al., *Selling Your Business to an ESOP*, 9th ed. (Oakland, CA: National Center for Employee Ownership, 2012).

Sample Statement of Election

I hereby irrevocably elect nonrecognition treatment under Section 1042(a) of the Internal Revenue Code of 1986 with respect to the sale of the following qualified securities:

1. (Number of Shares) shares of voting stock ("Shares") of ABC, Inc.
2. Date of sale of the Shares:_____, 20____.
3. Adjusted basis of Shares:_____
4. Amount realized upon sale of Shares: $_____
5. The Shares were sold to the ABC, Inc. Employee Stock Ownership Plan and Trust.

I have attached to this Statement of Election a verified Statement of Consent Executed by the _____ of ABC, Inc.

By: _____

Signature of the seller

Tax ID Number:_____

Sample Statement of Consent for ABC, Inc.

In connection with the sale of Shares of the common stock of ABC, Inc. by <u>Shareholder Name</u>, to the ABC, Inc. Employee Stock Ownership Plan and Trust, the Company hereby consents to the application of Section 4978 and 4979A of the Internal Revenue Code of 1986.

Date:_____   By:_____

Title: _____

Verification:

I hereby declare and under penalties of perjury that I am the duly elected _____ of ABC, Inc., that I have read the forgoing Statement of Consent, and that to the best of my knowledge and belief such Statement is true and correct.

Date:_____

Sample Statement of Purchase

I hereby declare that the securities described below constitute the Qualified Replacement Property (QRP) with respect to the sale of qualified securities under Section 1042 of the Internal Revenue Code of 1986.

Security Description	Number	Net Cost	Date Purchased

Date:_____

State of: _____)

) ss.

County of:_____)

I,_____, a notary public for the County aforesaid, in the State of_____, do certify that_____, whose name is signed in the writing above, bearing the date on the day of _____, 20_____.

    My term of office expires on the_____day of_____, 20_____.

                        By:_____

                      Notary's Signature

Chapter 4

Employee Stock Ownership Plan Transactions and C Corporations

This chapter illustrates many of the tax planning aspects previously described. An example company is described in sufficient detail to provide insights into structuring employee stock ownership plan (ESOP) transactions in C corporations. The same basic financial information is used for each type of ESOP transaction, and those factors significant to the various transactions are highlighted, as appropriate, in each example section.

Sample Facts—ABC, Inc. (C Corporation)

The hypothetical ESOP candidate, ABC, Inc. (ABC), has been selected to illustrate many attributes of successful installations. Abbreviated financial statements for ABC are presented for analysis purposes. An abbreviated analysis is presented of the fair market value (FMV) of the stock of ABC for the purposes of an ESOP.

The ownership of ABC is a single shareholder, Mr. Robert Smith (age 61), who is the founder, is active in the daily operations of the business, and currently serves as the president. Mr. Smith is the only member of the family active in the company. ABC is a well-established manufacturing company that has demonstrated consistent profitability and is recession resistant. Sales have grown consistently, but future growth is expected to be slightly ahead of inflation. ABC operates from two production facilities, and the company owns both facilities. The compensation to Mr. Smith is reasonable for valuation purposes.

These are the basic facts for each of the following illustrations, unless otherwise noted. The valuation summary is intended to serve as an illustration for planning purposes and is not intended to be a primer on business valuations. Business valuations for the purposes of an ESOP are often very complex, with myriad details that are beyond the scope of this book to examine in detail.

Abbreviated Financial Statements

Exhibit 4-1 shows the abbreviated income statement of ABC:

Exhibit 4-1: ABC (C Corporation) Abbreviated Income Statements

	20X1	20X2	20X3
Sales	$14,000,000	$15,000,000	$16,500,000
Cost of sales	9,800,000	10,600,000	11,500,000
Gross profit	4,200,000	4,400,000	5,000,000
Selling, general and administrative expenses	2,850,000	3,140,000	3,460,000
Interest expense	250,000	260,000	240,000
Subtotal	3,100,000	3,400,000	3,700,000
Pretax income	1,100,000	1,000,000	1,300,000
Income taxes (35%)	385,000	350,000	455,000
Net income	$715,000	$650,000	$845,000
Qualifying payroll for the purposes of an ESOP in year 20X3			$4,000,000

Exhibit 4-2 shows ABC's abbreviated balance sheet:

Exhibit 4-2: ABC (C Corporation) Abbreviated Balance Sheet at December 31, 20X2

Current assets	$5,500,000	Current liabilities	$2,000,000
		All debt	3,000,000
Plant and equipment	7,000,000		
Less: Depreciation	3,000,000	Common stock	500,000
Net fixed assets	4,000,000	Retained earnings	4,000,000
		Total equity	4,500,000
Total assets	$9,500,000	Total liabilities and equity	$9,500,000

The equity of the company consists of 100,000 shares of common stock authorized and 50,000 shares of common stock issued and outstanding. There is only one class of stock and no treasury stock. The company has been a C corporation from its founding.

FMV of Common Stock for the Purposes of an ESOP

ABC is an excellent candidate for an ESOP because of its established financial track record and predictable earnings. The senior management and owner of the company, Mr. Smith, will consider the ESOP as an exit vehicle. Stock will be sold to the ESOP over a period of time. Current valuation methodology assumes the candidate company for the ESOP is a C corporation, even if the company is already an S corporation. This assumption will be explained in more detail in chapter 7, "Valuation Issues and Considerations," that considers ESOP valuations. The general theory is that a hypothetical buyer is a C corporation. Remember that both the IRS and the Department of Labor have valuation oversight of ESOPs. For this example, the net income of ABC has ranged from a low of $615,000 in 20X2 to a high of $845,000 in 20X3. We have selected net income of $800,000 for this analysis. We will value ABC on both a minority position and control position. We will assume that an appropriate control premium is 10 percent. The discount for marketability is already reflected in the analysis, for ease of presentation.

Minority Position FMV

Selected net income for valuation purposes	800,000
Price earnings multiple applied in this case	x 7.5
Minority position FMV	6,000,000

Control Position FMV

Add premium for control: 10%	600,000
Control position FMV	6,600,000

Value Per Share

Minority position FMV per share (6,000,000/50,000)	$120/share
Control position FMV per share (6,600,000/50,000)	$132/share

Lack of Marketability

The preceding minority position multiple of 7.5 already includes a lack of marketability adjustment. The multiple of 7.5 is reasonable and already reflects the lack of marketability that is offset in part or total by the put option that ESOP participants have back to the company. We have assumed that a premium for control of 10 percent is reasonable. The control position value does consider a lack of marketability discount for ease of presentation. It is beyond the scope of this book to specifically quantify the lack of marketability adjustment for the purposes of an ESOP.

Common Entities in Transactions

Exhibit 4-3 identifies common parties of interest in ESOP transactions. The applicable components will be used to illustrate the steps and issues surrounding the various transactions in the examples that follow.

Exhibit 4-3: Common Parties of Interest in ESOP Transactions

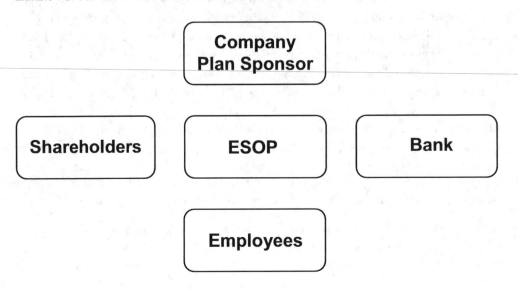

The following ESOP transactions will be covered in detail for C corporations:

- *Shareholders.* Shareholders represent the owners of the stock in the company (plan sponsor) prior to the ESOP acquiring stock.
- *Company (plan sponsor).* The company is also referred to as the employer or plan sponsor. The ESOP is established for the benefit of the employees of the company.
- *ESOP.* The employee stock ownership plan and trust is a separate legal entity that will acquire stock in the company. Once stock is acquired, the ESOP becomes a shareholder.
- *Employees.* They are ESOP participants with rights and interests protected by the Employee Retirement Income Security Act of 1974 and other applicable statutes.
- *Bank.* The bank typically represents a financial institution providing funds to the ESOP for the purchase of company stock.

The following ESOP transactions will be covered in detail for C corporations:

- Stock contributed to ESOP (capital formation ESOP)
- Leveraged ESOP with Internal Revenue Code (IRC) Section 1042 rollover
- Prefunded ESOP with IRC Section 1042 rollover
- Leveraged ESOP with IRC Section 1042 rollover and control
- Leveraged ESOP with IRC Section 1042 rollover, multiple classes of stock, and control

Example—Stock Contributed to ESOP (Capital Formation ESOP)

Significant Factors

Mr. Smith will authorize ABC to contribute stock to the ESOP for the upcoming year. The stock will come from authorized but unissued shares. There will be some dilution of the ownership percentage of Mr. Smith, but the dilution is deemed justified to determine if the ESOP will be embraced by the employees. At a later date, Mr. Smith may personally decide to sell more stock to the ESOP. The company will contribute $300,000 in stock to the ESOP, a minority position block of stock.

Illustration—Stock Contributed to ESOP (Capital Formation ESOP)

Exhibit 4-4 indicates conceptually the contribution of stock from the company to the ESOP:

Exhibit 4-4: Contribution of Stock From the Company to the ESOP

Step 1: The company is authorized to contribute $300,000 of common stock to the ESOP. The total value of the contributed stock is known—$300,000—but the number of shares this amount represents is not known. There will be dilution to the existing shareholder as a result of the contribution.

Step 2: The number of shares represented by the $300,000 contribution must be determined. The minority position FMV of the company is $6 million.

Dilution computation:

$$\text{Value per share} = \frac{\text{Aggregate FMV of company stock contribution}}{\text{Number of shares outstanding before contribution}}$$

$$\text{Value per share} = \frac{\$6,000,000 - \$300,000}{50,000}$$

Value per share = $114
Shares issued = $300,000/$114
Shares issued = $2,631 (Rounded to whole shares)

Step 3: New shares will be issued representing the stock contribution. The following schedule indicates the ownership of the company following the contribution. After the transaction, Mr. Smith now owns 95 percent of the outstanding stock, and the ESOP owns 5 percent of the stock.

Shareholder	Stock Before Contribution	Stock After Contribution
Mr. Smith	50,000 (100%)	50,000 (95%)
ESOP	0	2,631 (5%)
Total	50,000 (100%)	52,631 (100%)

Step 4: The stock contribution provides a tax deduction to the company without a corresponding cash outlay. The company has generated positive cash flow as a result of the stock contribution, to the extent of the tax savings.

Stock contribution	$300,000
Corporate tax rate (35%)	× 0.35
Enhanced cash flow	$105,000

(Continued)

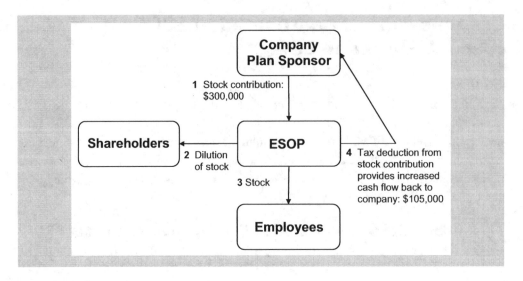

Strategic Tax Summary

- The company receives a tax deduction for the contribution to the ESOP: $300,000.
- The company shelters $105,000 of cash by the tax savings of the $300,000 noncash deduction ($300,000 × 35%).
- There is dilution to existing shareholders by the contribution of stock to the ESOP.
- The ESOP is currently a small percentage of the outstanding stock. The percentage of stock in the ESOP may be increased at the election of the controlling shareholders.

Example—Leveraged ESOP With IRC Section 1042 Rollover

Significant Factors

Mr. Smith will authorize the sale of 30 percent of his outstanding shares to the ESOP. This transaction will qualify for the IRC Section 1042 rollover. At this time, only 30 percent of the stock will be sold to the ESOP, with no future anticipated sales, a minority position. A bank will provide the financing for the entire transaction.

Illustration—Leveraged ESOP with Section 1042 Rollover

Exhibit 4–5 indicates conceptually a typical leveraged ESOP. In this example, the ESOP is going to borrow money from a bank and purchase stock of the company from Mr. Smith (shareholder). The following steps indicate the flow of funds from the bank to the selling shareholder:

Exhibit 4-5: Typical Leveraged ESOP

FMV of stock sold to the ESOP = Minority position FMV × Sale percentage
FMV of stock sold to the ESOP = $6,000,000 × 30% = $1,800,000
Loan amortization 5 years ($1,800,000/5) = $360,000/year

Step 1: The company arranges for the ESOP to borrow money from the bank to purchase stock from the shareholders: $1.8 million. The company guarantees the ESOP loan from the bank. The bank loans the money to the ESOP.

- More commonly, the bank loans the money directly to the company to have a greater security position in the transaction. The company has a "mirror" loan to the ESOP for the same amount. The company is directly liable for the loan.

Step 2: The ESOP takes the loan proceeds from the bank and buys the stock from the shareholder for $1.8 million. The shareholder sells stock to the ESOP and qualifies for the IRC Section 1042 tax-free rollover because the ESOP has acquired at least 30 percent of the outstanding stock.

- After the transaction, the ESOP owns the stock, but because of the ESOP-related debt, the stock is held in a suspense account, often referred to as unearned ESOP shares.

Step 3: The company repays the bank loan by advancing money to the ESOP in an amount to cover both loan interest and principal and by getting a deduction for the ESOP contribution. This effectively makes the principal of the bank loan deductible. The ESOP repays the bank loan with proceeds received from the company. As the ESOP debt is repaid, shares are released from the suspense account.

- The first-year ESOP obligation is as follows:

ESOP principle payment	$360,000
Interest expense ($1,800,000 × 7%)	126,000
Total	$486,000

- The entire amount is deductible to the company. The ESOP obligation is significantly below the allowable payroll contribution amount. The payroll contribution limit is 25 percent of qualifying payroll (excluding ESOP-related interest expense). The interest expense is deductible in full without counting against the 25 percent of payroll contribution limitation if less than one-third of the ESOP contribution is allocated to the highly compensated employees.

Contribution limit ($4,000,000 × 25%)	$1,000,000
ESOP contribution, excluding interest	$ 360,000

Step 4: When an employee leaves the ESOP, a distribution is made in stock or cash.

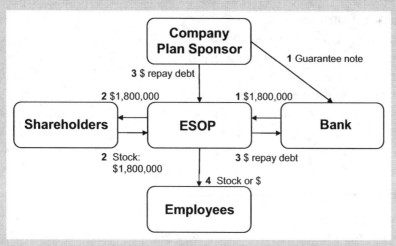

Note: The typical leveraged ESOP transaction may become more complex than the illustration discussed. Often, the bank may require additional collateral by the selling shareholder and a pledge of collateral of a part or all of the ESOP sale proceeds while the ESOP-related debt is amortized.

IRC Section 1042 Restrictions

Mr. Smith sells 30 percent of his stock to the ESOP for $1.8 million. The entire amount will be free of all taxes, providing the funds are fully reinvested in qualified replacement property (QRP) within the applicable 12-month period following the transaction and the 3 months before the transaction.

After the sale, restrictions apply regarding possible participation in the ESOP by certain family members and nonfamily 25 percent shareholders. We have assumed that Mr. Smith is the sole shareholder; therefore, the restriction to another 25 percent owner does not apply. Additionally, we assumed that Mr. Smith is the only member of his family active in the company; therefore, the restriction to other family members does not apply.

Strategic Tax Summary

- The company receives a tax deduction over time for the full stock purchase price of $1.8 million plus related interest expense.
- The ESOP acquires 30 percent of the outstanding stock, a minority position block. This percentage may be increased at a later date by the decision of the controlling shareholder.
- The transaction qualifies for the IRC Section 1042 tax-free rollover. The transaction price of $1.8 million is tax free to the selling shareholder, subject to proper reinvestment in QRP.
- IRC Section 1042 restrictions apply.
- Bank financing was used exclusively for the transaction. The bank may ask the selling shareholder to pledge QRP as additional loan collateral.

Example—Prefunded ESOP With IRC Section 1042 Rollover

Significant Factors

This illustration is similar to the previous example. Mr. Smith will authorize the sale of 30 percent of his outstanding shares to the ESOP. This transaction will qualify for the IRC Section 1042 rollover. At this time, only 30 percent of the stock will be sold to the ESOP, with no future anticipated sales, a minority position.

The company will prefund the ESOP with deductible contributions of cash to the ESOP for 3 years. Each year, the company will contribute $300,000 to the ESOP. A bank will fund the balance of the transaction price. The FMV of the stock is still assumed to be $1.8 million. The following schedule indicates the funding for the 30 percent block of stock:

Deductible cash contribution to ESOP 20X3	$ 300,000
Deductible cash contribution to ESOP 20X4	300,000
Deductible cash contribution to ESOP 20X5	300,000
Investment income on ESOP contributions	100,000
Bank financing	800,000
Total funds available	$1,800,000

Prefunding the ESOP transaction in this manner significantly reduces the amount of outside debt required. The yearly deductible cash contributions to the ESOP are below the payroll contribution limit ($4,000,000 × 25% = $1,000,000 contribution limit). It is assumed that prefunding the ESOP does not reduce the value of the company.

Illustration—Prefunded ESOP With IRC Section 1042 Rollover

Exhibit 4-6 indicates a typical leveraged ESOP combined with a portion of prefunding from the company to the ESOP. In this example, the ESOP is going to use a combination of funds borrowed from a bank, along with funds already in the ESOP. Stock of the company will be sold to the ESOP from Mr. Smith (shareholder). The following steps indicate the flow of funds to the selling shareholder:

Exhibit 4-6: Prefunded ESOP

FMV of stock sold to the ESOP = Minority position FMV x Sale percentage
FMV of stock sold to the ESOP = $6,000,000 x 30% = $1,800,000
Loan amortization of 3 years ($800,000/3) = $267,000/year

The loan amortization period is only three years, but the prefunding has significantly reduced the amount required from the bank.

Step 1: The company prefunds cash contributions to the ESOP for 3 years. Total prefunding amounts to $1 million. The entire cash balance is available for purchasing stock. The balance of the transaction price will be provided from a bank.

Step 2: The company arranges for the ESOP to borrow money from the bank to purchase stock from the shareholders: $800,000 ($1,800,000–$1,000,000). The company guarantees the ESOP loan from the bank. The bank loans the money to the ESOP.

- More commonly, the bank loans the money directly to the company to have a greater security position in the transaction. The company has a "mirror" loan to the ESOP for the same amount. The company still guarantees the loan.

Step 3: The ESOP takes the loan proceeds from the bank and the prefunded dollars in the ESOP and buys the stock from the shareholder for $1.8 million. The shareholder sells stock to the ESOP and qualifies for the IRC Section 1042 tax-free rollover because the ESOP has acquired at least 30 percent of the outstanding stock.

- After the transaction, the ESOP owns the stock, but because of the ESOP-related debt, a portion of the stock is held in a suspense account, often referred as unearned ESOP shares.
- A portion of the shares sold to the ESOP will be allocated directly to the participant account balances. The prefunded cash from the company ($1 million) will purchase stock from the shareholder, and that stock will be allocated to the accounts of the ESOP participants. The stock allocated to individual accounts will be subject to vesting.

Step 4: The company repays the bank loan by advancing money to the ESOP in an amount to cover both loan interest and principal and getting a deduction for the ESOP contribution. This effectively makes the principal of the bank loan deductible.

The ESOP repays the bank loan with proceeds received from the company. As the ESOP debt is repaid, shares are released from the suspense account.

- The first-year ESOP obligation is as follows:

ESOP principal payment	$267,000
Interest expense ($800,000 x 7%)	56,000
Total	$323,000

- The entire amount is deductible to the company. The ESOP obligation is significantly below the allowable payroll contribution amount. The payroll contribution limit is 25 percent of qualifying payroll (excluding ESOP-related interest expense).

Contribution limit ($4,000,000 x 25%)	$1,000,000
ESOP contribution, excluding interest	$ 267,000

Step 5: When an employee leaves the ESOP, a distribution is made (line from ESOP to Employees in the following chart) in stock or cash.

(continued)

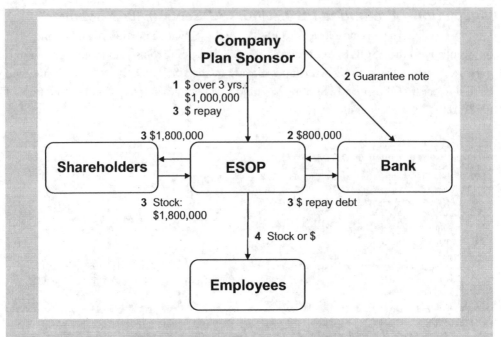

Note: The typical leveraged ESOP transaction may become more complex than the illustration discussed. Often, the bank may require additional collateral of the selling shareholder and a pledge of collateral of a part or all of the ESOP sale proceeds while the ESOP-related debt is amortized.

IRC Section 1042 Restrictions

Mr. Smith sells 30 percent of his stock to the ESOP for $1.8 million. The entire amount will be free of all taxes, providing the funds in full are reinvested in QRP within the applicable 12-month period following the transaction.

After the sale, restrictions apply regarding possible participation in the ESOP by certain family members and nonfamily 25 percent shareholders. We have assumed that Mr. Smith is the sole shareholder; therefore, the restriction to another 25 percent owner does not apply. Additionally, we assumed that Mr. Smith is the only member of his family active in the company; therefore, the restriction to other family members does not apply.

Strategic Tax Summary

- The company receives a tax deduction over time for the full stock purchase price of $1.8 million. The company previously deducted prefunding contributions to the ESOP. The company will also be able to deduct the $800,000 in bank debt plus related interest expense.
- The ESOP acquires 30 percent of the outstanding stock, a minority position block. This percentage may be increased at a later date by the decision of the controlling shareholder.
- The transaction qualifies for the IRC Section 1042 tax-free rollover. The transaction price of $1.8 million is tax free to the selling shareholder, subject to proper reinvestment in QRP.

- IRC Section 1042 restrictions apply.
- Bank financing was used for only a portion of the transaction: 44 percent ($800,000/$1,800,000 = 44%). The bank may ask the selling shareholder to pledge QRP as additional loan collateral. By prefunding a significant percentage of the transaction, the selling shareholder may be in a stronger position to negotiate terms with the bank.

Example—Leveraged ESOP With IRC Section 1042 Rollover and Control

Significant Factors

Mr. Smith will use the ESOP as his exit vehicle, and over time, he will sell 100 percent of his stock to the plan and receive a control position price. The company is currently a C corporation, so Mr. Smith will plan on utilizing the IRC Section 1042 rollover to provide valuable tax benefits as he sells all his stock to the ESOP. Bank financing will be used for the entire transaction.

Mr. Smith will sell his stock in three transactions. This strategy is elected because no single transaction will impose an unreasonable amount of ESOP-related debt on the company. It is unlikely that Mr. Smith could sell all his stock to the ESOP in a single transaction and negotiate loan terms acceptable to him. The following schedule indicates the ESOP transaction structure:

Transaction	Shares Sold	Transaction Amount
First transaction: 52%	26,000	$3,432,000 (0.52 × $6,600,000)
Second transaction: 24%	12,000	Control FMV at transaction date*
Third transaction: 24%	12,000	Control FMV at transaction date*
Total	50,000	

*Subject to proper documentation.

Issue: Receiving a Prorated Control Position Price

The intent of Mr. Smith is to sell all his stock to the ESOP: a control position. Mr. Smith wants to avoid the leverage placed on the company by selling all his stock in a single transaction. In this case, he will sell enough stock to the ESOP in a single transaction to pass control (over 50 percent of the stock) to the ESOP. In the preceding case, 52 percent of the stock is sold, just to simplify the example.

Mr. Smith will agree to sell a complete control position over time. The key point in this example is that Mr. Smith will execute an agreement granting the ESOP the authority to purchase enough stock to provide a control position with the first transaction. The first transaction will be linked to succeeding transactions as though they occurred on the same day and in a consistent manner. The mechanics of this type of transaction are often referred to as a serial sale. It is important to link the transactions in this manner because the ESOP is gaining a control position with the first purchase. Mr. Smith will want to be assured that future minority blocks of stock sold to the ESOP (in this case, 2 additional minority blocks of 24 percent) will qualify for the same control position valuation. Without the serial sale agreement in place, the ESOP may not be obligated to pay a control price for a future minority block of stock. Such agreements require informed consultation with experienced ESOP attorneys. If the prorated control price is to be realized in subsequent transactions, the selling shareholder must be willing to relinquish control with the initial transaction. Experienced ESOP attorneys will be able to provide insights on how best to achieve selling shareholder goals.

The first transaction, 52 percent, will be valued at the prevailing FMV on a control position basis: $3,432,000 ($6,600,000 × 52%). Succeeding transactions will be valued at the prevailing FMV on a control position basis on the date of the transaction. If the company continues to grow and remain profitable, it is probable that the value will increase.

The first transaction, 52 percent, will qualify for the IRC Section 1042 rollover. Succeeding transactions will also qualify because the percentage of stock in the ESOP will remain above 30 percent.

Illustration—Leveraged ESOP With IRC Section 1042 Rollover and Control

This illustration is similar to the prior example of a leveraged ESOP with the IRC Section 1042 rollover. In this case, the transaction will be repeated three times as the three blocks of stock are sold to the ESOP.

Exhibit 4–7 indicates conceptually a typical leveraged ESOP. In this example, the ESOP is going to borrow money from a bank and purchase stock of the company from Mr. Smith (shareholder). The following steps indicate the flow of funds from the bank to the selling shareholder:

Exhibit 4-7: ESOP Borrowing Money From a Bank to Purchase Shareholder Stock

FMV of stock sold to the ESOP = Control position FMV x Sale percentage

FMV of stock sold to the ESOP = $6,600,000 x 52% = $3,432,000

Loan principal amortization of 7 years rounded to nearest $1,000 ($3,432,000/7) = $490,000/year

The loan amortization is increased to seven years, so that the full ESOP obligation (both interest and principal) is manageable for the company.

Step 1: The company arranges for the ESOP to borrow money from the bank to purchase stock from the shareholder: $3,432,000. The company guarantees the ESOP loan from the bank. The bank loans the money to the ESOP.

- More commonly, the bank loans the money directly to the company to have a greater security position in the transaction. The company has a "mirror" loan to the ESOP for the same amount. The company is directly liable for the loan.

Step 2: The ESOP takes the loan proceeds from the bank and buys the stock from the shareholder. The shareholder sells stock to the ESOP and qualifies for the IRC Section 1042 tax-free rollover if this is a C corporation, and the ESOP has acquired at least 30 percent of the outstanding stock.

- After the transaction, the ESOP owns the stock, but because of the ESOP-related debt, the stock is held in a suspense account, often referred to as unearned ESOP shares.

Step 3: The company repays the bank loan by advancing money to the ESOP in an amount to cover both loan interest and principal and getting a deduction for the ESOP contribution. This effectively makes the principal of the bank loan deductible. The ESOP repays the bank loan with proceeds received from the company. As the ESOP debt is repaid, shares are released from the suspense account.

(continued)

- The first-year ESOP obligation is as follows:

ESOP loan principal payment	$490,000
Interest expense ($3,432,000 x 7%)	240,000
Total	$730,000

- The entire amount is deductible to the company. The ESOP obligation is significantly below the allowable payroll contribution amount. The payroll contribution limit is 25 percent of qualifying payroll (excluding ESOP-related interest expense).

Contribution limit ($4,000,000 x 25%)	$1,000,000
ESOP contribution, excluding interest	$490,000

Step 4: When an employee leaves the ESOP, a distribution is made in stock or cash.

Note: The typical leveraged ESOP transaction may become more complex than the illustration discussed. Often, the bank may require additional collateral of the selling shareholder and a pledge of collateral of a part or all of the ESOP sale proceeds while the ESOP-related debt is amortized.

IRC Section 1042 Restrictions

Mr. Smith sells 52 percent of his stock to the ESOP for $3.9 million. The entire amount will be free of all taxes, providing the funds are fully reinvested in QRP within the applicable 12-month period following the transaction and 3 months before the transaction.

After the sale, restrictions apply regarding possible participation in the ESOP by certain family members and nonfamily 25 percent shareholders. We have assumed that Mr. Smith is the sole shareholder; therefore, the restriction to another 25 percent owner does not apply. Additionally, we assumed that Mr. Smith is the only member of his family active in the company; therefore, the restriction to other family members does not apply.

Control Position Transaction

Mr. Smith is interested in selling control to the ESOP, thereby earning a higher value for his stock (the control position value: $6.6 million). The serial sale agreement will ensure that the ESOP has the ability to acquire a control position block of stock and that Mr. Smith will be able to sell all this stock to the ESOP at a control position value. The first sale of stock to the

ESOP is a control block of 52 percent, but future sales will be minority blocks: 2 blocks of 24 percent are anticipated in this example.

For the ESOP to pay the control position price, control must exist both in appearance and fact. The ESOP will acquire the control position block with the first purchase: 52 percent. This meets the first test of control in appearance. The ESOP will eventually purchase the remaining stock in 2 additional transactions of 24 percent each. For the purposes of this example, we have assumed that a block of stock in excess of 50 percent constitutes control of the company.

The ESOP must also be in control in fact. In this case, Mr. Smith will not serve as the sole ESOP trustee (serving as the sole trustee will not be considered passing control to the ESOP). Typically, a plan committee with several members will act as the ESOP trustee.

S Corporation Election

Almost certainly, the company will make the S corporation election following the third transaction. One hundred percent of the stock will be owned by the ESOP, and the S corporation election will mean the company will not have any exposure to federal income taxes. The company will still have significant ESOP repurchase obligations, but the repurchase exposure will be much easier to meet with federal income tax liability.

Strategic Tax Summary

- The company receives a tax deduction over time for the full stock purchase price on a control position basis. The first block of stock is $3,432,000 (52 percent).
- The ESOP acquires 52 percent of the outstanding stock in the first transaction. Two other transactions are planned to provide the ESOP with 100 percent of the stock over a reasonable time. A serial sale agreement is employed to provide the shareholder with a prorated control position price for the first transaction and all future transactions.
- The first transaction qualifies for the IRC Section 1042 tax-free rollover. The transaction price of $3.9 million is tax free to the selling shareholder, subject to proper reinvestment in QRP. Additional transactions will also qualify for the same tax treatment.
- IRC Section 1042 restrictions apply.
- Bank financing is used for the entire amount of the first transaction: $3.9 million. The bank may ask the selling shareholder to pledge QRP as additional loan collateral.
- The company will almost certainly elect S corporation status shortly after the last transaction that enables the ESOP to own 100 percent of the stock.

Example—Leveraged ESOP With IRC Section 1042 Rollover, Multiple Classes of Stock, and Control

Significant Factors

Mr. Smith will use the ESOP as his exit vehicle, and over time, he will sell 100 percent of his stock to the plan and receive a control position price. The company is currently a C corporation, so Mr. Smith will plan on utilizing the IRC Section 1042 rollover to provide valuable tax benefits as he sells all his stock to the ESOP. Bank financing will be used for the entire transaction.

Mr. Smith will sell his stock in three transactions. This strategy is elected because no single transaction will impose an unreasonable amount of ESOP-related debt on the company. It is unlikely that Mr. Smith could sell all his stock to the ESOP in a single transaction and negotiate loan terms acceptable to him. The following schedule indicates the ESOP transaction structure:

Transaction	Shares Sold	Transaction Amount
First transaction: 52%	26,000	$3,432,000 (52% × $6,600,000)
Second transaction: 24%	12,000	Control FMV at transaction date*
Third transaction: 24%	12,000	Control FMV at transaction date*
Total	50,000	

*Subject to proper documentation.

The actual mechanics of the ESOP transaction are similar to prior examples that employ the IRC Section 1042 rollover combined with outside bank debt. The one significant difference with this example is that a separate class of stock will be sold to the ESOP that pays a dividend rate. This second class of equity is developed, so that the company is able to make tax-deductible contributions to the ESOP in excess of payroll contribution limits.

The requirement for this type of ESOP transaction structure is typically attributed to the FMV of the company being relatively high in relation to the qualifying payroll. In the prior example of ABC, the overall FMV is lower in relation to the qualifying payroll; therefore, the ESOP-related obligations are comfortably met by retaining a single class of stock that does not have to pay dividends.

Issue: Receiving a Prorated Control Position Price

The intent of Mr. Smith is to sell all his stock to the ESOP: a control position. Mr. Smith wants to avoid the leverage placed on the company by selling all his stock in a single transaction. In this case, he will sell enough stock to the ESOP in a single transaction to pass control (over 50 percent of the stock) to the ESOP. In the preceding case, 52 percent of the stock is sold, just to simplify the example.

Mr. Smith will agree to sell a complete control position over time. The key point in this example is that Mr. Smith will execute an agreement granting the ESOP the authority to purchase enough stock to provide a control position with the first transaction. The first transaction will be linked to succeeding transactions as though they occurred on the same day and in a consistent manner. The mechanics of this type of transaction are often referred to as a serial sale. It is important to link the transactions in this manner because the ESOP is gaining a control position with the first purchase. Mr. Smith will want to be assured that future minority blocks of stock sold to the ESOP (in this case, 2 additional minority blocks of 24 percent) will qualify for the same control position valuation. Without the serial sale agreement in place, the ESOP may not be obligated to pay a control price for a future minority block of stock.

The first transaction, 52 percent, will be valued at the prevailing FMV on a control position basis: $3,432,000 ($6,600,000 × 52%). Succeeding transactions will be valued at the prevailing FMV on a control position basis on the date of the transaction. If the company continues to grow and remain profitable, it is probable that the value will increase.

The first transaction, 52 percent, will qualify for the IRC Section 1042 rollover. Succeeding transactions will also qualify because the percentage of stock in the ESOP will remain above 30 percent.

Creating a Second Class of Stock

The company will create a second class of stock for the ESOP transactions. The second class of stock in this example is super common stock paying a 6 percent dividend (super common stock). Because the company is a C corporation, dividends paid to the ESOP are deductible, if used to pay down ESOP-related debt. The dividend on the super common stock will be paid only while ESOP-related debt is outstanding. Once the ESOP debt is repaid, dividends will no longer be paid on the super common stock.

We will assume the following factors for this example:

- The FMV control position of ABC remains at $7.5 million.
- Fifty-two percent of the stock is sold on the first transaction.
- Qualifying payroll is only $2 million.
- The ESOP will purchase super common stock paying a 6 percent dividend.
- The entire transaction price is financed with bank debt.

Illustration — Leveraged ESOP With IRC Section 1042 Rollover, Multiple Classes of Stock, and Control

The company first authorizes the creation of a separate class of stock for the ESOP transaction: super common stock. The dividend rate must be reasonable. Mr. Smith exchanges his common stock for super common stock prior to the ESOP transaction on a tax-free basis. Mr. Smith then sells his super common stock to the ESOP. In this example, the ESOP is going to borrow money from a bank and purchase stock of the company from Mr. Smith (the shareholder). Exhibit 4-8 indicates the flow of funds from the bank to the selling shareholder:

Exhibit 4-8: Leveraged ESOP	
FMV of stock sold to the ESOP = Control position FMV x Sale percentage	
FMV of stock sold to the ESOP = $6,600,000 x 52%	$3,432,000
Amount of bank debt required (the entire transaction)	$3,432,000
Maximum deductible contribution to the ESOP based on qualifying payroll ($2,000,000 x 25%)	$ 500,000
Additional deductible contribution to the ESOP due to super common stock dividend (6% x $3,432,000)	$ 205,000
Total deductible contribution to ESOP	$ 705,000
Loan amortization ($3,432,000/$705,000)	4.8 years

The loan amortization period is approximately 4.8 years using both payroll contributions and the super common stock dividend. Without using the super common stock dividend, the loan amortization period for the first 52 percent block of stock is 6.8 years ($3,432,000/$500,000). The super common stock dividend accelerates the payment of the ESOP-related debt, often a requirement to meet a selling shareholder's timetable for withdrawing from the company.

(continued)

Step 1: The company arranges for the ESOP to borrow money from the bank to purchase stock from the shareholder: $3,432,000. The company guarantees the ESOP loan from the bank. The bank loans the money to the ESOP.

- More commonly, the bank loans the money directly to the company to have a greater security position in the transaction. The company has a "mirror" loan to the ESOP for the same amount. The company is directly liable for the loan.

Step 2: The ESOP takes the loan proceeds from the bank and buys the super common stock from the shareholder. The shareholder sells his or her super common stock to the ESOP and qualifies for the IRC Section 1042 tax-free rollover if this is a C corporation, and the ESOP has acquired at least 30 percent of the outstanding stock. The ESOP is acquiring 52 percent of the stock (for $3,432,000), so this requirement is met.

- After the transaction, the ESOP owns the stock, but because of the ESOP-related debt, the stock is held in a suspense account, often referred to as unearned ESOP shares.

Step 3: The company repays the bank loan by advancing money to the ESOP in an amount to cover both loan interest and principal. In this example, the company secures tax-deductible funding for the ESOP debt payment from contributions related to payroll limits and super common stock dividends. This effectively makes the principal of the bank loan deductible (line from Company Plan Sponsor to ESOP in the following chart). The ESOP repays the bank loan with proceeds received from the company (line from ESOP to Bank in the following chart). As the ESOP debt is repaid, shares are released from the suspense account.

- First-year ESOP obligation funded as follows:

Deductible payroll contribution ($2,000,000 x 25%)	$500,000
Super common stock dividend ($3,432,000 x 6%)	205,000
Total debt principal paid	$705,000
Interest expense ($3,432,000 x 7%)	240,000
Total ESOP-related obligations	$945,000

The ESOP-related obligations, as presented in this example, will consume a significant percentage of the company's pretax income (estimated to be approximately $1.3 million, substantially the same as 20X3, as stated earlier): 72% ($945,000/$1,300,000). This is a very high percentage, and if the company suddenly has a significant drop in earnings, the ESOP-related debt could hamper operations.

Step 4: When an employee leaves the ESOP, a distribution is made in stock or cash.

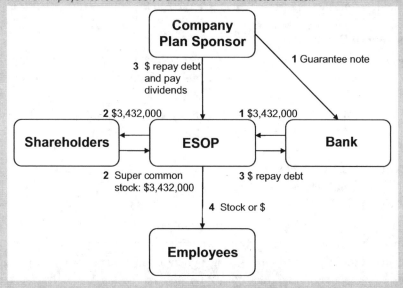

Note: The typical leveraged ESOP transaction may become more complex than the illustration discussed. Often, the bank may require additional collateral of the selling shareholder and a pledge of collateral of a part or all of the ESOP sale proceeds while the ESOP-related debt is amortized.

IRC Section 1042 Restrictions

Mr. Smith sells 52 percent of his stock to the ESOP for $3,432,000. The entire amount will be free of all taxes, providing the funds are fully reinvested in QRP within the applicable 12-month period following the transaction and 3 months prior to the transaction.

After the sale, restrictions apply regarding possible participation in the ESOP by certain family members and nonfamily 25 percent shareholders. We have assumed that Mr. Smith is the sole shareholder; therefore, the restriction to another 25 percent owner does not apply. Additionally, we assumed that Mr. Smith is the only member of his family active in the company; therefore, the restriction to other family members does not apply.

Control Position Transaction

Mr. Smith is interested in selling control to the ESOP, thereby earning a higher value for his stock (the control position value: $6.6 million). The serial sale agreement will ensure that the ESOP has the ability to acquire a control position block of stock and that Mr. Smith will be able to sell all his stock to the ESOP at a control position value. The first sale of stock to the ESOP is a control block of 52 percent, but future sales will be minority blocks: 2 blocks of 24 percent are anticipated in this example.

For the ESOP to pay the control position price, control must exist both in appearance and fact. The ESOP will acquire the control position block with the first purchase: 52 percent. This meets the first test of control in appearance. The ESOP eventually purchases the remaining stock in 2 additional transactions of 24 percent each. For purposes of this example, we have assumed that a block of stock in excess of 50 percent constitutes control of the company.

The ESOP must also be in control in fact. In this case, Mr. Smith will not serve as the sole ESOP trustee (serving as the sole trustee will not be considered passing control to the ESOP). Typically, a plan committee with several members will act as the ESOP trustee. It is important for Mr. Smith to initiate steps to pass control to the ESOP with the first transaction.

S Corporation Election

Almost certainly, the company will make the S corporation election following the third transaction. One hundred percent of the stock will be owned by the ESOP, and the S corporation election will mean the company will not have any exposure to federal income taxes. The company will still have significant ESOP repurchase obligations, but the repurchase exposure will be much easier to meet with federal income tax liability.

Strategic Tax Summary

- The company receives a tax deduction over time for the full stock purchase price on a control position basis. The first block of stock is $3,432,000 (52 percent).
- The ESOP acquires 52 percent of the outstanding stock in the first transaction. Two other transactions are planned to provide the ESOP with 100 percent of the stock over a reasonable time. A serial sale agreement is employed to provide the shareholder with a prorated control position price for the first transaction.
- The first transaction qualifies for the IRC Section 1042 tax-free rollover. The transaction price of $3,432,000 is tax free to the selling shareholder, subject to proper reinvestment in QRP. Additional transactions will also qualify for the same tax treatment.

- IRC Section 1042 restrictions apply.
- As a C corporation, the company is able to create a second class of stock that is sold to the ESOP (super common stock) and that pays a tax-deductible dividend. The dividend paid on the super common stock will be used to repay ESOP-related debt.
- Bank financing is used for the entire amount of the first transaction: $3,432,000. The bank may ask the selling shareholder to pledge QRP as additional loan collateral.
- The company will almost certainly elect S corporation status shortly after the last transaction that enables the ESOP to own 100 percent of the stock.

Summary

The examples illustrate the various tax incentives for ESOPs, as they relate to C corporations. With proper structure, all qualifying contributions to an ESOP are tax deductible. ESOP-related debt principal becomes deductible for taxes. Dividends may even become deductible under certain circumstances. Finally, a selling shareholder in a C corporation may qualify for the IRC Section 1042 tax-free rollover. The tax savings on leveraged ESOPs are substantial and typically warrant a close examination by business owners contemplating strategic transition planning.

Chapter 5

Employee Stock Ownership Plan Transactions and S Corporations

This chapter illustrates many of the tax planning aspects previously described. An example company is described in sufficient detail to provide insights into structuring employee stock ownership plan (ESOP) transactions in S corporations. The examples in chapter 4, "Employee Stock Ownership Plan Transaction and C Corporations," largely parallel the examples in this chapter, with the key difference being the income tax election of the company.

Sample Facts—ABC, Inc. (S Corporation)

The hypothetical ESOP candidate, ABC, Inc. (ABC), has been selected to illustrate many attributes of successful installations. Abbreviated financial statements for the company are presented for analysis purposes. An abbreviated analysis is presented of the fair market value (FMV) of the stock of the company for the purposes of an ESOP.

The ownership of ABC is a single shareholder, Mr. Robert Smith (age 61), who is the founder, is active in the daily operations of the business, and currently serves as the president. Mr. Smith is the only member of the family active in the company. ABC is a well-established manufacturing company that has demonstrated consistent profitability and is recession resistant. Sales have grown consistently, but future growth is expected to be slightly ahead of inflation. ABC operates from two production facilities, and the company owns both facilities. The compensation to Mr. Smith is reasonable for valuation purposes.

These are the basic facts for each of the following illustrations, unless otherwise noted. The valuation summary is intended to serve as an illustration for planning purposes and is not intended to be a primer on business valuations. Business valuations for the purposes of an ESOP are often very complex, with myriad details that are beyond the scope of this book to examine in detail.

Abbreviated Financial Statements

Exhibit 5-1 shows the abbreviated income statement of ABC:

Exhibit 5-1: ABC (S Corporation) Abbreviated Income Statements

	20X1	20X2	20X3
Sales	$14,000,000	$15,000,000	$16,500,000
Cost of sales	9,800,000	10,600,000	11,500,000
Gross profit	4,200,000	4,400,000	5,000,000
Selling, general and administrative expenses	2,850,000	3,140,000	3,460,000
Interest expense	250,000	260,000	240,000
Subtotal	3,100,000	3,400,000	3,700,000
Pretax income	1,100,000	1,000,000	1,300,000
Less: Distribution percentage (40%)	440,000	400,000	520,000
Balance to company AAA	$ 660,000	$ 600,000	$ 780,000

Mr. Smith is in a marginal personal tax rate of 40 percent. The company must distribute a minimum of 40 percent of its pretax income to Mr. Smith accordingly.

Qualifying payroll for the purposes of an ESOP in year 20X3 = $4,000,000

Exhibit 5-2 shows ABC's abbreviated balance sheet:

Exhibit 5-2: ABC (S Corporation) Abbreviated Balance Sheet at December 31, 20X3

Current assets	$5,500,000	Current liabilities	$2,000,000
		All debt	3,000,000
Plant and equipment	7,000,000		
Less: Depreciation	3,000,000	Common stock	500,000
Net fixed assets	4,000,000	AAA	4,000,000
		Total equity	4,500,000
Total assets	$9,500,000	Total liabilities and equity	$9,500,000

The equity of the company consists of 100,000 shares of common stock authorized and 50,000 shares of common stock issued and outstanding. There is only one class of stock and no treasury stock. The company has been an S corporation from its founding.

S Corporation Consideration

Note that the S corporation equity of the company consists of both contributed capital, as indicated by the common stock ($500,000), and the balance in the accumulated adjustment account (AAA) ($4 million). The AAA represents previously taxed income to the share-holder, Mr. Smith. From a tax-planning standpoint, the AAA may be paid out to Mr. Smith with no further federal income tax liability. The distribution of the AAA prior to the installation of an ESOP is often a common planning point.

FMV of Common Stock for the Purposes of an ESOP

ABC is an excellent candidate for an ESOP because of its established financial track record and predictable earnings. The senior management and owner of the company, Mr. Smith, will consider the ESOP as an exit vehicle. Stock will be sold to the ESOP over a period of time. Current valuation methodology assumes the candidate company for the ESOP is a C corporation, even if the company is already an S corporation, as in this example. The general theory is that a hypothetical buyer is a C corporation. Remember that both the IRS and the Department of Labor have valuation oversight of ESOPs. For this example, assuming a C corporation (refer to chapter 4 on C corporations) and a 35 percent C corporation income tax, net income of ABC ranges from a low of $615,000 ($1,000,000 × 65%) in 20X2 to a high of $845,000 ($1,300,000 × 65%) in 20X3. We have selected net income of $800,000 for this analysis. We will value ABC on both a minority position and control position. We will assume that an appropriate control premium is 10 percent. The discount for lack of marketability is already reflected in the analysis, for ease of presentation.

Minority Position FMV

Selected net income for valuation purposes	800,000
Price earnings multiple applied in this case	x 7.5
Minority position FMV	6,000,000

Control Position FMV

Add premium for control: 10%	600,000
Control position FMV	6,600,000

Value per Share

Minority position FMV per share (6,000,000/50,000)	$120/share
Control position FMV per share (6,600,000/50,000)	$132/share

Lack of Marketability

The preceding minority position multiple of 7.5 already includes a lack of marketability adjustment. The multiple of 7.5 is reasonable and already reflects the lack of marketability that is offset in part or total by the put option that ESOP participants have back to the company. We have assumed that a premium for control of 10 percent is reasonable. The control position value does consider a lack of marketability discount for ease of presentation.

It is beyond the scope of this book to specifically quantify the lack of marketability adjustment for the purposes of an ESOP.

Common Entities in Transactions

Exhibit 5-3 identifies common parties of interest in ESOP transactions. As in chapter 4, the applicable components will be used to illustrate the steps and issues surrounding the various transactions in the examples that follow.

Exhibit 5-3: Common Parties of Interest in ESOP Transactions

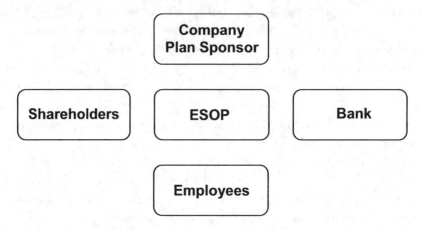

- *Shareholders*. Shareholders represent the owners of the stock in the company (plan sponsor) prior to the ESOP acquiring stock.
- *Company (plan sponsor)*. The company is also referred to as the employer or plan sponsor. The ESOP is established for the benefit of the employees of the company.
- *ESOP*. The employee Stock ownership plan and trust is a separate legal entity that will acquire stock in the company. Once stock is acquired, the ESOP becomes a shareholder.
- *Employees*. They are ESOP participants with rights and interests protected by the Employee Retirement Income Security Act of 1974 (ERISA) and other applicable statutes.
- *Bank*. The bank typically represents a financial institution providing funds to the ESOP for the purchase of company stock.

The following ESOP transactions will be covered in detail for S corporations:

- Stock contributed to ESOP (capital formation ESOP)
- Leveraged ESOP (paying capital gains)
- Prefunded ESOP with no bank debt
- Convert to C corporation—Leveraged ESOP with Internal Revenue Code (IRC) Section 1042 rollover and control

Example—Stock Contributed to ESOP (Capital Formation ESOP)

Significant Factors

This example is substantially the same as the corresponding example in chapter 4 on C corporations. Many of the issues are identical. The full narrative is reproduced to keep the example in chapter 5 comparable with the examples in chapter 4.

Mr. Smith will authorize ABC to contribute stock to the ESOP for the upcoming year. The stock will come from authorized but unissued shares. There will be some dilution of the ownership percentage of Mr. Smith, but the dilution is deemed justified to determine if the ESOP will be embraced by the employees. At a later date, Mr. Smith may personally decide to sell more stock to the ESOP. The company will contribute $300,000 in stock to the ESOP, a minority position block of stock.

Illustration—Stock Contributed to ESOP (Capital Formation ESOP)

Exhibit 5–4 indicates conceptually the contribution of stock from the company to the ESOP:

Exhibit 5-4: Contribution of Stock From the Company to the ESOP

Step 1: The company is authorized to contribute $300,000 of common stock to the ESOP. The total value of the contributed stock is known—$300,000—but the number of shares this amount represents is not known. There will be dilution to the existing shareholder as a result of the contribution.

Step 2: The number of shares represented by the $300,000 contribution must be determined. The minority position FMV of the company is $6 million.

Dilution computation:

$$\text{Value per share} = \frac{\text{Aggregate FMV of company stock contribution}}{\text{Number of shares outstanding before contribution}}$$

$$\text{Value per share} = \frac{\$6,000,000 - \$300,000}{50,000}$$

Value per share = $114

Shares issued = $300,000/$114

Shares issued = $2,631 (Rounded to whole shares)

Step 3: New shares will be issued representing the stock contribution. The following schedule indicates the ownership of the company following the contribution. After the transaction, Mr. Smith now owns 95 percent of the outstanding stock, and the ESOP owns 5 percent of the stock.

Shareholder	Stock Before Contribution	Stock After Contribution
Mr. Smith	50,000 (100%)	50,000 (95%)
ESOP	0	2,631 (5%)
Total	50,000 (100%)	52,631 (100%)

Step 4: Assuming the company distributes earnings to Mr. Smith to cover any personal tax liability, the stock contribution provides a tax deduction to the company without a corresponding cash outlay. The company has generated positive cash flow as a result of the stock contribution, to the extent of the tax savings.

Stock contribution	$300,000
Mr. Smith tax rate (40%)	× 0.40
Enhanced cash flow	$120,000

(continued)

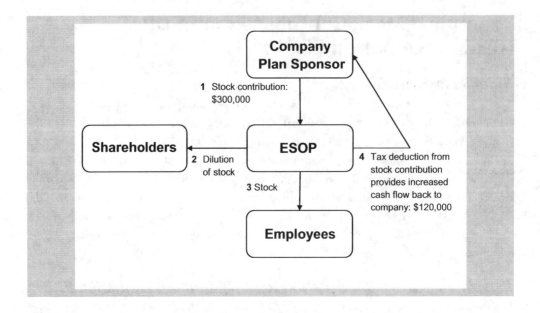

Strategic Tax Summary

- The company receives a tax deduction for the contribution to the ESOP: $300,000.
- The company shelters $120,000 of cash by the tax savings of the $300,000 noncash deduction ($300,000 × 40%).
- There is dilution to existing shareholders by the contribution of stock to the ESOP.
- The ESOP is currently a small percentage of the outstanding stock. The percentage of stock in the ESOP may be increased at the election of the controlling shareholders.

Example—Leveraged ESOP (Paying Capital Gains)

Significant Factors

This example shares a number of similar considerations as a leveraged ESOP in a C corporation. Unlike the C corporation example, if the shareholder in an S corporation elects to sell shares to the ESOP, the gain on the transaction is taxable to the shareholder. Typically, the gain on the sale is taxed as capital gain. Unlike the C corporation, there are no IRC Section 1042 restrictions. The shareholder is not required to sell 30 percent of stock to the ESOP because all the gain is taxable, in any event.

Mr. Smith will authorize the sale of 20 percent of his outstanding shares to the ESOP. Without the IRC Section 1042 restrictions, Mr. Smith does not have to be concerned with the 30 percent test. At this time, only 20 percent of the stock will be sold to the ESOP, with no future anticipated sales, a minority position. A bank will provide the financing for the entire transaction.

Illustration—Leveraged ESOP (Paying Capital Gains)

Exhibit 5-5 indicates conceptually a typical leveraged ESOP. In this example, the ESOP is going to borrow money from a bank and purchase stock of the company from Mr. Smith (shareholder). The following steps indicate the flow of funds from the bank to the selling shareholder:

Exhibit 5-5: Typical Leveraged ESOP

FMV of stock sold to the ESOP = Minority position FMV × Sale percentage
FMV of stock sold to the ESOP = $6,000,000 × 20% = $1,200,000
Loan amortization 5 years ($1,200,000/5) = $240,000/year

Step 1: The company arranges for the ESOP to borrow money from the bank to purchase stock from the shareholders: $1.2 million. The company guarantees the ESOP loan from the bank. The bank loans the money to the ESOP.

- More commonly, the bank loans the money directly to the company to have a greater security position in the transaction. The company has a "mirror" loan to the ESOP for the same amount. The company, in effect, still guarantees the loan.

Step 2: The ESOP takes the loan proceeds from the bank and buys the stock from the shareholder: $1.2 million. Shareholder gain on the sale of the stock is subject to capital gain tax.

- After the transaction, the ESOP owns the stock, but because of the ESOP-related debt, the stock is held in a suspense account often referred to as unearned ESOP shares.

Step 3: The company repays the bank loan by contributing money to the ESOP in an amount to cover both loan interest and principal and by getting a deduction for the ESOP contribution. This effectively makes the principal of the bank loan deductible. The ESOP repays the bank loan with proceeds received from the company. As the ESOP debt is repaid, shares are released from the suspense account.

- The first year ESOP obligation is as follows:

ESOP principal payment	$240,000
Interest expense ($1,200,000 × 7%)	84,000
Total	$324,000

- The entire amount is deductible to the company. The ESOP obligation is significantly below the allowable payroll contribution amount. The payroll contribution limit is 25 percent of qualifying payroll (including ESOP-related interest expense).

Contribution limit ($4,000,000 × 25%)	$1,000,000
ESOP contribution, including interest	$ 324,000

- A key distinction is the S corporation payroll contribution limit of 25 percent must include the interest expense on the loan.

Step 4: When an employee leaves the ESOP, a distribution is made from the ESOP in stock or cash.

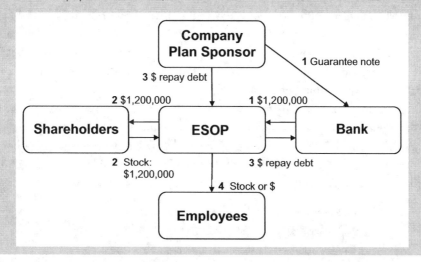

S Corporation Issues

The selling shareholder, in this case, will be paying taxes (likely capital gain taxes) on the gain from the sale of stock to the ESOP. Although the prospect of paying taxes is unfortunate, a number of other aspects to the transaction moderate the tax impact.

Mr. Smith will be permitted to participate in the ESOP. He is selling stock to the ESOP, but because he will remain active in the company for a period of time, ESOP contributions allocated to his account will help offset the taxes he will pay on the sale.

The IRC Section 1042 restrictions do not apply regarding family member attribution rules and other 25 percent shareholders. In this example, neither of those issues applies. However, if the company did employ family members, or there was a 25 percent shareholder, then freedom from the IRC Section 1042 restrictions would be a significant benefit.

Care must be taken, however, to avoid allocating so much stock to family members that a possible tax penalty is incurred under IRC Section 409(p), discussed in chapter 3, "Employee Stock Ownership Plan Transaction Mechanics."

Strategic Tax Summary

- The company receives a tax deduction over time for the full stock purchase price of $1.2 million plus related interest expense.
- The ESOP acquires 20 percent of the outstanding stock, a minority position block. This percentage may be increased at a later date by the decision of the controlling shareholder.
- The gain on the transaction is taxable to the selling shareholder. Most likely, the shareholder is exposed to capital gain tax.
- Bank financing was used exclusively for the transaction. The bank may ask the selling shareholder to pledge the cash received by the shareholder as additional loan collateral.

Example—Prefunded ESOP With No Bank Debt

Significant Factors

This example is similar to the previous one. Mr. Smith will authorize the sale of 20 percent of his outstanding shares to the ESOP. Because the IRC Section 1042 tax deferral is not available, Mr. Smith is free to sell any percentage of stock to the ESOP he wishes because all the gain will be taxable to him. In this case, Mr. Smith wishes to sell enough stock to obtain significant cash payment, but he also wants to avoid bank debt.

The company will prefund the ESOP with deductible contributions of cash to the ESOP for 3 years. Each year, the company will contribute $350,000 to the ESOP. Projections indicate that after 3 years of prefunding, the ESOP will have sufficient cash to purchase the 20 percent block of stock. The FMV of the stock is still assumed to be $1.2 million. The following schedule indicates the funding for the 20 percent block of stock:

Deductible cash contribution to ESOP 20X3	$ 350,000
Deductible cash contribution to ESOP 20X4	350,000
Deductible cash contribution to ESOP 20X5	350,000
Investment income on ESOP contributions	150,000
Total funds available	$1,200,000

Prefunding the ESOP transaction in this manner eliminates the requirement for bank-related debt. The yearly deductible cash contributions to the ESOP are below the payroll contribution limit ($4,000,000 × 25% = $1,000,000 contribution limit).

Illustration—Prefunded ESOP With No Bank Debt

Exhibit 5-6 indicates the prefunded ESOP in which only the cash in the ESOP will be used to acquire company stock. Mr. Smith could elect to sell $350,000 of stock to the ESOP each year at the prevailing FMV. The gain on the stock transaction each year will be taxed to Mr. Smith. The following steps indicate the flow the funds to the selling shareholder:

Exhibit 5-6: Prefunded ESOP With No Bank Debt

FMV of stock sold to the ESOP = Minority position FMV × Sale percentage
FMV of stock sold to the ESOP = $6,000,000 × 20% = $1,200,000

Step 1: The company prefunds cash contributions to the ESOP for 3 years. The cash contributions are deductible to the company. Total prefunding with investment income amounts to $1.2 million. The entire cash balance is available for purchasing stock.

- The ESOP prefunding obligation is significantly below the allowable payroll contribution amount. The payroll contribution limit is 25 percent of qualifying payroll (excluding ESOP-related interest expense).

Contribution limit ($4,000,000 × 25%)	$1,000,000
ESOP contribution	$ 350,000

Step 2: The ESOP takes proceeds from the prefunded ESOP and buys the stock from the shareholder: $1.2 million. The shareholder sells stock to the ESOP, and any gain will be taxable to the shareholder, typically as capital gain.

- After the transaction, the ESOP owns the stock, and the stock will be allocated directly to the accounts of the ESOP participants. The stock allocated to individual accounts will be subject to vesting.

- The cash contributions to the ESOP effectively allow the company employees to gain an equity stake in the business with tax-deductible dollars. If the employees had to purchase the stock, they would do so with after-tax dollars (dollars on which they already paid taxes).

Step 3: When an employee leaves the ESOP, a distribution is made in stock or cash.

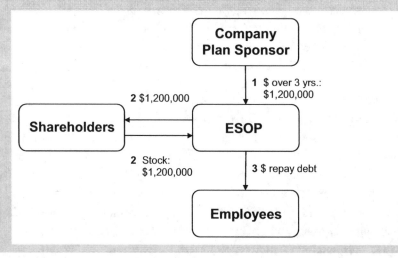

Strategic Tax Summary

- The company receives a tax deduction over time for the contributions to the ESOP, which represents most of the purchase price. The company previously deducted prefunding contributions to the ESOP.
- The ESOP acquires 20 percent of the outstanding stock, a minority position block. This percentage may be increased at a later date by the decision of the controlling shareholder.
- The gain on the transaction is taxable to the selling shareholder. Most likely, the shareholder is exposed to capital gain tax.
- The use of prefunding enables the company to purchase stock without the use of bank-related debt. If the shareholder wishes to eliminate or reduce the reliance on outside debt, the prefunding strategy is a solid option.

Example—Convert to C Corporation—Leveraged ESOP With IRC Section 1042 Rollover and Control

Significant Factors

The company is currently an S Corporation, but Mr. Smith wants to benefit from the IRC Section 1042 rollover. The tax deferral on the IRC Section 1042 is significant in this example because Mr. Smith wants to sell 100 percent of his stock to the ESOP and obtain the control position value.

The strategy in this case is to have the company make the election to immediately become a C corporation. This election will enable Mr. Smith to employ the IRC Section 1042 rollover on the sale of stock to the ESOP. Bank financing will be used for the entire transaction.

At the time of this publication, the federal capital gain rate of 15 percent is legislated to expire by January 1, 2013, and it will be reset to 20 percent at that time. Additionally, a proposed capital gain surtax of approximately 3.5 percent is part of nationalized health care. When maximum state capital gain taxes are considered (in such jurisdictions as California, New York, and New Jersey), the combined federal and state capital gain tax rate may approach 30 percent or even higher. With combined marginal rates that high, many business owners may consider the tax attractions of the IRC Section 1042 tax deferral.

Tax Planning Strategy
Conversions Between S and C Corporations

This ESOP installation assumes the company will first convert from an S corporation to a C corporation. The company will use bank debt to finance the stock transaction, which should significantly increase deductible interest expenses and ESOP-related debt repayment. The company will have a limited exposure to C corporation federal income taxes as a result. After the last block of stock is sold to the ESOP, and the ESOP becomes a 100 percent shareholder, the company will elect to return to being an S corporation.

Once the C corporation election is completed, the company must wait five years before electing to become an S corporation again. The five-year wait, in this case, is not likely to be a significant drawback. The company will have significant ESOP-related obligations for several years that will sharply reduce any C corporation–related federal income taxes. The company will elect to become an S corporation after the last transaction that takes the ESOP to 100 percent.

AAA Distribution

Because Mr. Smith is selling all his stock to the ESOP, it is advised that the AAA be distributed to him. The AAA is previously taxed income to him, and the company may distribute the balance to Mr. Smith free of all personal federal income taxes. It is essential that the AAA be distributed within one year after the C corporation election. The AAA balance becomes retained earnings of the company after one year and no longer may be distributed to shareholders tax free. The AAA may be reclassified as a shareholder note payable in part or total to preserve the option of making the distribution to Mr. Smith tax free as the cash flow of the company permits.

The AAA distribution is being completed just prior to the sale of stock to the ESOP. We assume the company does not have the cash to pay the AAA. Mr. Smith will take a shareholder note for the total amount: $4 million (shareholder note). This shareholder note will be offset against the FMV control position amount. (Some significant adjustment to the FMV is appropriate because the company is replacing $4 million in equity with an equal amount of debt.) Here we have simply offset the shareholder note against the FMV of the stock for ease of presentation.

Shareholder Note

This strategy makes good tax planning because as the shareholder note of $4 million is repaid, the debt principal proceeds are tax free to Mr. Smith. (Interest income will be taxable to Mr. Smith as ordinary income.) If the AAA was left in the company (and not deducted from the FMV of the stock), the amount of the AAA would increase the basis of the qualified replacement property (QRP) purchased by Mr. Smith, pursuant to the IRC Section 1042 rollover provisions. This would benefit Mr. Smith only if he disposed of QRP by reducing the realized gain. The shareholder note will likely have a very long amortization period because the repayment of the ESOP note will have the higher priority. The bank will almost certainly insist that the shareholder note be subordinate to the ESOP debt.

In this case, Mr. Smith is providing a significant degree of seller financing on this transaction by taking back the shareholder note. He could also negotiate with the bank and have it provide a percentage of the funds for a partial immediate payment for the AAA.

Stock Transactions

Mr. Smith will use the ESOP as his exit vehicle and, over time, sell 100 percent of his stock to the plan and receive a control position price. The company will convert to a C corporation, so that Mr. Smith will be able to use the provisions of IRC Section 1042.

Mr. Smith will sell his stock in three transactions. This strategy is elected because no single transaction will impose an unreasonable amount of ESOP-related debt on the company. It is unlikely that Mr. Smith could sell all his stock to the ESOP in a single transaction and negotiate loan terms acceptable to him.

The following schedule indicates the allocation of the transaction value between the shareholder note (formerly the AAA) and ESOP:

FMV control position	$6,600,000
Less: AAA reclassified as shareholder note	4,000,000
FMV control position to the ESOP	$2,600,000

Transaction	Shares Sold	Transaction Amount
First transaction: 52%	26,000	$1,352,000 (0.52 × $2,600,000)
Second transaction: 24%	12,000	Control FMV at transaction date*
Third transaction: 24%	12,000	Control FMV at transaction date*
Total	50,000	

*Subject to proper documentation.

Mr. Smith is both selling a 52 percent block to the ESOP for $1,352,000 and receiving a $4 million note for his AAA balance. The total of $5,352,000 is being received.

Issue: Receiving a Prorated Control Position Price

The intent of Mr. Smith is to sell all his stock to the ESOP: a control position. Mr. Smith wants to avoid the leverage placed on the company by selling all his stock in a single transaction. In this case, he will sell enough stock to the ESOP in a single transaction to pass control (over 50 percent of the stock) to the ESOP. In the preceding case, 52 percent of the stock is sold, just to simplify the example.

Mr. Smith will agree to sell a complete control position over time. The key point in this example is that Mr. Smith will execute an agreement granting the ESOP the authority to purchase enough stock to provide a control position with the first transaction. The first transaction will be linked to succeeding transactions as though they occurred on the same day and in a consistent manner. The mechanics of this type of transaction are often referred to as a serial sale. It is important to link the transactions in this manner because the ESOP is gaining a control position with the first purchase. Mr. Smith will want to be assured that future minority blocks of stock sold to the ESOP, in this case 2 additional minority blocks of 24 percent each, will qualify for the same control position valuation. Without the serial sale agreement in place, the ESOP may not be obligated to pay a control price for a future minority block of stock. If the selling shareholder wishes to receive a control position value for his or her stock sold to the ESOP, care must be taken to ensure the ESOP is gaining the control it is buying. It is advisable to consult with an experienced ESOP attorney when structuring such a transaction.

The first transaction, 52 percent, will be valued at the prevailing FMV on a control position basis: $1,352,000 ($2,600,000 × 52%). Succeeding transactions will be valued at the prevailing FMV on a control position basis on the date of the transaction. If the company continues to grow and remain profitable, it is probable that the value will increase.

The first transaction, 52 percent, will qualify for the IRC Section 1042 rollover. Succeeding transactions will also qualify for the IRC Section 1042 rollover because the percentage of stock in the ESOP will remain above 30 percent.

Illustration—Convert to C Corporation—Leveraged ESOP With IRC Section 1042 Rollover And Control

This illustration is similar to the example of a leveraged C corporation ESOP in the prior chapter with the IRC Section 1042 rollover. In this case, the transaction will be repeated 3 times as the 3 blocks of stock are sold to the ESOP. Additionally, the company will amortize the shareholder note for $4 million over a longer period of time.

Exhibit 5-7 indicates conceptually a typical leveraged ESOP. In this example, the ESOP is going to borrow money from a bank and purchase stock of the company from Mr. Smith (shareholder). The following steps indicate the flow of funds from the bank to the selling shareholder:

Exhibit 5-7: ESOP Borrowing Money From a Bank to Purchase Shareholder Stock

FMV of stock sold to the ESOP = Control position FMV × Sale percentage
FMV of stock sold to the ESOP = $2,600,000 × 52% = $1,352,000
Loan amortization ESOP note of 5 years ($1,352,000/5) = $270,000/year
Loan amortization shareholder note of 20 years ($4,000,000/20) = $200,000/year

Step 1: The company makes a distribution of the AAA to the shareholder in the amount of $4 million. The company does not have the cash for the payment, so the shareholder accepts a $4 million note that will be subordinate to the bank debt.

Step 2: The company arranges for the ESOP to borrow money from the bank to purchase stock from the shareholder: $1,352,000. The company guarantees the ESOP loan from the bank. The bank loans the money to the ESOP.

- More commonly, the bank loans the money directly to the company to have a greater security position in the transaction. The company has a "mirror" loan to the ESOP for the same amount. The company is directly liable for the loan.

Step 3: The ESOP takes the loan proceeds from the bank and buys the stock from the shareholder. The shareholder sells stock to the ESOP and qualifies for the IRC Section 1042 tax-free rollover because the ESOP has acquired at least 30 percent of the outstanding stock.

- After the transaction, the ESOP owns the stock, but because of the ESOP-related debt, the stock is held in a suspense account often referred as unearned ESOP shares.

Step 4: The company repays the bank loan by advancing money to the ESOP in an amount to cover both loan interest and principal and by getting a deduction for the ESOP contribution. This effectively makes the principal of the bank loan deductible. The ESOP repays the bank loan with proceeds received from the company. As the ESOP debt is repaid, shares are released from the suspense account.

- The first-year ESOP note and shareholder note obligation are as follows:

ESOP principal payment	$270,000
ESOP interest ($1,352,000 × 7%)	95,000
Shareholder note principal	200,000
Shareholder note interest ($4,000,000 × 6%)	240,000
Total	$805,000

- A significant amount of the $805,000 is deductible for taxes to the company. The deductible amounts include all the interest and the ESOP principal payment: $605,000 ($270,000 + $95,000 + $240,000).

- The company will also have to repay the shareholder note of $4 million. The repayment of the shareholder note principal will not be tax deductible to the company like the ESOP note principal. Interest expense on the shareholder note will be tax deductible. If the company has additional cash after taxes, it may accelerate repayment of the shareholder note because a 20-year amortization in this illustration will likely be unacceptable to the seller.

- The ESOP obligation is significantly below the allowable payroll contribution amount. The payroll contribution limit is 25 percent of qualifying payroll (excluding ESOP-related interest expense).

(continued)

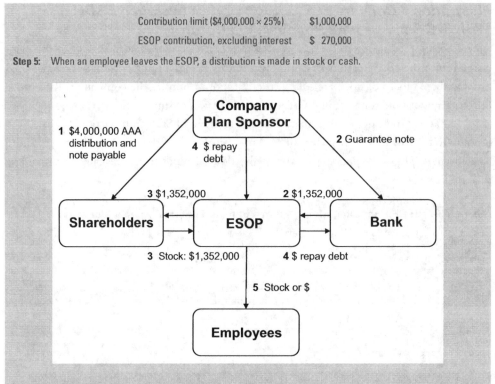

Contribution limit ($4,000,000 × 25%) $1,000,000

ESOP contribution, excluding interest $ 270,000

Step 5: When an employee leaves the ESOP, a distribution is made in stock or cash.

Note: The typical leveraged ESOP transaction may become more complex than the illustration discussed. Often, the bank may require additional collateral of the selling shareholder and a pledge of collateral of a part or all of the ESOP sale proceeds while the ESOP-related debt is amortized.

IRC Section 1042 Restrictions

Mr. Smith sells 52 percent of his stock to the ESOP for $1,352,000. The entire amount will be free of all taxes, providing the funds in full are reinvested in QRP with the applicable 12-month period following the transaction and 5 months prior to the transaction.

After the sale, restrictions apply regarding possible participation in the ESOP by certain family members and nonfamily 25 percent shareholders. We have assumed that Mr. Smith is the sole shareholder; therefore, the restriction to another 25 percent owner does not apply. Additionally, we assumed that Mr. Smith is the only member of his family active in the company; therefore, the restriction to other family members does not apply.

Control Position Transaction

Mr. Smith is interested in selling control to the ESOP, thereby earning a higher value for his stock: $2,600,000 (control position value of $6,600,000 − $4,000,000 AAA). The serial sale agreement will ensure that the ESOP has the ability to acquire a control position block of stock and that Mr. Smith will be able to sell all his stock to the ESOP at a control value. The first sale of stock to the ESOP is a control block of 52 percent, but future sales will be minority blocks: 2 blocks of 24 percent are anticipated in this example.

For the ESOP to pay the control position price, control must exist both in appearance and fact. The ESOP will acquire the control position block with the first purchase: 52 percent. This meets the first test of control in appearance. The ESOP will eventually purchase the remaining stock in 2 additional transactions of 24 percent each. For the purposes of this example, we have assumed that a block of stock in excess of 50 percent constitutes control of the company.

The ESOP must also be in control in fact. The structure of the ESOP trustee is important in this instance. In this case, Mr. Smith will not serve as the sole ESOP trustee (because serving as the sole trustee will not be considered passing control to the ESOP). Typically, a plan committee with several members will act as the ESOP trustee. Another option for the company is to engage an outside independent trustee, often a trust department in a financial institution. It is important for Mr. Smith to initiate steps to pass control to the ESOP with the first transaction.

S Corporation Election

Almost certainly, the company will make the S corporation election following the third transaction. One hundred percent of the stock will be owned by the ESOP, and the S corporation election will mean the company will not have any exposure to federal income taxes. The company will still have significant ESOP repurchase obligations, but the repurchase exposure will be much easier to meet with no federal income tax liability.

The company was originally an S corporation that changed to a C corporation. ABC will have to wait a minimum of five years before it can elect to be an S corporation again. In this case, waiting five years will not likely be burdensome from a federal corporate income tax standpoint. The company will be heavily leveraged following the first ESOP transaction and the AAA conversion to the shareholder note.

Strategic Tax Summary

- The company receives a tax deduction over time for the full stock purchase price on a control position basis. The first block of stock is $1,820,000 ($3,500,000 × 52%).
- The ESOP acquires 52 percent of the outstanding stock in the first transaction. Two other transactions are planned to provide the ESOP with 100 percent of the stock. A serial sale agreement is employed to provide the shareholder with a prorated control position price for the first transaction and all subsequent transactions.
- The first transaction qualifies for the IRC Section 1042 tax-free rollover. The transaction price of $1,820,000 is tax free to the selling shareholder, subject to proper reinvestment in QRP. Additional transactions will also qualify for the same tax treatment.
- IRC Section 1042 restrictions apply.
- Prior to the C corporation election and the sale of stock to the ESOP, the AAA from the S corporation is distributed to the shareholder: $4 million. The company does not have the cash to pay the AAA; therefore, the shareholder takes a shareholder note for $4 million. As the shareholder note principal is repaid by the company, the proceeds will pass to the shareholder free of all federal income tax. The company will not receive a tax deduction for the repayment of the shareholder note principal but will get a tax deduction for interest. A key point in planning is that when the company is 100 percent ESOP, and the applicable waiting period has passed to reelect the S corporation, the S corporation election is very beneficial. An S corporation that is 100 percent ESOP will be able to repay the balance of the shareholder note with pretax dollars because the S corporation will not have any current-year federal income tax exposure.

- Bank financing is used for the entire amount of the first transaction: $1,820,000. The bank may ask the selling shareholder to personally guarantee the loan or pledge QRP as additional loan collateral.
- The company will almost certainly elect S corporation status shortly after the last transaction that enables the ESOP to own 100 percent of the stock.

Example—Leveraged Sale of 100 Percent to the ESOP in a Single Transaction

Significant Factors

Increasingly, this transaction structure is being considered because the company becomes an income tax-free entity immediately upon the completion of the sale. Remember that ABC is an S corporation, and as an S corporation, it is a pass-through entity for income tax purposes. ABC does not pay federal or state income taxes; rather, the taxable income is passed through to its shareholders and taxed to them at their individual tax rates annually. In this case, following the transaction, the only shareholder is the ESOP (100 percent owner). The ESOP is a qualified retirement plan under ERISA, and the plan pays no current-year income taxes. As employees leave the plan, and distribution are made to them, those distributions may be rolled over into another qualified plan (generally free of all income taxes), or the funds may be withdrawn under the various ERISA options and will be taxed to the individual as ordinary income when received. Following the sale of 100 percent of the stock to the ESOP, ABC is an income tax-free company. Remember, although the company does not have exposure to current-year income taxes, a substantial long-term stock repurchase option is being assumed.

The 100 percent ESOP S corporation ESOP does hold attractive attributes for repaying acquisition-related debt entirely with pretax cash flow. This fact often indicates that acquisition debt principal is often repaid in half the time because the corporate level or individual level (as in S corporation shareholders) do not have to be considered.

There is a significant issue with such a transaction: the substantial amount of debt being assumed by the company. From a pragmatic standpoint, it is highly unlikely that third-party financing will be secured for such a transaction. In our example, ABC is an attractive ESOP candidate because of its profitability and strong beginning balance sheet, but the debt capacity of the company for the purposes of a 100 percent buyout are limited. If such a transaction is to occur, it is a virtual certainty that the shareholder, Mr. Smith, will have to provide substantial financial assistance in the form of a seller note.

For ease of presentation, we will assume Mr. Smith will provide all the financing for this transaction in the form of a seller note. Mr. Smith has agreed to this structure knowing he could have obtained some funding from a bank, but any seller note would be subordinate to the bank, so he concluded to just be the sole banker for this transaction. He realizes the debt principal will be repaid with pretax cash flow, which is attractive. The seller note carries a blended rate between the senior bank lending rate (say 6 percent) and a mezzanine rate that is significantly higher. Mr. Smith agrees to a blended rate of 8 percent on the seller note. This blended rate is very attractive in comparison with long-term Treasury yield under 3 percent, and a highly volatile public equity market. Although it is possible Mr. Smith could have negotiated a higher interest rate, the interest is taxable to him as ordinary income, and he would rather have ABC repay the debt principal as fast as possible because that is subject to capital gain tax liability. Further, the taxable gain on the sale is $2.6 million (the purchase price on a control basis of $6.6 million less the AAA account of $4 million). Mr. Smith's exposure to capital gain taxes is limited by the gain of $2.6 million.

Illustration — Leveraged Sale of 100 Percent to the ESOP in a Single Transaction

Exhibit 5-8 indicates conceptually the leveraged ESOP transaction. In this case, Mr. Smith is providing all the seller financing. Certainly, ABC has some debt capacity, and a bank could have been used, in part, for a portion of the transaction price. Because Mr. Smith would have to subordinate his note to the bank and possibly guarantee the bank note, he determined to simply finance the transaction at a blended rate of 8 percent.

Exhibit 5-8: Leveraged Sale of 100 Percent to the ESOP in a Single Transaction

FMV of stock sold to ESOP control position = $6,600,000

Loan amortization permits the full application of the pretax income of ABC because there will be no income tax liability. During the most recent fiscal year, the pretax income (earnings before interest and taxes) is $1,540,000. (Remember, there is preexisting debt in ABC, and there was $240,000 of interest expense; the existing debt was assumed by the ESOP.) In general terms, we will assume the company has approximately $1.3 million of pretax cash flow to service the acquisition-related debt.

Step 1: Mr. Smith loans the full purchase price of $6.6 million to the company in return for a seller note at 8 percent (the outside loan). The cash flow analysis suggests the seller note to Mr. Smith will be repaid in 8 years or less. Taking a more conservative position, the seller note is for 10 years, with no prepayment penalty. It is likely the company will be able to repay the note in substantially less time than 10 years, especially if ABC posts a few years of strong profitability. The company guarantees the seller note to Mr. Smith.

Step 2: The company loans the full purchase price of $6.6 million to the ESOP (the inside note). The inside note is not recorded on the books of the company. The amortization of the inside note will be used to release the stock from collateral. The company elects to amortize the inside loan over 15 years, a deliberately different (and extended) amortization period than the outside loan. The inside loan will cause the stock to be allocated to the employees' ESOP accounts over the next 15 years. This has the effect of providing an ESOP contribution to the employees over a longer period of time and delaying the repurchase obligation.

Step 3: The ESOP acquires the stock from Mr. Smith for the $6.6 million in seller notes. This example is somewhat circular in that Mr. Smith has sold all his stock to the ESOP in return for a seller note, and he has not received any cash. He could have arranged for some bank financing up to the debt capacity of the ABC. Legal counsel for Mr. Smith ensures that he is well-protected as a creditor to the company. The legal protections are beyond the scope of this example.

Step 4: The company will repay the $6.6 million seller note over time by making contributions of both debt principal and interest to the ESOP. The ESOP, in turn, pays Mr. Smith the appropriate amounts to amortize the seller note. The diagram indicates the ESOP is repaying the seller note, and that is technically the case. The real source of funding for the note payments is the company.

The preexisting debt in ABC (see example balance sheet: $3 million) following the sale of stock to the ESOP will also be repaid with pretax cash flow. Assume the bank holding this debt agrees to a 2-year interest-only payment program; the company will have approximately $1.3 million in cash flow to service the ESOP acquisition note at 8 percent. Interest the first year is approximately $530,000 ($6,600,000 × 8%), enabling ABC to repay approximately $770,000 in acquisition debt principal ($1,300,000 − $530,000). In a similarly aggressive manner, the ESOP acquisition debt principal may be reduced. Due to the ability to repay debt principal with pretax dollars, approximately $2.5 million in debt may be repaid within 36 months, or almost 38 percent of the acquisition price ($2,500,000/$6,600,000).

(continued)

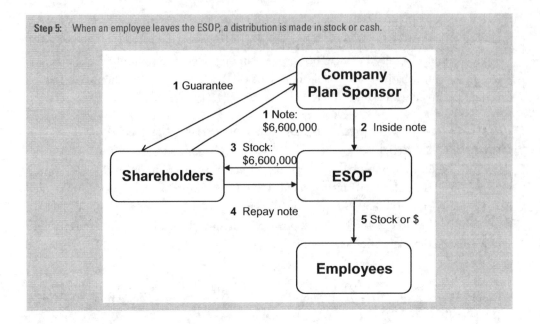

Step 5: When an employee leaves the ESOP, a distribution is made in stock or cash.

Strategic Tax Summary

- Mr. Smith sells all his stock to the ESOP in a single taxable transaction. The purchase price by the ESOP is $6.6 million, and we have assumed a tax basis of $4 million (the amount of the AAA account), for a taxable gain of $2.6 million. Assuming a 15 percent federal capital gain tax rate, the federal capital gain tax liability to Mr. Smith is $390,000 ($2,600,000 × 15%). Because there is seller financing, Mr. Smith could elect installment sale treatment on the gain. State and local capital gain taxes may apply.

- Mr. Smith sold all the stock to the ESOP and received a control position price for the transaction. He engaged a fully discretionary independent outside trustee to represent the ESOP in the sale of stock. Following the sale of stock to the ESOP, the outside trustee was retained to assist in corporate governance. The outside trustee was joined by a select number of senior officers to form a trust committee. Mr. Smith is not serving in any trustee capacity. This section is included to illustrate best practices and what we often find in practice. Mr. Smith is not advised to serve in any trustee capacity because he sold the stock in ABC on a control position basis.

- The 100 percent S corporation ESOP pays no income taxes (but is subject to the longer-term repurchase obligation that is significant). All ESOP acquisition debt principal is repaid with pretax cash flow. Additionally, all existing debt principal in the company is repaid with pretax cash flow.

- This example has focused on the ability of ABC to repay the outside seller note to Mr. Smith with pretax dollars. The annual contribution to the ESOP is typically limited to 25 percent of qualifying payroll, and that percentage includes interest on the acquisition debt in an S corporation. The S corporation contribution limit to employees will be acknowledged with the amortization of the inside loan. The inside loan amortization period in this example is 15 years. Having a protracted amortization period delays the time when the repurchase obligation begins, and it ensure there will be an allocation of ESOP stock into the account balances of the employees over the 15 years. New employees added during this time will have an opportunity to participate in the ownership of ABC.

- Mr. Smith has agreed to provide seller financing in this case. Selling to an ESOP takes time and the assistance of the selling shareholder, in most instances. It is likely that the total debt of the company could be refinanced at some point (say in five years), and Mr. Smith could be in a position to walk away and let the successor management team run the business.

Summary

The examples illustrate the various tax incentives for ESOPs as they relate to S corporations. With proper structure, all qualifying contributions to an ESOP are tax deductible. ESOP-related debt principal becomes deductible for taxes. Shareholders selling to an S corporation ESOP are exposed to taxes on the recognized gain on the stock. One technique is to switch the S corporation to a C corporation to utilize the IRC Section 1042 deferral. The higher the marginal capital gain tax rate (including federal and state taxes), the more attractive the IRC Section 1042 deferral becomes. Increasingly, companies with strong cash flow will elect to go 100 percent ESOP immediately. Although this election offers substantial tax advantages, it also places a very high amount of acquisition debt on the company. Given the recent economic volatility, highly leveraged transactions should only be considered with great care and analysis to avoid the risk of default. The tax savings on leveraged ESOPs are substantial and typically warrant a close examination by business owners contemplating strategic transition planning.

Chapter 6

Advanced Employee Stock Ownership Plan Applications

This chapter is intended to provide a brief overview of the range of employee stock owner-ship plan (ESOP) applications in closely held companies. This range of illustrations is not intended to be all-inclusive; rather, it is a sampling of the flexibility ESOPs may provide in meeting various requirements. ESOPs may become very complex, with myriad issues and complexities as the transactions grow in both size and sophistication. It is beyond the scope of this book to describe such applications in any appreciable detail. Rather, by providing an overview of such applications, the intent is to leave the impression that ESOPs are often a viable option for consideration in transition planning.

This book is oriented to the discussion of ESOPs in closely held companies. ESOPs or other types of equity participation plans have been installed in many publicly held corpo-rations, as well. The dynamics of ESOPs in public companies are often much different than ESOPs in closely held firms. With public companies, the securities markets will determine the value of the stock. The public markets are often notorious for their short-term orien-tation and volatility. Correspondingly, ESOP-related issues in publicly held companies often have different dynamics. ESOPs in publicly held companies are not considered in this chapter.

Mergers and Acquisitions—Buying a Target Company With Pretax Dollars

This particular illustration is easiest to understand with the S corporation that is 100 percent ESOP owned. The S corporation has no federal income tax liability because it is a pass-through entity for tax purposes. The only shareholder of the company is the ESOP, a qualified benefit plan that has no federal income tax liability to pay. The company is profit oriented, but it pays no federal income taxes.

- Remember, however, the 100 percent ESOP company has a significant stock repurchase obligation that must be funded eventually. When the ESOP participant leaves the plan, the stock will be redeemed at that point, and the company will have to provide cash for the stock purchase. This is a deferral of the federal income tax only because the ESOP participant will eventually pay ordinary income on the distribution.
- If the ESOP company (acquirer) identifies a suitable acquisition candidate (target), the target may be purchased with pretax dollars. The acquirer pays no federal income taxes; therefore, all its income may be retained in the company for business purposes. Additionally, any debt incurred by the acquirer for whatever reason may be repaid with pretax dollars. These factors are critical to understanding the unique tax position of the acquirer. Any available company cash or outside debt used by the acquirer for an acquisition represents pretax dollars, and the debt principal is repaid with pretax dollars.

Purchase of Stock

This strategy is most useful, for example, if the acquirer offers to buy the stock of the target. Typically, one significant disadvantage of buying stock in the target is that the acquirer must accept the existing depreciation schedule of the target. The purchase price of the stock in the target becomes merely the new basis of the stock, not subject to amortization, depreciation, or any other form of capital recovery.

- In a typical stock purchase, the acquirer will not be able to recover or deduct its purchase price for tax purposes, except to the extent there is depreciation and amortization available from the target.
- This common disadvantage of buying stock disappears in the case of the acquirer. The acquirer does not require depreciation or amortization to provide a form of capital recovery (or the recovery of the purchase price) because the purchase price is repaid with pretax dollars.
- Another common and legitimate disadvantage of buying stock is that all known and unknown liabilities of the target company are also acquired. For discussion purposes, we assume hidden liabilities are not attached to the purchase of the stock of the target company.

The ability of the acquirer to repay the acquisition price with pretax dollars is potentially a strong negotiating point. The acquirer may offer to purchase the stock of the target and extend capital gain tax treatment on the sale of the stock by the shareholder(s) of the target. Most acquisitions of closely held companies are asset sales with unfavorable tax consequences to the selling shareholders. In return for agreeing to purchase the stock of the target, the acquirer may be able to negotiate a portion of the tax savings for itself in the form of a reduced purchase price. Note that the target will have to be an S corporation to pass income up to the parent and receive tax-free treatment.

Purchase of Assets

The tax standing of the acquirer is also useful, even if a more common asset sale of the target is proposed. The asset sale will enable the acquirer to recover its purchase price by depreciation and amortization of the acquired assets. This point may be less relevant in this case if the acquirer is a 100 percent ESOP S corporation. The acquirer does not pay federal income taxes; therefore, the acquirer may be unwilling to pay a higher price to the target because the target owners may be subject to double taxes, which is often the case.

- The acquirer will typically recover its purchase price more rapidly than the depreciation and amortization schedules available under applicable tax regulations because any acquisition-related debt will be repaid with pretax dollars.
- It is noteworthy to emphasize that the income of the target subject to taxation will be converted to the same tax status as the income of the acquirer. In this case, the income of the combined entities—the acquirer and target—is not subject to federal income taxes. This will almost certainly enable the acquirer to recover its purchase price much faster.

Mergers and Acquisitions—Extending the Internal Revenue Code Section 1042 Rollover to a Target Company

In IRS Private Letter Ruling (PLR) 200052023, the Internal Revenue Code (IRC) Section 1042 rollover was extended to the shareholders of an acquisition target. In this PLR case, an existing ESOP company (acquirer) sought to acquire another company (target) and extend the tax benefits of the IRC Section 1042 rollover to the shareholders of the target. The target does not have an ESOP prior to discussions with the acquirer.

The target adopts an ESOP, and all the shareholders of the target sell their stock to the newly formed ESOP. The target itself becomes a 100 percent ESOP company. The acquirer may help arrange the financing for the target ESOP to acquire all the stock from the selling shareholders. After the sale of stock to the target ESOP, the target is merged into the acquirer in a type B reorganization, and the ESOPs of both companies are merged. The result is that both the target and acquirer are owned by the acquirer's ESOP.

In this case, the shareholders of the target realize the advantage of receiving the IRC Section 1042 rollover for the value of their stock. The acquirer arranged for the financing of the target ESOP, and after the tax-free reorganization, the acquirer will assume responsibility for that financial obligation.

Obviously, the actual details of the transaction are more complex than this brief summary, but the key point is that it is possible to extend the IRC Section 1042 rollover benefits to the selling shareholders of an acquisition target with proper structure. In this case, the professional fees must be considered because an ESOP is being created in the target just prior to the reorganization with the acquirer. In addition to legal fees, the fair market value of the stock of each company must be determined. Finally, it takes time to obtain a PLR. Considerable planning and expense is required to complete a transaction with this amount of detail.

Extending the IRC Section 1042 Rollover to an Investment in Another Closely Held Company

The selling shareholder to an ESOP making the IRC Section 1042 election must reinvest the funds in qualified replacement property (QRP) within the applicable reinvestment period to qualify for the tax deferral. The QRP is subject to a number of qualifying conditions.

For this analysis, the QRP must be a security in a domestic operating corporation in which 50 percent or more of the assets are used in the active conduct of the business, and the QRP does not have passive investment income in excess of 25 percent of gross receipts in the preceding taxable year in which the purchase occurs. The QRP may be the stock of a closely held company, if the applicable conditions are satisfied. Note that the QRP may not be a subsidiary of the original ESOP company.

It is possible for the shareholder electing the IRC Section 1042 rollover to invest the proceeds in the equity of a qualifying closely held corporation (replacement corporation). The basis of the stock in the replacement corporation is the same basis of the stock sold to the original ESOP. If the replacement corporation stock is sold, the shareholder is subject to applicable taxes (most likely capital gain tax) at the time of sale. If the replacement corporation is also a candidate for an ESOP, a properly structured sale to the replacement corporation ESOP may qualify for an IRC Section 1042 rollover. In this manner, the shareholder may again defer the gain on the sale of the replacement corporation stock to the ESOP.

Multiple Investor ESOPs

In certain larger ESOP-related transactions, the overall complexity may increase significantly if there are a number of investors. These transactions are referred to as multi-investor ESOPs for the purposes of this book. One common example of a multi-investor ESOP is the purchase of a company by a consortium of investors, including management, investment bankers, other investors, and the ESOP.

Typically, multi-investor ESOPs are found in larger transactions in which there is often a significant amount of debt. The multiple investors may be contributing equity with varying levels of future participation in the increases in the value of the company. The future participation is typically linked to such attributes as the risk of loss of an individual investment, dividend preferences, liquidation preferences, the actual cash that is contributed, and other issues that are negotiated between the shareholders. Commonly, not all shareholders participate equally. Depending on an interpretation of relative risk assumed and other market factors, the future equity appreciation is allocated differently among the shareholders.

An independent appraiser may be solicited to allocate the fair market value of the company to the different shareholders or opine to the fairness of an equity allocation methodology. The Department of Labor (DOL) has not offered any formal guidelines on the matter of equity allocation, and there is minimal case law in this area.

- In transactions involving multiple investors, the issue of allocating equity may become a contested matter if the shareholders are not treated equally.
- The argument for not treating the shareholders equally involves the fact that different investors are perceptually assuming different amounts of risk and responsibility. For example, management is typically expected to provide the leadership to enable the company to repay all the purchase-related debt (assuming a leveraged buy-out in this case). If there is an investment banker, the investment banker is often contributing a percentage of capital and, perhaps, additional financing. The ESOP typically is borrowing funds to purchase stock, but typically, no equity is being contributed initially. The ESOP is bringing to the transaction some tax advantages, but those tax advantages will only be realized if the ESOP-related debt is repaid. In such circumstances, the parties to the transaction participate at different levels, and equity allocations are computed.
- The merits of each transaction should be considered individually. Proponents of equity allocations frequently state that such allocations reflect the reality of the financial markets.

An opposite argument believes all shareholders should participate equally per dollar of equity investment. This position was adopted by the DOL in the instance of the Western/Scott Fetzer Company. This position by the DOL has merit from the standpoint of fairness to all shareholders, particularly the ESOP. The position, unfortunately, does not typically reflect the dynamics of the financial markets that tend to reward investors based on both the relative abilities to negotiate more or less favorable allocations and the level of risk being assumed.

There is little formal guidance on the matter of equity allocations. This is an area that is technical and potentially very involved. Generally, such assignments are reserved only for those financial advisers with the resources to support positions and willingness to litigate.

Charitable Giving and ESOPs

Contributions of Closely Held Stock to Charities

Some business owners will consider gifting a portion of stock in their closely held company to a favorite charity. Under current gift tax regulations, the donor may deduct the fair market value of the gift from income subject to federal income taxes. If the gift happens to be stock in a closely held company, the donor must have the stock appraised at fair market value, and a tax-deductible donation may be made based on the determination of fair market value.

Often, the problem is that the charity will be unwilling to accept the gift of stock in a closely held company because there is no market for the equity. There often is no readily established method for the charity to transform the stock into cash other than the company purchasing the stock.

A solution to this issue is having an ESOP installed in the company prior to the charitable gift. The ESOP will make a market for the stock. The charity may enter into an agreement in which a certain specified percentage of the stock may be sold to the ESOP each year or according to some other methodology. The charity is assured that a market exists for the stock, although the ESOP may only pay fair market value at the time the stock is actually purchased. The proceeds received by the charity for the stock will typically be tax free by definition of what constitutes a charity for tax purposes.

This structure may offer advantages to the donor. First, the donor receives a tax deduction for the fair market value of the gift: stock, in this case. The donor deducts the full fair market value, and the charity will sell the stock to the ESOP for its fair market value. The charity will likely have more cash after the ESOP transaction than if the donor had to sell stock first, pay taxes on the sale, than contribute the balance after taxes to the charity.

Charitable Remainder Income Trusts and ESOPs

A business owner, for example, may have an interest in providing a significant contribution to a charity. An ESOP may be used to accomplish the goal of providing a significant gift to the charity while the business owner receives income during his or her life.

The shareholder establishes a charitable remainder income trust (CRIT) for the favored charity. A key advantage to a CRIT is that it is exempt from income taxes. The shareholder then contributes a block of stock to the CRIT. The shareholder receives an income tax deduction for the present value or the remainder interest of the gift that will eventually pass to the charity. The shareholder may use the tax deduction for the gift to provide the funding for life insurance. The life insurance eventually will become part of the overall estate of the family (not necessarily for tax purposes) and replace the value of the stock contributed to the CRIT.

The CRIT sells the stock to an ESOP in the shareholder's company and takes back a note for the purchase price. The note held by the charity will be repaid by the company's tax-deductible contributions to the ESOP. The funds received by the charity to repay the ESOP note are used to provide the lifetime income promised by the charity to the shareholder based on the provisions of the CRIT. Upon the death of the shareholder, the charity will receive the balance of the accumulated assets in the CRIT.

Summary

The preceding illustrations of the flexible uses of an ESOP are abbreviated summaries of strategies that may be considered. In reality, the application of the strategy is likely to be complex, with many legal issues that have to be addressed. Anyone with a serious interest in such strategies is advised to retain the advice of experienced legal counsel before acting.

Chapter 7

Valuation Issues and Considerations

This chapter undertakes a discussion of many of the significant issues related to employee stock ownership plan (ESOP)-based valuations for closely held companies. Such valuations have unique attributes that must be understood by professionals and business owners.

The AICPA has issued Statement on Standards for Valuation Services (SSVS) No. 1, *Valuation of a Business, Business Ownership Interest, Security, or Intangible Asset* (AICPA, *Professional Standards*, VS sec. 100). The AICPA Consulting Services Executive Committee has written this standard to improve the consistency and quality of practice among AICPA members performing business valuations. AICPA members will be required to follow this standard when they perform engagements to estimate value that culminate in the expression of a conclusion of value or a calculated value. SSVS No. 1 is effective for engagements accepted on or after January 1, 2008. SSVS No.1 is mentioned by reference only because it is beyond the scope of this chapter to discuss valuation standards.

The AICPA also supports the professional designation accredited in business valuation (ABV) that requires the holder to be both a CPA and a member of the AICPA. This valuation credential is popular among CPAs providing business valuations who are members of the AICPA. The ABV credential is not a requirement for CPAs providing business valuations because several professional valuation organizations provide business valuation accreditations, including the American Society of Appraisers (ASA), the National Association of

Certified Valuators Analysts (NACVA), and the Institute of Business Appraisers (IBA). Even if an AICPA member provides business valuations, that member is not obligated to obtain the ABV credential, but as an AICPA member, he or she will be required to adhere to SSVS No. 1. In addition to SSVS No. 1, AICPA members who hold other business valuation accreditations by other organizations may be required to adhere to those organizations' professional standards, as well. It is beyond the scope of these materials to consider the organizations granting business valuation accreditations.

Issues Regarding ESOP-Based Valuations

This section considers a number of valuation issues specifically related to closely held companies that either are considering an ESOP or already have one installed. The items are not presented in any specific order. The points discussed often relate to the valuation of closely held companies in general, with applications to ESOPs specifically noted.

Many generally accepted practices and procedures relating to ESOP valuations are discussed, but there are ongoing and often significant differences of opinion on specific treatments of many topics. Those differences arise among a wide range of interested parties, including, but not limited to, valuation practitioners, the IRS, federal courts, plan participants, and the Department of Labor (DOL). The valuation process often contains elements of both judgment and science, and informed individuals may disagree on specific applications. Litigation could result from the application of processes and methodologies contained in these materials. ESOP sponsors and plan fiduciaries should discuss such items with appropriate legal counsel and experienced financial advisers.

Identify the Client

When providing an ESOP valuation, the client is typically the ESOP trustee or ESOP trust committee, both of which are plan fiduciaries. Generally, the ESOP fiduciary is engaging a valuation professional to provide a fair market valuation of the common stock of the company or plan sponsor. The ESOP fiduciary typically seeks the financial advice of the independent valuation professional.

- It is essential to note that the client is not the plan sponsor (the company is the plan sponsor), and the client is not any of the company shareholders or officers.
- The company, its officers, and its shareholders may have conflicts of interest with the ESOP fiduciary; therefore, the client must be the ESOP fiduciary. From a practical point of view, the company will usually be paying the professional fees relating to the valuation.
- The valuation professional should always document that the client is the ESOP fiduciary, even during the feasibility stage prior to the installation of the ESOP and, perhaps, prior to the formal appointment of the ESOP fiduciary.
- From a practical standpoint, the ESOP fiduciary may also serve as an officer or be a shareholder of the company. If the same individual is serving in multiple capacities, that individual must be aware of the significant duties related to being an ESOP

fiduciary. Should conflicts arise between ESOP fiduciary duties and other obligations, Employee Retirement Income Security Act of 1974 (ERISA) standards will typically prevail. Increasingly, company shareholders selling to an ESOP are encouraged not to serve as an ESOP fiduciary because of the possibility of conflicts of interest. When such conflicts arise, an independent fiduciary may be an appropriate solution.

Standard of Value

We have previously discussed how the ESOP falls under the jurisdiction of both the IRS and the DOL. Each agency has its own standard of value. Although the agencies basically agree on many points, the DOL has its own issues beyond the understanding of the IRS. We will examine the standards of value for the IRS and the DOL.

IRS

The IRS standard of value is fair market value. This definition is most extensively defined and documented in Revenue Ruling 59-60. The standard of value has been enhanced over time with other revenue rulings, but we will only consider Revenue Ruling 59-60 because of its importance.

- *Definition of* fair market value. The price at which the asset would change hands between a willing buyer and willing seller, neither being under any compulsion to buy or sell and both having reasonable knowledge of relevant facts and being able to enter into the transaction.
- Additional fair market value considerations:
  - Fair market value is a hypothetical standard.
  - Financial buyer is assumed, not a strategic or specific buyer.
  - Terms are assumed to be for cash.

Revenue Ruling 59-60 establishes a number of key items that must be considered in the determination of fair market value. Those items are briefly summarized, with additional considerations noted for ESOP valuations:

- *The nature of the business and the history of the enterprise from its inception.* It is appropriate to consider a longer-term time horizon for an ESOP because it is intended, in part, to be a retirement benefit. Correspondingly, the long-term prospects for the subject company are an appropriate consideration in assessing the relative risk factors in estimating fair market value.
- *The economic outlook in general and the condition and outlook of the specific industry in particular.* Although it is essential to consider short-term prospects for the subject company, a longer-term assessment is likely to be more applicable for the purposes of an ESOP. Industry trends are very important in this regard.
- *The book value of the stock and the financial condition of the business.* Although the book value of the company is often not the best indicator of fair market value, it is frequently an indication of the financial strength of the business. The long-term viability of the

business is often a function of financial strength as reflected in the book value. Correspondingly, the book value and relative amount of anticipated long-term debt are important determinants in estimating the risk environment of the business.

- *The earnings capacity of the company.* The earnings capacity is most often the key determining factor in estimating the fair market value of a closely held stock. For the purposes of an ESOP, it is perhaps even more important in the long term. A closely held ESOP company is obligated to make a market for its own stock, and the ability to honor this market-making requirement in the long term is a function of a sustainable earnings capacity.
  - The ERISA statutes require the employer to redeem the shares of stock allocated to a participant's account, if requested, when that individual leaves the plan, for example, through retirement or termination of employment. This requirement to purchase the stock is what is meant by the concept of making a market for the security.
- *The dividend-paying capacity.* For closely held companies, this is often not a critical factor. Although the dividend capacity needs to be addressed, smaller companies rarely pay dividends but may have the ability to pay them.
- *Whether the enterprise has goodwill or other intangible value.* For the purposes of an ESOP, the earnings capacity of the business is critical. The earnings capacity over the long term will reflect the existence of goodwill and other intangible value by the company's ability to earn profits. For an ESOP company, long-term profitability is crucial to meeting the market-making mandate of ERISA.
- *Sales of the stock and the size of the block of stock to be valued.* In a closely held company, prior sales of stock that meet the standards of an arm's-length transaction are rare. There may be shareholder agreements stating the terms and processes for consummating sales of stock among investors in a closely held company, but those agreements rarely establish *fair market value*, as defined by the IRS, as the basis for the stock price. What is significant for the purposes of an ESOP is the size of the block.
  - Many stock transactions in closely held companies are minority positions, or blocks of stock under 50 percent of the outstanding shares. Such transactions are valued on a minority basis and typically subject to minority position discounts and risk factors.
  - When the block of stock being transacted is over 50 percent, an additional set of factors must be considered because the block is potentially a controlling interest for the purposes of an ESOP. The DOL specifically addresses this point, and it will be considered shortly.
- *The market prices of the stock of corporations engaged in the same or a similar line of business having their stocks actively traded in a free and open market, either on an exchange or over the counter.* This is the basis of a market-based approach in determining fair market value. The advantage to this analysis is the relative abundance of information on publicly traded stocks. The challenge is to find publicly traded companies that are considered comparable to the closely held company with an ESOP. It is rare to establish a high degree of comparability between publicly held companies and smaller closely held

businesses. The public stock market is often a volatile and unstable environment in the short term. Wide swings in individual company stock prices and even entire industry segments are common.

- It is important to consider both short-term and longer-term financial performance when determining the comparability of publicly held companies to a closely held company for the purposes of an ESOP.
- A closely held company with an ESOP must make a market for its stock. This requirement of marketability is specifically considered by the DOL and will be discussed shortly.

DOL

Guidance for valuing the shares of a closely held company in an ESOP came primarily from the IRS. The IRS requires that the ESOP be prohibited from paying more than the fair market value for the securities of the employer.

The IRS and the DOL generally cooperated on the valuation of ESOP securities, but the DOL issued its own *Proposed Regulation Relating to the Definition of* Adequate Consideration, as published in the *Federal Register* on May 17, 1988.[1] A final regulation has not been issued to date, but professionals must consider this regulation carefully in discharging their responsibilities.

- *DOL Proposed Regulation Relating to the Definition of* Adequate Consideration (four parts)
  - Definition of *adequate consideration*
  - Definition of *fair market value*
  - Requirements for acting in good faith
  - Requirements for written documentation

Definition of Adequate Consideration

The first part of the proposed regulation applies to securities when no well-established market exists. The concept of adequate consideration means the fair market value of the asset as established in good faith by the ESOP trustee or named fiduciary. An ESOP is prohibited from paying more than the adequate consideration for the securities it receives. Two main criteria must be met for a valid determination of adequate consideration:

- The assigned value of the asset must reflect its *fair market value*, as defined by the regulations.
- The assigned value must be the result of the fiduciary acting in *good faith*, as defined by the regulations. Clearly, the DOL wants to link the determination of fair market value and good faith to ensure that the valuation reflects all appropriate market considerations.

---

[1] The Department of Labor's (DOL's) *Proposed Regulation Relating to the Definition of* Adequate Consideration was originally referred to as Title 29 U.S. *Code of Federal Regulations* (CFR) Part 2510, as published in the *Federal Register*, on May 17, 1988. An examination today of 29 CFR 2510 does not disclose the *Proposed Regulation Relating to the Definition of* Adequate Consideration because the regulation has not been finalized. The proposed regulation is considered as the view of the DOL, as referenced in employee stock ownership plan valuation reports and Employee Retirement Income Security Act of 1974 litigation.

Definition of Fair Market Value

The second part of the proposed regulation defines *fair market value*. Generally stated, *fair market value*, as defined by the DOL, is substantially the same as the definition established by the IRS that was previously discussed.

The DOL recognizes that the fair market value of an asset is likely to be a range of value rather than a single figure. The DOL requires that the value established for an asset falls within an acceptable range of fair market value.

Requirements for Acting in Good Faith

The third part of the proposed regulation addresses the requirement for the ESOP trustee or fiduciary to make a determination of adequate consideration in good faith. This good faith requirement is intended to establish an objective standard of conduct. Two main factors must be present to establish good faith:

- First, the fiduciary must apply sound business principles of evaluation and conduct a prudent investigation of the appropriate circumstances prevailing at the time of the valuation.
- Second, good faith may only be demonstrated when the valuation is made by persons who are both qualified and independent of the parties to the transaction (other than the plan). This means that the valuation must be made by an independent fiduciary or a fiduciary relying on the report of an independent appraiser.

If the fiduciary does not have the personal experience or expertise to make the valuation under consideration, the fiduciary should not undertake the assignment. Most commonly, fiduciaries rely on the valuation reports of professionals. The proposed regulation notes that the fiduciary or appraiser must in fact be independent of all parties in the transaction, other than the plan.

Independence

The independence of the appraiser is, in part, established by factors such as having the appraiser appointed by the fiduciary, the fiduciary maintaining the right to terminate the appointment, and establishing that the ESOP plan is the appraiser's client. The impact of the Sarbanes–Oxley Act of 2002 (SOX) will be considered shortly.

- There are separate understandings of independence by the DOL, the IRS, CPAs, and other valuation practitioners. Generally, CPA practitioners have standards of independence that are part of the professional rules of conduct and ethics.
- The Securities and Exchange Commission (SEC) emphasized its own understanding of independence in 2001. It looked at certain relationships within the general area of publicly held companies and concluded that some traditional relationships are not to its standard of independence. An example of a problematic circumstance is the relationship between investment bankers and brokerage houses when both are related associates under a common parent. Another example is the relationship among the audit firm, the audit firm's consulting division, and the audit client when consulting revenue billed to the client is substantial. In those examples, independence appears compromised to the SEC.

- The Government Accountability Office (GAO) is active in examining the relationship among interests such as professional service providers, their clients, government reporting, and regulatory compliance. New and more restrictive interpretations of independence are being considered by the GAO as a result of the actions initiated by the SEC. The important point to emphasize is that many traditional interpretations of independence are being questioned. The appearance of independence is an important consideration.
- With regard to ESOP valuations, most CPA practitioners take the position that they are not independent if they (or their firm) provide both the ESOP valuation and other significant services to the employer, shareholders, or officers. These significant services are understood to include preparing financial statements; issuing an opinion on financial statements; providing attest services; or providing tax services (for example, preparing tax returns).
- The appraiser (individual or firm) must also be qualified to complete the valuation assignment.
- The appraiser normally provides business valuations. Professional business valuation designations by appraisers responsible for the ESOP valuation may include, among others, the
  - ABV designation by the AICPA.
  - certified valuation analyst designation by NACVA.
  - accredited senior appraiser designation by the ASA.
  - certified business appraiser designation by the IBA.
  - chartered financial analyst designation by the Association for Investment Management and Research.
- The appraiser has significant experience with ESOPs. Membership in organizations, such as the ESOP Association (EA) and the National Center for Employee Ownership (NCEO), is recommended. Attending ESOP industry conferences and participating in ESOP meetings also indicates an intention to understand the specific requirements of an ESOP-based valuation assignment.

Requirements for Written Documentation

The fourth part of the proposed regulation establishes the requirements for written documentation when the determination of fair market value is being made. The DOL has adopted substantially all the requirements of Revenue Ruling 59-60 due to the DOL's wide familiarity with plan fiduciaries, professionals, and the business community. The general parameters of Revenue Ruling 59-60 were briefly discussed previously. The DOL has added a number of other reporting requirements specific to ESOP valuations. Those requirements include the following items:

- A summary of the qualifications of the person(s) making the valuation
- A statement of the asset's value, a statement of the methods used in determining value, and the reasons for the valuation in light of those methods
- A full description of the asset being valued

- The factors taken into account in making the valuation, including any restrictions, understandings, agreements, or obligations limiting the disposition of the asset
- The purpose for which the valuation was made
- The relevance or significance accorded to the valuation methodologies taken into account
- The effective date of the valuation
- The signature of the person making the valuation and the date the report was signed, in cases when a valuation report has been prepared

The fourth part of the proposed regulation also includes a discussion of valuation considerations specific to ESOPs. These are considerations in addition to the elements mentioned under the parameters for Revenue Ruling 59-60:

- *Marketability of the security.* First, the valuation must consider the marketability, or lack thereof, of the securities of the plan sponsor. Typically, the plan purchases securities that are subject to put rights on the part of plan participants (that is, plan participants can elect to sell the stock back to the ESOP when trigger events occur).
  - A lack of marketability discount for the securities of a closely held company is typically considered.
  - The DOL also wants considered the extent to which such put rights are enforceable, as well as the company's ability to meet its obligations with respect to the put rights. This means some consideration must be given to the ability of the plan sponsor to make a market for the ESOP shares.
  - If it is determined that there is a question about the ability of the plan sponsor to meet its put obligation, consideration should be given to applying an additional discount, often referred to as a discount for lack of liquidity.
- *Control premium.* Second, another consideration is the ability of the selling shareholder to obtain a control premium with regard to the block of securities being valued. A control premium is permissible to the extent a third party is willing to pay for the control. In the case of a shareholder selling to an ESOP, there is a two-part standard to determine if a control premium is appropriate, as detailed in the proposed regulation.
  - Control must exist in form or appearance, generally meaning the ESOP has more than 50 percent of the outstanding stock.
  - Control must exist in substance or fact. The ESOP, over time, must be able to exercise the prerogatives of control.
  - The purchaser's control should not dissipate within a short period of time subsequent to the acquisition. The DOL is interested in ensuring that ESOPs paying a control premium receive the benefits that a control position confers on the owner of the stock.

The proposed regulation offers insights into a range of issues of specific interest to the DOL. Over time, most of the key issues contained in the proposed regulation have been upheld by the federal courts. The trend in federal courts is to hold those with fiduciary responsibilities to increasingly stringent standards of conduct.

Valuation Independence and SOX

As previously discussed, both the IRS and the DOL call for the valuation in an ESOP-related assignment to be completed by a qualified independent appraiser. The DOL proposed regulation discusses the independence of the appraiser in ESOP assignments. ESOP fiduciaries meet the requirements of adequate consideration in determining fair market value in good faith if they engage someone who is independent of all parties to the transaction.

The DOL proposed regulation imposes a substantial obligation on the ESOP fiduciary to ensure that an independent valuation is obtained. Although the proposed regulation provides little specific guidance for CPAs, it is generally believed that the understanding of independence in the DOL proposed regulation is more narrowly defined than the understanding of independence as defined by the IRS.

Considering that there are two understandings of independence, the valuation practitioner is advised to interpret the issue of independence with caution.

Impact of SOX

This watershed legislation was largely the result of a series of financial scandals in the late 1990s and early 2000s. Perhaps the most infamous case involved Enron Corporation. SOX is very broad in establishing more transparent relationships in the public company arena. Among its many provisions, the legislation redefines the relationship between publicly held companies and their auditors:

- In Section 201, the legislation identifies a number of activities that are prohibited between auditors and publicly held clients.
- Section 201 says it will be unlawful for a registered public accounting firm to provide any nonaudit service to an issuer contemporaneously with the audit, including appraisal or valuation services, fairness opinions, or contribution-in-kind reports. This abbreviated statement does not list all the prohibited services, but clearly, SOX is aimed at sharply curtailing the relationship between auditors and their publicly held clients.

Although Section 201 specifically addresses the relationship between auditors and publicly held clients, it is currently unclear if such activities are prohibited between auditors and closely held clients. Many in the public accounting profession think it is only a matter of time until the spirit of SOX is extended to closely held businesses.

AICPA Newsletter: *CPA Expert*, Summer 2003

CPA Expert is a newsletter published by the AICPA for providers of business valuation and litigation services. "The Impact of Auditor Independence Rules on Business Valuation and Litigation Services" is the lead article in the summer 2003 issue of *CPA Expert*.

An informative dialog is on page 4 of the same issue: "Providing Business Valuation Services to an Attest Client: Q&A." This discussion relates to the relationship between all CPAs and their attest clients not publicly held. The third question asks, "Can the CPA firm value the shares of an attest client held in an ESOP?" The response is, "No, when the value of the shares has a material effect on the company's financial statements."

Valuation Perspective on the Repurchase Obligation and the Put Option

We have listed the repurchase obligation and put option together; they are separate but related issues in ESOP valuations.

The existence of the repurchase obligation mandated by applicable federal legislation is a defining element of ESOP valuations in closely held companies. The longer-term prospects of the plan sponsor, the company, must be considered when an ESOP valuation is being completed because of this market-making mandate.

Under IRC Section 409(h), departing ESOP participants have the option of either keeping the stock in their individual account or requiring the company to redeem the company stock allocated and vested in their individual account. The ESOP participant may put the company stock back to the company, and the company must repurchase it. The company may redeem the stock either back to the ESOP or company treasury.

- Most closely held companies require that individuals leaving the ESOP must sell their stock back to the company (the company often has the option of directing the ESOP fiduciary to redeem the stock). Having minority shareholders with small blocks of stock is often a very negative scenario. ESOP companies often override federal statutes and have a call provision on the company stock. The call provision is typically accomplished by stating in company bylaws that only the ESOP or company employees may own stock. In this manner, departing employees may not have the option of taking company stock as part of their distribution.
- The employer is required to make a market for its stock. As the stock in the ESOP becomes vested in participants' accounts, the sum total of the value of the stock often becomes a significant future obligation to the company. This outstanding liability is often referred to as the repurchase obligation.
- The repurchase obligation is not disclosed on the financial statements as a specific liability. However, sometimes, the repurchase obligation in total is disclosed in financial statement footnotes, depending on the standard of financial reporting adopted by the company.
- The determination of fair market value for the purposes of an ESOP must consider the ability of the company to make a market for the stock over time. The requirement to make a market for the stock stays with the company as long as the ESOP holds company stock. This time period will likely span both market expansions and recessions. Therefore, this mandate has to be considered over a broad range of business activity scenarios.
  - When the company is repaying ESOP-related debt, the issue of making a market for the stock is often deferred until the debt is repaid, and the company typically has greater resources available to honor puts or enforce calls.

- As the company matures, ESOP-related debt is repaid, and ESOP account balances become increasingly vested. It is appropriate to examine the plans the company has to service the repurchase obligation.
- Some ESOP companies have formal repurchase obligation studies. Such studies frequently involve benefit administration companies and commonly have a degree of statistical validity over a range of assumptions.
- From a practical viewpoint, smaller ESOP companies do not typically have formal repurchase obligation studies. They often anticipate the potential departure of a few key individuals with larger account balances and plan accordingly. They may fund the repurchase obligation on a pay-as-you-go basis, or they may provide a measure of liquidity in the plan by contributing cash. If the ESOP is provided with liquidity, the amount may depend on the vulnerability of the company to business cycles and other significant risks. It is a recommended practice, however, for all ESOP companies to study their repurchase obligation and be financially prepared for the future.

- The proposed DOL regulation previously discussed requires an assessment of the employer's ability to make a market for the stock. It is therefore appropriate for the appraiser to consider in the determination of fair market value the long-term ability of the employer to continually make a market for the stock.
  - The situation may occur when short-term considerations may raise questions about the ability of the employer to make a market for the stock. Examples of such situations may be the unexpected loss of a major account or a sudden natural disaster, such as a fire. In the near term, significant unanswered questions may exist about the financial stability of the employer. In such instances, it is often appropriate to consider applying an additional discount in the valuation process.
  - Many appraisers consider this discount, which is typically applied until the issue giving rise to the uncertainty is resolved, a lack of liquidity. The application of an additional discount for a lack of liquidity is typically at the judgment of the appraiser.

Valuation Report Date and Events

The valuation report typically establishes the opinion of value at a specific date. Often, the first valuation report for ESOP companies establishes the value of the company at some point during the fiscal year rather than at a fiscal year-end date. If the ESOP is installed, subsequent annual updates are typically provided on the fiscal year-end date of the plan. Additionally, there may be subsequent sales or redemptions of stock with the ESOP that require an additional midyear update.

- It is common to perform an initial valuation of the company to determine if an ESOP is economically feasible. This initial valuation is often performed in the middle of a plan year, rather than at a plan year-end, so the report carries an interim or a midyear date. After the initial valuation report is completed, the ESOP may be installed. It is essential to have the value of the stock established on the date of the actual ESOP transaction (in this case, the initial sale).

- If the initial report is issued within a reasonable time from the formal installation of the ESOP, there is often no need to formally issue another full report at the date of ESOP installation. If there have been no events that would have a significant impact (either positive or negative) on the valuation, it is common practice to update a valuation report with a letter affirming the price of the stock at the date of the actual ESOP transaction. Generally, a period of 60–90 days is considered a reasonable period of time. Prior to issuing the valuation update, the valuation professional should take appropriate steps to ensure himself or herself that the opinion of value in the preceding valuation report is still valid.

- If the amount of time between the initial valuation report and the installation of the ESOP exceeds the 60–90 day range, the requirement for a full updated report will depend on the circumstances of the situation. Generally, the more time that passes and the more activity that occurs that may impact the value of the company, the greater the likelihood a full valuation report may be necessary. Individual circumstances are the determining factors that decide what level of reporting is appropriate at the date of the ESOP transaction.

Once an ESOP is installed, and the ESOP owns shares of stock of the plan sponsor, then the requirement for an annual update exists. The annual updates are typically dated the day of the fiscal year-end of the plan. For example, if the fiscal year-end of the ESOP is December 31, the annual valuation is dated on December 31 of the year. Occasionally, there are different fiscal year-ends for the ESOP and plan sponsor, and typically, the year-end of the ESOP is the determining date for the stock value.

It is common practice to obtain a stock valuation when significant transactions with the ESOP occur:

- One frequent transaction after the ESOP is installed is that another block of stock from an outside shareholder is sold to the plan. If the selling shareholder is also a controlling shareholder, it is appropriate to have the stock valued on the date of the transaction. Generally, significant transactions with the ESOP should be valued by an independent source at the date of the transaction.

- Occasionally, the plan sponsor will redeem a block of stock from the ESOP. One common justification for this action is to provide both a degree of liquidity and diversification for the plan participants. If the plan sponsor is redeeming stock from the ESOP directly, it is recommended that the reasoning for the transaction be documented. Like other significant transactions, it is recommended that the stock be valued at the date of the transaction.

Generally, when the ESOP is repurchasing the stock from a departing plan participant, the plan documents need to be referenced to determine the participant's options regarding the redemption of the stock. In most cases, the annual stock valuations are used to establish prices.

Opinion of Value at a Point in Time

The initial valuation is often completed in contemplation of a significant ESOP transaction. However, assuming the transaction is completed, and the ESOP owns stock in the closely held company, the stock will then be subject to annual updates. Due to the dynamic nature of the ESOP assignment and the recurring valuation requirement, many valuation professionals adopt a longer-term time horizon when establishing value. This is done to minimize the impact of short-term market conditions that may have a temporary impact on the value of the company at a specific date.

A longer-term time horizon is also more appropriate to provide consistency in the valuation process between years.

Approaches to Establishing Value

Generally, there are three broadly understood approaches to establishing value for the purposes of an ESOP. Indeed, the same three broad valuation approaches apply to most business valuations. Those three approaches are

1. income approach.
2. market approach.
3. asset approach.

It is beyond the scope of this material to discuss these three approaches in significant detail, but a limited number of observations regarding these concepts will be offered as they relate specifically to ESOP assignments. It is emphasized that an ESOP may only exist in either a C corporation or an S corporation. This distinction is specifically addressed first.

Initial Valuation: C Versus S Corporation Considerations

Historically, the standard of value, fair market value, was understood to define a valuation amount between a hypothetical buyer and hypothetical seller. This definition was previously discussed in this chapter.

The hypothetical buyer traditionally was understood to be a C corporation. This makes inherent sense because C corporations comprise the vast percentage of corporate wealth in this country because all publicly held firms are C corporations. Additionally, the S corporation requires the unanimous vote of all shareholders to make the election to be taxed in that manner. The tax attributes of an S corporation, correspondingly, have no value to the hypothetical C corporation buyer because such tax attributes would be lost upon purchase.

The implications of the preceding discussion suggest that, for the purposes of an ESOP valuation, the company will be interpreted as being a C corporation. If an S corporation is considering an ESOP, it is common practice to assume the company is a C corporation for valuation purposes. The earnings of the S corporation would be adjusted for the implied C corporation tax exposure (that is to say the earnings are tax affected [C corporation taxes applied]).

There is significant support for the assumption that the candidate ESOP company is a C corporation for valuation purposes. The Valuation Advisory Committee of the EA released Advanced Issue Brief #22, *Valuation Issues for ESOPs in S Corporations* (issue brief). This issue brief concludes that for ESOP valuation purposes in a privately held company, the appraiser should assume the candidate company is a C corporation. The NCEO published the book *ESOP Valuation: Third Edition* that includes the chapter "Valuation S Corporation ESOP Companies" by Kathryn F. Aschwald and Donna J. Walker. The authors conclude that a candidate ESOP company that is privately held assumes a C corporation for valuation purposes. Both the EA and the NCEO have published articles that support the C corporation assumption. I have not seen any authoritative articles that contradict this valuation assumption.

- Recent IRS court cases
  - The IRS recently and suddenly challenged the notion of the hypothetical buyer in a number of valuation cases involving gifts, not ESOPs. Under a limited number of court cases involving gifts of stock, the IRS has prevailed with the theory that S corporation earnings will not be tax effected (that is, the subject company's S earnings will not be adjusted for the imputed C corporation income taxes).
  - *Walter L. Gross, Jr. and Barbara H. Gross (Petitioner) vs. Commissioner* (TC Memo 1999-254) is the recent, high-profile court case in which the IRS established that the earnings of the subject S corporation are not adjusted by imputed C corporation income taxes (the earnings are not tax affected). It is beyond the scope of this book to detail the analysis of this particular case, but it is emphasized that the specific facts of the case contributed to the court's decision. Additionally, it is emphasized that the case involves gifting, not the sale of stock to an ESOP.
- DOL and IRS valuation considerations
  - Although the IRS has made an adjustment to the understanding of fair market value in a limited number of gift tax applications, the IRS is not necessarily the final determinant of value in ESOP applications.
  - The DOL also has an understanding of value, adequate consideration, as previously discussed. Although the DOL has not published an official position on this matter at the time of this book's publication, most experienced ESOP valuation practitioners believe it is appropriate to tax effect S corporation earnings for the purposes of an initial ESOP installation. Correspondingly, this interpretation assumes the hypothetical buyer is a C corporation for the purposes of an ESOP valuation assignment.
- Practical summary
  - Most experienced ESOP valuation professionals currently think it is appropriate to tax effect S corporation earnings for the purposes of ESOP valuation analysis, particularly for the sale of stock to an ESOP. Although there is no definitive federal pronouncement on this matter, the weight of historical valuation practices and an understanding of the DOL proposed regulation strongly support the tax effecting of S corporation earnings.

Income Approach

This approach is typically the most appropriate selection for initial ESOP valuations. Significantly, when an ESOP acquires stock, the company is obligated to make a market for the stock as plan participants depart (this is the repurchase obligation previously discussed). The plan sponsor will best be able to meet mandated repurchase obligations from future income.

There are many definitions of earnings, including net income; pretax income; free cash flow; earnings before interest and taxes; earnings before interest, taxes, depreciation, and amortization; and so on. Collectively, these concepts are summarized for discussion purposes as earnings.

The value of stock is typically a function of future expected financial returns. Those future financial returns may be measured or computed in many ways. Two common measurements include

1. capitalizing historic earnings.
2. projecting or forecasting future earnings and discounting them to a current time period.

The key distinction is the difference between historical results and future or projected results. A brief analysis of historical and projected considerations is appropriate for ESOP purposes:

- *Capitalizing historic earnings.* One primary advantage of analyzing historic earnings within an ESOP context is that they represent a standard of financial performance that the company has actually attained. Such results are verifiable and less subject to being second-guessed in the future. Reliance on the analysis of historical results, for example, is most often appropriate when the company is well-established, and historical results are a reasonable proximate indicator of future potential.

  Another advantage of historical results is that such results may be capitalized by employing verifiable and readily available determinants of costs of capital (such as Ibbotson and Associates). By applying a capitalization rate specifically determined for the subject ESOP company, an overall value may be developed.

  A major issue to consider with this approach is that historical results may not reflect the future earnings potential of the company. If this is the case, an alternate method of analysis may be employed.

- *Projected earnings—discounted cash flow (DCF).* Perhaps the strongest case for embracing projected or forecasted earnings is that this method reflects a specific financial benefit to stakeholders during the projection period. In theory, the argument for projected earnings has solid appeal. The pragmatic issue is that preparing projections is often a very complex task, especially for the purposes of an ESOP, in which you're subject to perfect hindsight due to the recurring nature of the assignment.

  The DCF approach is a valid valuation method when used properly and in the right application. DCF requires a substantial understanding of the company and projections of both the income statement and balance sheet if the approach is used properly.

  Perhaps the most pronounced criticism of DCF in ESOP applications is the ease with which multiple variables may be adjusted to produce almost any desired result.

Projections may be employed to mask historical problems. Additionally, projections supplied by selling shareholders have to be viewed with a degree of suspicion as perhaps being too self-serving. If projections are being considered, it is appropriate to explore the history of how accurate prior projections have been. If there is no history of accurate prior projections, reliance on this method must be undertaken with the greatest care.

- The appraiser should be aware of ESOP-based litigation when projections later determined to be unrealistic were an integral part of determining the fair market value of the employer's stock. If the projections are overly optimistic, a frequent bias with the DCF method, the ESOP is paying more than fair market value. The appraiser is reminded that anyone reviewing the projections will likely have the benefit of perfect hindsight years after the report in question was completed.

- CPAs in particular are advised to be knowledgeable about the AICPA Guide *Prospective Financial Information*. There may be some question whether the DCF method of valuation is prospective financial information, as defined and understood in the Guide *Prospective Financial Information*. If the DCF method is embraced in a valuation report, many valuation professionals will insist that the client provide the projected financial results.

- *Adjustments to historical financial statements.* An ESOP valuation is similar to many other determinations of fair market value involving closely held companies. It is appropriate to consider making adjustments to the historical financial statements to have them reflect a clearer picture of what is economically happening in the company.

  Adjustments to the financial statements typically are classified into a number of common areas, including

  - changes in accounting and reporting methods. Changes in accounting may include a change in reporting taxes, a change in reporting inventories, a change in accounting for certain deferred credits, and so on. For the purposes of determining fair market value, if there is a significant impact on the financial statements in the period in which the change is reported, it is often appropriate to make an adjustment to normalize the impact of the change over the proximate period of time to which it applies.

  - nonrecurring or unusual events. Nonrecurring or unusual events may include litigation settlements, unusually large professional fees related to a single event, and start-up expenses related to opening a new location, among others. Most nonrecurring events are represented as costs to the company. Occasionally, the reverse is true, and the company realizes a nonrecurring gain, such as an insurance settlement. Adjusting historical financial results requires a thorough understanding of the circumstances, and such adjustments may be appropriate as an integral step in determining value.

    ○ Most commonly, such adjustments result in increases in pretax income for income statement purposes and an increase in net worth for balance sheet analysis. The circumstances of the nonrecurring event need to be thoroughly understood.

  - discretionary items. Discretionary costs may include expenses over which management has a high degree of judgment. Such costs may include substantial bonuses to officers, shareholders, and others that effectively reduce the reported pretax income of the company to a nominal amount. Another example of an expense often with a significant degree of discretion is the contribution to a profit sharing plan. Adjusting historical financial statements for such discretionary costs requires a thorough understanding of the company.

- Adjustments to the financial statements, particularly the income statement, are most appropriate when the discretionary costs are going to be significantly curtailed or eliminated after the installation of the ESOP.
- Perhaps one of the areas that causes the most discussion among appraisers is adjustments related to the compensation of owners and officers. Any adjustment for compensation depends on the specific circumstances in each application.
- If an ESOP is being installed, things such as nonessential assets are often phased out or simply eliminated.

Market Approach

Traditionally, the market approach embraces two general methods of analysis. First, it is appropriate to consider publicly held companies actively traded on stock exchanges. The benefit of this analysis is that publicly traded companies demonstrate current value by the daily transactions on stock exchanges and other market-making vehicles. A second market-based method is to consider actual sale transactions of similar companies:

- *Publicly held companies.* If publicly held companies comparable to the subject ESOP company exist in sufficient quantities, this approach has a number of positive attributes. Publicly traded companies establish actual indexes of value among investors. These indexes of value may be useful in establishing a valuation for ESOP purposes.

  There are a number of significant issues with this analysis. Finding comparable publicly held companies may be, at best, a daunting challenge. Many publicly held companies are so large in relation to the closely held ESOP company that making comparisons is very difficult. Markets for publicly held companies are often subject to sharp swings in value, typically a function of the short-term orientation of many stakeholders in public companies. One may question the appropriateness of relying on the relative short-term focus of the public markets in general for ESOP applications in closely held businesses.

- *Closely held company transactions.* This method is helpful if there are a sufficient number of private company transactions within recent history to determine a number of valuation indexes. The source for such transaction data is often from business brokers or regulatory filings of publicly held companies that acquire closely held businesses.

  Although this source of data may be helpful as a reasonableness check on value, there are a number of concerns with this approach as a primary driver of determining value. Often, the buyers are strategic buyers, which are not comparable to hypothetical buyers, the appropriate consideration when determining fair market value for ESOP purposes.

  The transactions often do not fully disclose the terms of the deal, and the terms may have a significant impact on the overall consideration being exchanged.

- *Auction process of valuation.* There may be situations when the company has received an offer from an outside entity or investor to purchase the business. It is appropriate to consider such offers as one indication of value, but the ESOP is under no obligation to match it. It is important to understand the full terms of the specific proposal and determine if it has an impact on the ESOP valuation. There is a considerable difference between a letter of intent from a serious prospective buyer and a prospecting marketing letter from a business broker.

  Typically, such offers are for a controlling interest in the company, and the offer comes from a specific and, often, strategic buyer. Additionally, frequently, terms in the offer have the current shareholders financing a portion of the price. Terms in the offer often involve earn-out provisions in which the selling shareholders are at considerable risk of nonpayment if certain events fail to occur.

  The standard of value for an ESOP transaction is fair market value, and an offer to purchase the company from an outside investor is typically a different standard of value.

- *Prior transactions in the company stock.* Prior sales of stock in a closely held company may be considered. Typically, such transactions are not arm's length. The parties to the transaction are often related or do not have balanced negotiating strength. Most typically, such transactions are not very helpful in determining value for ESOP purposes.

Asset Approach

The underlying assets of an ESOP company should be considered in the valuation process. It is important to emphasize that the fundamental driver of value from an ESOP perspective is future anticipated financial earnings. It must also be remembered that, ultimately, the plan sponsor has to pay for the stock being purchased by the ESOP. The ability to pay for the stock is most commonly related to earnings of the business, not necessarily its assets.

Generally, you would expect to have the assets employed in the business to provide a reasonable rate of return. If such a return is not realized, one has to question whether the assets are effectively utilized.

Example 7-1

An example of an inappropriate consideration of the asset approach for ESOP purposes involves the case in which the asset value is high in relation to the earnings of the business. Assume the fair market value of the company assets is $10 million (consisting of assets such as plant and equipment), and the business generates only $200,000 of earnings. For ESOP purposes, the overall value, in this case, is likely to be a function of the earnings, not the assets. With only $200,000 in earnings, the ESOP company could not afford the assets in the business. Additionally, the assets in the business do not seem to provide a reasonable rate of return ($200,000 / $10,000,000 = 2%). Although this example is deliberately simplified, the key point is that assets should be analyzed with a consideration of the anticipated future benefits they might provide.

Lack of Marketability Adjustment (Discount)

Clearly from the standpoint of the ESOP participants, the existence of the put option requires the employer to make a market for the stock. This requirement, combined with the resources to adequately repurchase ESOP stock, has an impact on the fair market value analysis.

Generally, the put option helps create a market for the employer's stock. Arguably, this favorable factor should help increase the value of the stock. Typically, the value is enhanced by adjusting the lack of marketability discount that theoretically exists between publicly held stock and stock in a closely held company. In this case, any adjustment for a lack of marketability must be viewed from the baseline established for valuation analysis. If public company comparisons are applicable, then it is appropriate to consider reducing a lack of marketability discount to reflect the impact of the put option. The reduction of the marketability discount increases the overall value of the stock.

Remember, the ESOP company must make a market for the stock over a wide range of conditions in the future, including both economic recessions and expansions. When the total circumstances are assessed, great care is required when considering reducing or eliminating a marketability discount. The particular facts and circumstances of each assignment will be guidelines on decisions relating to any adjustment for lack of marketability.

Ownership Characteristics

Minority and Control Positions

There is a difference in valuation theory between a minority interest and controlling interest in a company. A controlling interest is generally deemed to be more valuable because of prerogatives of control that have value. Prerogatives of control include setting compensation levels, hiring and firing, selecting vendors, declaring dividends, selling assets, and changing articles of incorporation and bylaws.

The proposed DOL regulation discussed earlier in this chapter permits the ESOP to pay a controlling premium for a controlling interest in a company, to the extent that a third party would be willing to pay a control premium, when two conditions are met:

- First, the ESOP must be in control in appearance or voting control. Generally, the ESOP has to have more than 50 percent of the outstanding stock; typically, it has much more than 50 percent of the stock if it is in a control position.
- Second, the ESOP must be in control in fact. The ESOP must be in a position to exercise the prerogatives of control over time and in accordance with corporate governance. This standard is often addressed by determining the ESOP trustee. The trustee may be one individual or a committee. Alternatively, the trustee may be an independent organization, such as a bank. What is important with this standard is that a good faith attempt is made to have the ESOP in control.
  - Generally, when a sole controlling shareholder sells a majority of the stock to the ESOP and also serves as the sole trustee to the ESOP, the ESOP is not in control. Correspondingly, it is not advised under such circumstances for the ESOP to pay a control premium for the majority block of the stock.

- When the ESOP is in a minority position, it is common to find a controlling shareholder also serving as the ESOP trustee. This situation is different because the ESOP is in a minority position, and the ESOP has very little power, according to corporate governance. The ESOP has only paid a minority position price that reflects the relative lack of control.
- The appraiser should clearly state in the report if the stock is valued on a minority basis or control basis.

Assuming the ESOP meets the DOL standards for a control position valuation, the issue may arise regarding the appropriate control premium to be applied. As in so many theoretical valuation issues, the correct response is that it depends on the individual facts and circumstances of the application.

- The degree of control assumed by the ESOP is typically reflected in the determination of fair market value when the stock is purchased. When assessing the degree of control, a factor such as the percentage ownership of the ESOP is a significant matter. There is a difference between an ESOP with just over 50 percent of the stock and 100 percent ESOP ownership. That difference and the appropriate quantification of a control premium are the responsibility of the appraiser to determine. Professional judgment must be exercised.

There are situations when the ESOP begins as a minority shareholder and, over time, purchases a majority of the stock. Assume that when the ESOP acquires the majority percentage of the outstanding stock, the ESOP also meets the DOL requirements for a control position valuation. Also assume that all the ESOP purchases have been on a minority position basis (the ESOP attained the current ownership percentage though a series of smaller transactions). In this case, an important issue is should the ESOP be valued on a control basis:

- This is an issue with many interpretations and no absolutely correct answer. If this issue arises, it is advisable to obtain the advice of an experienced ESOP adviser.
  - One key piece of information is the fact that the ESOP has never paid a control position price for any of the stock it owns. The issue of consistency may be applicable, suggesting that the ESOP continue to be valued on a minority position basis.
  - A second interpretation of these factors favors the ESOP being valued on a control position basis because that is the reality of the power base in the company. Changing from a minority position valuation to a control position valuation represents an immediate gain to the ESOP participants.
  - A third interpretation suggests that the value of the company reflect a migration to a control position on a phased-in basis over time.

Multistage Transactions

One common issue in ESOP installations is the intent of the controlling shareholder(s) to sell a controlling interest to the plan, but the company currently can only afford to purchase a minority position block of stock. Over time, it is likely the company will be able to afford purchasing the controlling interest as intended. The ESOP, under these circumstances, may still pay a prorated control position price for the stock if certain conditions are present. One transaction technique is referred to as a multistage transaction:

- Staged transactions are very technical and potentially complex transactions. There is little formal guidance on how to structure such a transaction from either the IRS or the DOL. There should be a binding written agreement that provides the right of the ESOP to acquire enough stock to give it the control that is intended within a reasonable period of time. Additionally, the ESOP should not have the control it is buying dissipated shortly after the transaction.
- Staged transactions require the passing of control to the ESOP. Issues on interpretation may arise regarding matters such as when and how much effective control passes, does control pass within a reasonable amount of time, is the premium paid for the control consistent with the control being acquired, and so on. Clearly, such issues should only be addressed by practitioners familiar with such transactions.
- It is beyond the scope of this book to offer definitive guidance on structuring such transactions. If such a transaction is being contemplated, it is highly recommended that only experienced professionals be retained to structure the sale. Recent reading on this topic may be found in the article "An Update on Multi-Stage ESOP Transactions" in the fall 2003 issue of the *Journal of Employee Ownership Law and Finance*.
- From a practical standpoint, if the owner wants to sell a controlling interest to the ESOP in order to gain the prorated control position price, it is best to structure a transaction so the ESOP acquires over 50 percent of the outstanding stock. This may be accomplished by a number of strategies, including prefunding the ESOP for a period of time to build equity in the plan or simply providing a seller note in an amount sufficient for the ESOP to acquire a controlling interest immediately.

Dilution Considerations and Outstanding Shares

It is important that items having a dilutive impact on the value of the company on a per share basis be fully reflected in the ESOP valuation. The ESOP is prohibited from paying more than adequate consideration for company stock. Correspondingly, items that have a dilutive impact on the number of shares outstanding, thereby lowering the price of the stock on a per share basis, must be adequately considered in the report.

For the purposes of an ESOP, outstanding shares include issued shares owned by investors outside the ESOP and all shares purchased by the ESOP, both in the suspense account and those released to participants' accounts.

- Dilutive items may include stock options, warrants, convertible stock, and preferred stock. They have to be individually analyzed for the impact on the value of the company.
- Determining the dilutive impact of a type of security may become a complex analysis. Typical considerations include the overall number of shares that may become outstanding, determining exercise prices for the shares, examining vesting schedules, determining if there is a specified market with a repurchase obligation for the shares

if they are issued, and what impact the inflow of capital will have on the value of the company if new shares are issued.

- Once the impact of the securities has been determined, it is appropriate to compute the value of the stock per share on a fully diluted basis. It is beyond the scope of this book to consider how to compute the dilution that may occur.

Dilution With the ESOP Contribution of Newly Issued Stock

Another form of dilution occurs when the employer contributes stock to the plan. The stock may be newly issued shares or treasury shares. Typically, the employer accrues the ESOP contribution at the end of the fiscal year in a designated dollar amount, but the number of shares that dollar amount represents is unknown. Then, based on the valuation of the company, the number of shares represented by the accrued ESOP contribution must be determined. A formula is commonly used to compute the number of new shares to be issued. This formula and an example illustrate the computation:

Example 7-2   Example Computation Dilution With Newly Issued Stock to the ESOP

Formula to compute the number of new shares to be issued:

$$\text{Value per share} = \frac{\text{(Value of company stock)} - \text{(Current-year ESOP contribution)}}{\text{Number of shares outstanding prior to ESOP contribution}}$$

Example: Facts as presented

- ABC Company has fair market value of $5.2 million
- ESOP contribution is $200,000 (to be in newly issued stock)
- Before the ESOP contribution, 20,000 shares are outstanding
- Determine the price per share after the ESOP contribution

Applying the preceding facts to the formula, we have the following:

$$\text{Value per share} = \frac{\$5,200,000 - \$200,000}{20,000}$$

Value per share = $250

Based on the preceding facts, 800 shares of stock will be issued (200,000 / 250)

Proof of math:

20,000 + 800 = 20,800 shares outstanding

20,800 shares × $250 per share = $5,200,000

(continued)

Summary: In this example, the value of ABC Company is established at $5.2 million. An ESOP contribution of $200,000 in newly issued stock indicates that 800 shares will be issued at a price per share of $250. The new number of shares outstanding is 20,800. The outstanding number of shares (20,800) multiplied by the price per share ($250) must equal the established overall valuation, which it does.

The following schedule summarizes the dilution that occurs as a result of the stock contribution:

Shareholder	Stock Before Contribution	Percent	Stock After Contribution	Percent
Outside shareholders	20,000	100%	20,000	95.2%
ESOP	0	0%	800	3.8%
Total	20,000	100%	20,800	100.0%

Leveraged ESOPs—Initial Valuation and Annual Updates

The ESOP is considered to be leveraged when it borrows money to purchase employer stock. If an ESOP is installed, the process of valuation typically includes issuing an initial report prior to the installation of the plan. This valuation report often establishes the viability of the ESOP as an option for the company. After the initial report, the ESOP purchases stock in the company. In many cases, the ESOP purchases stock from selling shareholders, and the source of the funds to buy the stock is from a bank loan. This is the traditional leveraged ESOP.

- The EA has published the booklet *Valuing ESOP Shares* (revised 2005) that is an excellent general overview of ESOP valuation issues.
- The EA has released the booklet *Report on Valuation Considerations for Leveraged ESOPs*, prepared in 1998 by The EA's Advisory Committee on Valuation. The booklet is an excellent source for a survey of the current thinking regarding the interpretation of reporting and valuation issues relating to leveraged ESOPs. The ideas in the booklet are informative, but they are not the authority on the matter. Within the ranks of experienced valuation authorities (the IRS and the DOL), there is often disagreement on many issues. The appropriate valuation analysis depends on the facts and specific circumstances of each case.
- The initial valuation is often intended to value the company for the purposes of an ESOP just prior to the transaction. Typically, the leveraged ESOP is going to borrow money to purchase stock of the employer. The initial valuation does not consider the structure of the ESOP-related debt.

- Prior to the installation of the ESOP, the valuation of the company should not consider how the ESOP will finance the purchase of the stock. The value of the company's stock is a separate issue from financing the ESOP transaction.

When the company incurs ESOP-related debt to purchase company stock, there is at least one significant difference between the initial report and subsequent annual updates. The initial report does not consider the ESOP-related debt that is going to be incurred, whereas the annual updates will reflect financial statements that report the ESOP-related debt. The balance sheet will report the ESOP-related debt as a liability, with a corresponding offset to the company equity. The income statement will reflect the interest and compensation expense that the company incurred as a result of the ESOP-related debt.

As a result of the ESOP-related debt, the subsequent annual update valuations consider the changed capital structure of the company from the time just prior to the ESOP installation. It is common in such circumstances for the valuation of the common stock to decrease following the installation of a leveraged ESOP.

The most common reason for the reduction in value is that the succeeding reports now account for the ESOP-related debt. The capital structure of the company has been changed as a result of the ESOP-related debt, and the increased debt often significantly changes the risk environment of the company while the debt is being repaid. This higher risk affects the value of the company for ESOP purposes. Additionally, the company has higher interest payments as a result of the ESOP-related debt.

Clients should be informed that the value of the stock will likely fall after the installation of the ESOP, due to the additional debt in the company. When the leverage is substantial, the fall in value may be a significant percentage of the value in the initial report. The drop in the value applies to all shares outstanding, including those investors outside the ESOP.

- This point is critical to communicate to the client because the drop in price may have an impact on the relative acceptance of the ESOP. If the drop in value is significant, other investors not selling to the ESOP at the initial transaction may take exception to the preferential treatment accorded the stockholders selling to the ESOP initially.
- Once the ESOP-related debt is repaid, the balance sheet and income statement no longer report the impact of the debt. The value of the company is typically fully restored. Investors outside the ESOP may be unwilling to wait for the debt to be repaid and the value to increase.

Annual ESOP Update Issues

Fluctuations in Value Between Years

Generally, sudden, substantial, and frequent swings in the value of the stock for ESOP purposes between years are not appropriate. The value of the stock may fluctuate over a longer period of time depending on market conditions and the specific performance of the company. Certainly, market forces have an impact on the value of the stock in a closely held company. That is a risk of being in business, and the value of the stock may, in fact, rise or decline.

- The fluctuation of the stock is most appropriately attributable to longer-term trends impacting the ESOP company. The price of stock in publicly held companies is typically more vulnerable to short-term market pressures. Investors in public companies have almost instant liquidity and virtually infinite investment options. Investment dollars in that arena are free to migrate to better investment options with few barriers. This is not the case with the stock in a closely held company in which liquidity is often a significant issue.
- Frequent and substantial swings in the value of the ESOP company stock typically indicate that the long-term nature of the assignment is misunderstood by the valuation professional. Unforeseen and unusual circumstances may cause significant swings in the value of the stock, but those circumstances are not likely to be the norm.
- Using a number of valuation approaches spanning a range of operating results will often provide an adequate baseline of analysis to help ensure a more stable assessment of the company's fair market value.

There are circumstances when a sudden change in the value of the stock is appropriate, but this is not the normal situation. Some examples of situations that may have a significant short-term impact on the value of the stock include the unanticipated loss of a major customer, the unanticipated default by a major supplier, the closing of a military base, a disastrous natural event (fire or flood), and an unanticipated product liability or product warranty issue. The severe recession beginning in 2007 and exacerbated with the Wall Street financial disaster in September 2008 is another example of a sharp and likely unanticipated jolt to the valuation of many privately held companies. If such an event occurs, it is still appropriate to consider the longer-term impact on the company for the purposes of the valuation.

Valuation Methodology—Issue of Consistency

It is customary to consider a number of different valuation approaches when determining the fair market value of company stock for the purposes of an ESOP. The analysis will often include a consideration of three basic valuation approaches or variations of them. The three overall approaches are market based, income based, and asset based. The valuation professional may consider any number of approaches in arriving at an opinion of value. Although not mandatory, there is an implied obligation that future reports will include an analysis similar to the methodology that was used in the first report.

There is an issue of consistency between years when determining value for an ESOP application. Although it is appropriate to be consistent in valuation methodology, it is also a practical consideration that facts and circumstances change for companies. Appropriate valuation methodology in one year may be inappropriate in later years as markets and products evolve.

- The valuation professional should not be blind to such changing conditions. It is important to document reasons for adjustments in the valuation approaches used.
- One practical method given the changing nature of business conditions is to consider a range of valuation approaches in the report and provide a well-reasoned

weighting of the approaches. This is not intended to suggest that a straight averaging of approaches is appropriate. Rather, if a weighted average is considered, the reasoning behind such weights should be detailed. If conditions warrant adjusting the weights, the reasons for such adjustments should be documented.

- It is not appropriate to use formula approaches in determining fair market value opinions. Formulas typically are incapable of adequately considering changing business conditions or qualitative factors in assessing the relative risk associated with a particular equity.

Increasing Value With Time

As a general observation, the value of the ESOP company may grow over time primarily as a result of increasing earnings and increasing the underlying value of assets. Earnings may increase as a result of a number of factors, such as reducing costs, increasing sales, and improving margins. The essential point is that value grows when company resources are deployed in a manner to increase shareholder wealth.

- If the company is not growing, or costs are not being significantly reduced, the value of the stock under such a mature market scenario is unlikely to grow appreciably.
- Increases in the price of the stock are typically related to the increasing earnings of the company. Without increasing earnings over time, the value of the company will typically stabilize.
- If earnings decrease over time, the value of the stock is almost certainly going to be negatively impacted.
- Remember that employee ownership has its own inherent rewards, and a steadily increasing rise in the value of the stock is not always a driving goal for the company. Increases in the value of the stock may contain implications for growth in the company sales, facilities, and employment base that are negative risk factors. Typically, when the growth in the value of the company stock stabilizes, the employer often introduces another benefit plan, such as a 401(k) plan, so that employee retirement funds are more diversified and continue to accumulate.

Multi-Investor ESOPs and Allocation Considerations

In certain larger ESOP-related transactions, the overall complexity may increase significantly if there are a number of investors. These transactions are referred to as multi-investor ESOPs for the purposes of this book. One common example of a multi-investor ESOP is the purchase of a company by a consortium of investors including participants such as management, investment bankers, other investors, and the ESOP.

Typically, multi-investor ESOPs are found in larger transactions when there is often a significant amount of debt. Equity is contributed to the transaction, but the participation in the future increases in company value is established by negotiation among shareholders. Commonly, not all the shareholders participate equally. Depending on an interpretation of relative risk assumed and other market factors, the future appreciation in value is allocated differently among the shareholders.

- The appraiser may be asked to allocate the fair market value of the company to the different shareholders or opine to the fairness of an equity allocation methodology. The DOL has not offered any formal guidelines on the matter of equity allocation, and there is minimal case law in this area.
- In transactions involving multiple investors, the issue of allocating equity may become a contested matter if the shareholders are not treated equally.
- The argument for not treating the shareholders equally involves the fact that, perceptually, different investors are assuming different amounts of risk and responsibility. For example, management is typically expected to provide the leadership to enable the company to repay all the purchase-related debt, assuming a leveraged buy-out in this case. If there is an investment banker, the investment banker is often contributing a percentage of capital and, perhaps, additional financing. The ESOP typically is borrowing funds to purchase stock, but there is typically no equity being contributed initially. The ESOP is bringing to the transaction some tax advantages, but those tax advantages will only be realized if the ESOP-related debt is repaid. In such circumstances, the participants to the transaction participate at different levels, and equity allocations are computed.
- The merits of each transaction should be considered individually. Proponents of equity allocations frequently state that such allocations reflect the reality of the financial markets.
- The DOL has informally expressed the opposite argument that all shareholders should participate equally per dollar of equity investment. This position is generally referred to as the dollar-for-dollar allocation. This position by the DOL has merit from the standpoint of fairness to all shareholders, particularly the ESOP. For example, this position holds that if an ESOP invests 90 percent of the total dollars invested, then the ESOP should receive 90 percent of the common shares after the conversion of all subordinated classes of stock. The position, unfortunately, does not typically reflect the dynamics of the financial markets that tend to reward investors based on both risk assumed and relative abilities to negotiate more favorable allocations.
- There is little formal guidance on the matter of equity allocations and few court decisions. This is an area that is technical and potentially very contentious. Generally, such allocation assignments are reserved only for those appraisal firms with the resources and experience to support positions.

Multiple Classes of Stock in C Corporation ESOP Transactions

This section considers the situation in which a second class of stock in addition to the common stock is created specifically for the ESOP transaction. With closely held companies, the creation of a special class of stock for the ESOP transaction is not the norm, but it has applications.

The most common application of creating a second class of stock in addition to the common stock occurs when few constraints are on the ESOP transaction as a result of a lack of qualifying payroll. For a leveraged ESOP in a C corporation, the contribution limit is 25 percent of qualifying payroll. In certain situations, this 25 percent ceiling is a barrier to the installation of the ESOP because the value of the company in relation to the qualifying payroll is higher. This may happen with companies that have a large asset base in relation to the payroll, such as in natural resource industries.

Currently, S corporations can only have a single class of stock; therefore, the creation of an additional equity is not an option at this time.

One common practice in these circumstances is to create a separate class of stock owned only by the ESOP. The most common types of equity created for this application are convertible preferred stock and senior common stock:

- Convertible preferred stock pays a dividend, and the dividend is typically used to repay ESOP-related debt. The dividend does not count toward the 25 percent payroll limit; therefore, the convertible preferred stock is a vehicle that is useful in the design of the ESOP when there are payroll constraints. The dividend payment is also deductible for income tax purposes, but the dividend is a consideration in determining the corporate alternative minimum tax.
- Common attributes of the convertible preferred stock created for the ESOP include the following:
  - Dividends are paid on the convertible preferred stock, but the dividends are intended to be paid only while the ESOP debt is being amortized. Upon the amortization of the ESOP debt, the convertible preferred stock is typically converted to common stock at an established conversion rate.
  - Dividends are typically stated as either a percentage of the par value or fixed dollar amount. Dividends are declared by the board of directors.
  - The dividends on the convertible preferred stock are typically cumulative, meaning that the dividends in arrears have to be both paid prior to any dividends being paid on other classes of stock and paid prior to conversion or redemption.
  - The dividend rate specified on the convertible preferred stock must be reasonable in relation to dividends on other similar equities. Guidance on the reasonableness of the dividend rate is typically obtained from information in the public markets.
  - The convertible preferred stock often has a liquidation preference over the common stock.
  - The convertible preferred stock for the purposes of the ESOP must have the highest level of voting rights. Upon conversion, the converted stock typically becomes common stock with the highest voting and dividend rights.
- Revenue Ruling 83-120 provides guidance on the valuation of preferred stock and has applications in the case of convertible preferred stock created for ESOP purposes. For valuation purposes, consideration is given to the particular rights and privileges of the convertible preferred stock. In addition to the factors mentioned in Revenue Ruling 83-120, other factors relating to a closely held company, such as voting control

and liquidation rights, are appropriately considered. The intent of the creation of the convertible preferred stock is also considered.

- It is also possible to create another equity referred to as senior common stock. The senior common stock is similar to preferred stock, with a number of common attributes, such as a dividend and preference rights. Typically, the senior common stock is not callable, and it is not converted into another class of stock. The dividend rights and preference attributes of the senior common stock may likely warrant a valuation premium over regular common stock.
  - The application of senior common stock is typically associated with more complex ESOP installations.

Practical Valuation Considerations

This section includes observations and insights gained over time. Usually, there are very few hard and fast rules with ESOP valuations. The individual facts and circumstances of each situation must be carefully analyzed:

- Generally, closely held companies that are either losing money or in industries that are rapidly declining make relatively poor candidates for an ESOP. The long-term orientation of the ESOP makes such an investment a questionable endeavor. The facts may change somewhat when the ESOP is proposed as one acceptable way to preserve jobs:
  - Saving jobs is a harsh reality that likely means employees will be making compensation concessions to provide the resources the company requires to service acquisition-related debt. Under such circumstances, the company stock must be valued for the purposes of an ESOP, but a significant amount of caution should accompany the valuation analysis. If the company fails for any reason, the price paid for the stock will be questioned, and those questioning the value of the stock will have the benefit of perfect hindsight.
- Companies in cyclical industries should be analyzed over at least one full business cycle, if practical, to assess the relative risk environment. Operating results should be considered over a longer term. If the ESOP is installed, there is a high likelihood that the company will go through additional business cycles in the future. The company must be able to meet ESOP-related obligations over a range of financial results.
- Companies in a start-up mode may install an ESOP as an employee benefit. It is unusual under such circumstances for the company to make a market for a retiring shareholder by purchasing a large block of stock because the company is relatively new, and the employees are often younger. Due to the lack of historical financial track record, valuation methods that project future prospects are often more seriously considered.
- When presented with an optimistic future outlook that is inconsistent with historically attained results, caution should be exercised when assessing the value of the stock. Generally, if the company is successful, it is practical to allow the value of the stock to increase as the company demonstrates financial success.

Chapter 8

Administration and Transaction Considerations

Employee stock ownership plan (ESOP) transactions often appear to be very complex because of the substantial planning that is entailed with the initial installation and the significant amount of detail that must be addressed by the company long term. This chapter will briefly examine a number of the major administrative issues to be addressed as the ESOP is being considered. The topics include performing a feasibility study (always advised), planning executive compensation, obtaining a stock valuation, and considering the stock repurchase obligation.

Initial Considerations and ESOP Feasibility Study

Most typically, business owners are attracted to the idea of an ESOP because they have heard about the tax incentives centered on their creation. Another leading source for interest is that business owners are attracted to the idea of passing an equity interest to their employees. Regardless of the reasons, when initial inquiry turns into more serious analysis, the issues surrounding the installation of an ESOP can become complex. There are many points of interest in an ESOP installation, including those of the business owner, the employees, and federal oversight agencies.

Team of Advisors

An ESOP installation is often a complex transaction that requires a number of professional service disciplines. It is emphasized that some professionals are able to provide more than one of the services required for the ESOP. In other instances, a single service provider is engaged for the specific function. A listing of the most typical service providers and the various functions commonly found with ESOP transactions is listed (the functions will be briefly described):

- *CPA firm*. Financial adviser and ESOP feasibility
- *Attorney*. Legal adviser and ESOP feasibility
- *ESOP stock appraiser*. Independent valuation adviser and ESOP feasibility
- *Benefits administration*. Recordkeeping and ESOP feasibility
- *Trustee (plan fiduciary)*. Serves as ongoing fiduciary
- *Independent fiduciary*. Serves as transaction fiduciary
- *Investment adviser*. Investing Internal Revenue Code (IRC) Section 1042 proceeds
- *Financial institution (banker)*. Provides funding and ESOP feasibility
- *Communications*. Employee education

The following is a listing of the various professional disciplines that may be provided for an ESOP installation. We note that when an ESOP installation is in a large company, the number of service providers may be significant because each of the disciplines is very specialized:

- *CPA*. Most ESOP candidates are well-established companies with a number of long-term professional advisers. One of the most frequently encountered advisers is a CPA firm. Typically, a principal in the firm is the lead contact with the business owner. The CPA is often regarded as the most trusted financial adviser to the company and its shareholders and is frequently one of the first advisers consulted regarding a potential ESOP.

  The CPA needs to have a working understanding of such broad topics as tax code, tax incentives, financial reporting issues, qualified benefit plans, and financing mechanics and an overview of strategic financial planning.

  CPAs need to be specifically aware of all applicable reporting and tax issues. If the company has over 100 ESOP participants, for example, the ESOP itself requires an audit. The audit of the plan will entail a detailed examination of the assets in the plan and the review of account balance computations, among a wide range of other applicable concerns.

  Candidates for ESOPs often already have financial statements that are either audited or reviewed by the CPA firm. After an ESOP installation, the standard of reporting is typically a reviewed financial statement at a minimum and, often, an audited financial statement. Fiduciary concerns often drive a desire to have a higher level of financial reporting for the company. Note that there is no formal requirement to have audited or reviewed financial statements for the company, but good business practices suggest the higher standards are appropriate.

- *Attorney.* Most ESOP candidate companies have corporate counsel, but the individual attorney for the company often does not have significant specific expertise in the Employee Retirement Income Security Act of 1974 (ERISA) and ESOPs. If the attorney is part of a larger law firm, the firm may have the in-house expertise to provide the legal work surrounding the installation of the ESOP.

  It is crucial that a law firm with significant ERISA and ESOP expertise be engaged for the assignment. The regulatory and compliance environment regarding ESOP transactions is complex. Possible penalties for improperly installed ESOPs may be severe. Mistakes may be exceedingly costly to the ESOP fiduciaries. ESOP fiduciaries ultimately bear personal responsibility for the management of the plan. This is a serious obligation.

  The attorney will be instrumental in drafting a number of documents related to the installation of the ESOP, such as the employee stock ownership trust agreement (ESOT) and the ESOP. Depending on the complexity of the transaction, there may be a wide range of additional documents required, such as employment contracts, noncompetition agreements, loan documents, and shareholder agreements, to mention a few.

  Additionally, an experienced ESOP attorney will be a good resource for insights on fiduciary responsibilities for the plan trustee. Adhering to ERISA-based transaction procedures and protocols is an important obligation of the trustee.
- *ESOP stock appraiser.* As previously discussed, the requirements are to have an independent appraiser provide the valuation of the stock for the purposes of an ESOP. There are many understandings of what constitutes independence, but the safest position for the ESOP fiduciary is to engage a valuation firm that has no other relationship to either the company or its shareholders.

  The appraiser should be knowledgeable about both the valuation of stock in a closely held company and the specific requirements of an ESOP-based assignment. Valuation firms are frequently asked to provide a feasibility study based on an estimate of value or to serve as an adviser regarding the possibility of an ESOP.

  Once the valuation adviser is selected, many companies tend to stay with the initial valuation firm for the purposes of consistency.
- *Benefits administration.* Once the ESOP is installed, the plan will typically require an administration firm to provide a range of services, such as timely filing all tax reports (particularly Form 5500), keeping accurate records of participant account balances, preparing participant account balance statements, and communicating the mechanics of the ESOP to participants. Some benefit administration firms offer capabilities for many types of qualified plan recordkeeping. Examples of commonly found plans are pensions, profit sharing plans, 401(k) plans, and ESOPs.

  It is our experience that ESOPs often have multiple qualified benefit plans. The most common combination is the ESOP and a 401(k) plan. Benefits administration is a highly technical field, and the arena is becoming highly fractured.

  When selecting an ESOP administration firm, be sure the firm has extensive specific ESOP administration experience. ESOPs are not the same as the more common 401(k) plans from an administrative standpoint. There are a number of unique aspects with ESOPs. Failure to engage a firm with specific ESOP administration expertise has occasionally resulted in disastrous results when the participant account balances are computed incorrectly.

- *Trustee (plan fiduciary)*. The ESOP, by definition, is qualified under the tax code and must have a trustee. The trustee may literally be anyone, but the trustee must understand the obligations of serving in the fiduciary capacity. In many closely held companies, the selling shareholder(s) or company officers serve as the trustee. The trustee may be an individual, or a number of individuals may serve as a plan committee. Such inside trustee candidates must be mindful of the significant obligations imposed on them by ERISA and court case precedent.

  An independent (outside) trustee may be considered. An independent trustee is often an institution with a trust department. The independent trustee may serve as a directed trustee or discretionary trustee. If an institution is selected to provide a trustee function, typically, a cost is associated with the service. Companies will have to balance the benefit of having the independent trustee against the expense of such a function. In this instance, the outside trustee is assumed to have an ongoing relationship with the company.

- *Independent fiduciaries*. Related to the trust function with an ESOP, an independent fiduciary typically serves as the ESOP fiduciary for just the stock transaction, including the establishment of an ESOP or any ongoing issues involving a conflict of interest. This role is intended to be short term in duration and to provide a layer of considerable protection to selling shareholders.

  The case for the independent fiduciary is enhanced when the ESOP transaction entails such attributes as a large dollar amount transaction (often in excess of many millions of dollars), a complex transaction that spans multiple investors, and side agreements for employment contracts and management incentive programs. When the transaction issues become more complex, the case for retaining an independent fiduciary is stronger. This fiduciary function can be served by individuals inside the company, individuals outside the company, a corporation subject to meeting certain requirements, or a trust company.

  - Regarding ESOP transactions, the role of the fiduciary is to act in the interests of the plan participants. This requires the fiduciary to actively participate in the exercise of diligence in such matters as establishing the ESOP; assessing the value of the shares being purchased; and negotiating on behalf of the ESOP, as appropriate.

  - If the selling shareholder is also serving as the fiduciary in a transaction, such an individual is often perceived to be conflicted. The shareholder, in this case, is both the selling party receiving the proceeds from a stock transaction and the ESOP fiduciary. The fiduciary standards of conduct in ESOP transactions are strict, and great care must be taken to fulfill the letter of the regulation. In such an environment, independent fiduciaries are often retained for the stock transaction.

- *Investment Adviser.* Typically, the investment adviser is required after the ESOP transaction. The most common scenario is that the selling shareholder has sold stock to the ESOP and now has received a large amount of cash. If the ESOP transaction is oriented to an IRC Section 1042 rollover, the need for an investment adviser with specific ESOP rollover experience is critical. Failure to properly structure the investment of qualified replacement property can result in terrible tax consequences for the shareholder.

  The investment adviser may also be instrumental in discussing the option of having the business owner self-finance an ESOP transaction. The mechanics of self-financing an ESOP transaction are often similar to the IRC Section 1042 rollover with the use of long-term debt and a margin account.

- *Financial institution (banker).* Many ESOPs are leveraged, and there is a need for a financial institution that understands the mechanics of ESOP transactions. Banks or financial institutions with considerable ESOP experience are an asset in providing helpful insights on structuring the ESOP transaction. If the ESOP is leveraged, and the assistance of a bank is required, there is a wide range of items to be considered. Naturally, the bank will provide funding for the proposed transaction, but terms and conditions are related to the loan, including guarantees and collateral.

- *Communication.* This is often one of the least appreciated disciplines, but it is typically the one key element that is a hallmark of successful ESOP installations. The best advice this author can provide to an ESOP candidate is to have someone (or a team) designated to communicate the ESOP and the philosophy of employee ownership to the employees in the company.

  There are a number of sources for the communications effort. Senior management may undertake the mission. If the senior management communicates the ESOP with conviction and persistence, there is often high acceptance by the employees. Outside consultants will also communicate the ESOP to the employees. Such outside specialists will often touch on issues not always apparent to the inside managers.

  The essential point is to make sure communication of the ESOP is an ongoing process. The advantages and obligations of employee ownership need to be continually reinforced and championed if the potential of the plan is to be achieved.

Team of Advisers Summary—Have a Transaction "Quarterback"

It is a best practice in ESOP installations to have one of the professional advisers serve as a transaction "quarterback." From the listing of potential advisers, it clearly can be a daunting challenge for the business owner to coordinate an ESOP installation with so many potential outside points of interest.

A common source of frustration for business owners is that conflicting advice may be received from the various advisers. It is critical to have an experienced ESOP specialist coordinating the entire transaction to ensure the myriad details are properly addressed. Often, the professionals have worked with one another, and one will assume the mantle of transaction coordination.

Feasibility Study

Prior to an ESOP being adopted by a company, there will be some form of a feasibility study performed to determine if the installation is practical. The feasibility study may range from informal discussions with professional advisers to a complete written plan. The degree to which the planning takes place is often a function of the complexity of the issues involved.

Informal Planning Process

In many instances, the planning process is more informal, with discussions between professional advisers and business owners. This is done to help minimize professional fees. In smaller transactions, the planning is typically more informal without a written study. It is helpful, however, to have at least one professional adviser serving as an ad hoc ESOP transaction coordinator to ensure that all proper elements of the transaction are completed. Typically, this function is managed by an ESOP adviser who either specializes in such transactions or has substantial experience in this area of practice. ESOP transactions are often complex due to the legal documents that are required and the myriad of issues that must be addressed. Having an experienced coordinator is integral to a successful installation.

Written ESOP Feasibility Study

In larger-dollar ESOP transactions or transactions with a number of complicating features, it may be desirable to have a written study that ensures all the significant issues relating to the ESOP transactions have been thoroughly considered.

An *ESOP feasibility study* (study) typically is a written report addressed to a potentially diverse audience that includes the shareholders of the company considering the ESOP, the board of directors, senior management, the acting fiduciary for the proposed ESOP, or some combination thereof. The study is often viewed as a deal book or decision package.

There are no standards regarding the study, but those charged with the review of the study will certainly consider the experience of the author before making a decision to commit to the work. Typically, only professional service providers with extensive ESOP and transaction experience are qualified to write such a study. ESOP transactions often are complex, and the purpose of the study is to address the many complexities that may arise.

The elements of a comprehensive study will typically contain the following general topics (the list is not all-inclusive but indicates the major issues).

Transaction Structure
- Determine if C corporation or S corporation issues apply (particularly with regard to S corporation anti-abuse regulations).
- Determine the percentage of stock to be sold overall.
- Determine if stock will be sold in stages to reach the overall target percentage.
- Plan for the IRC Section 1042 rollover if a C corporation.
- Consider accumulated adjustment account if an S corporation.
- Identify the sources of funding for the transaction: internal, seller, or third party.

- Determine if a minority price or control price for the stock applies.
- Have a preliminary range of value for analysis.
- Model the transaction to see if the plan's cash flows.

ESOP Design

- Determine who will participate in the ESOP.
- In a C corporation, do attribution rules related to IRC Section 1042 apply?
- In an S corporation, do new attribution rules apply?
- Is there sufficient qualifying payroll for the proposed transaction?
- Does the ESOP get integrated with other qualified plans?
- Determine such things as vesting, participation, voting rights, distributions, and so on.

Key Employee Incentives

- Determine if key employees require additional incentives during transition.
- Design key employee incentives, as required.

Administration Issues

- Select ESOP trustee(s): internal or external
  - External trustee: directed trustee or full discretion trustee.
  - Select an independent fiduciary if no external trustee is appointed, or the external trustee does not have full discretion.
- Select ESOP professional service providers:
  - Independent valuation firm
  - ESOP legal counsel
  - Financial institution (if leveraged)
  - Plan administrator
- Determine roles for other professional advisers:
  - Company CPA
  - Company legal counsel (if different from the ESOP counsel)
  - Investment adviser
  - Insurance agent
  - Other advisers
- Consider repurchase obligation
- Communications with employees

Feasibility Summary

A review of the preceding list indicates that the installation of an ESOP is an involved process with many components. Such a list of items to consider often contributes to the notion that ESOP transactions are complicated. Professional advisers must remind business owners that any major transaction regarding the closely held company is likely to entail a significant amount of detail.

An offsetting aspect to the perceived complexity of ESOPs is the far-ranging flexibility they provide in meeting the requirements of business owners and employees.

Strategic ESOP Design Considerations

The purpose of this section is to highlight a limited number of planning opportunities for ESOPs. Many considerations are part of installing the ESOP, but many are related to routine compliance with ERISA and IRC regulations and are clearly beyond the scope of this book. The points mentioned in this section are oriented to refinements in optimizing the tax benefits of the ESOP.

Contribution and Addition Limits to Qualified Plans Expanded

The Economic Growth and Tax Relief Reconciliation Act of 2001 (EGTRRA) has significant implications for companies either considering an ESOP or having an ESOP and expanding employee benefits. These provisions have been described in detail elsewhere in the book; they are summarized briefly for review.

Annual contributions and additions to qualified plans have been significantly expanded. The contribution limit to defined contribution plans (including an ESOP) is 25 percent of qualifying payroll, with the maximum covered compensation set per employee at $250,000 for 2012. The maximum covered compensation will be indexed in increments of $5,000. The annual addition limit (which includes forfeitures) is the lesser of 100 percent of qualifying pay per person or $50,000 per person. The $50,000 limit will be indexed in the future in $1,000 increments. Annual additions to an ESOP account balance may be significantly higher than traditional contribution constraints without placing the plan in noncompliance with regulations and, in some cases, excludes contributions used to pay interest on a loan to buy stock for an ESOP of a C corporation.

The expansion of annual addition limits is important in such circumstances when a leveraged ESOP with debt service requirements is likely to be at or near the 25 percent contribution limit.

Maintaining Both an ESOP and a 401(k) Plan

With the EGTRRA, elective deferrals by employees (employee contributions) into 401(k) plans will not count against the ESOP contribution limits. It is now much easier to have both the ESOP and 401(k) plan. Employees typically will make the contribution to the 401(k) without an employer match because the ESOP is an employer–provided benefit.

- Prior to the EGTRRA, the 401(k) contributions (and all other qualified plan contributions) counted against the ESOP contribution percentage. When the ESOP was leveraged, and ESOP debt obligations consumed virtually all the qualifying payroll contribution limit, this often meant that the employees had an existing 401(k) plan frozen. There was not enough allowable contribution limit to permit employees to have both the ESOP and 401(k). Losing the ability to contribute funds into a diversified plan, the 401(k) plan, while gaining an interest in only the stock of the employer (the ESOP) was, in some cases, a significant drawback. The ESOP was viewed as an investment with no diversification.

- The potentially significant drawback to an ESOP installation that is freezing an existing 401(k) plan may be reduced or eliminated. The careful study of projected contributions to all qualified plans by an experienced benefit administration firm is recommended. It is essential to make sure appropriate legislative compliance is maintained.

Creation of a Preferred Stock or Super Common Stock for the ESOP in a C Corporation

This consideration applies only to C corporations because they are permitted to have multiple classes of stock. As previously mentioned, limits on qualifying payroll may be addressed by the creation of another class of stock that is typically only owned by the ESOP. This strategy is useful when the value of the stock is high in relation to qualifying payroll.

The most common application of this strategy is the creation of a convertible preferred stock or super common stock that carries a stated dividend rate. The ESOP typically only owns this stock, and the stock exists to enable the company to declare a dividend. The dividend is paid only on this class of stock, and as the dividend is paid (contributed) to the ESOP, the company receives a tax deduction for the dividend if it is used to repay the acquisition debt. Note that the dividend is not deductible for the alternative minimum tax. This is the unique instance in the IRC in which a C corporation dividend is tax deductible in this manner.

Common design considerations include a number of items:

- A separate class of stock is created for the ESOP to own. In this case, the stock class is created to have a dividend that other non–ESOP stock will not receive. The intent is to expand ESOP contributions beyond payroll contribution limitations. The goal typically is to repay ESOP-related debt on a faster amortization schedule.
- The separate class of stock must typically have the following attributes: the highest voting rights, the highest dividend rights, and the highest liquidation preference. Generally, stock owned by the ESOP must have the most senior rights, per ERISA Section 404(a)(2).
- The dividend rate must be reasonable, according to IRC Section 404(k). The actual dividend may be stated as part of the security, or it may be more discretionary, as declared by the board of directors. There is only general guidance from the regulatory agencies regarding what constitutes a reasonable dividend. The facts and circumstances of each individual case will be examined to meet this standard.
  - The reasonableness test for dividends is examined in light of dividends paid on other comparable financial instruments.
  - Will the dividend seem reasonable when all other forms of compensation are considered?
  - Extraordinary dividends or unusually large nonrecurring dividends are likely to come under federal challenge.
- The stock is always convertible into common stock. The usual consideration is that the ESOP requires this separate class of stock while ESOP-related debt is repaid. Once the debt is repaid, the dividend feature is no longer required. At this point, the stock is converted, at the election of the board of directors, into common stock,

assuming this is in the best interest of the ESOP participants and meets applicable fiduciary standards.

The company may be able to skirt the issue of having a separate class of stock owned by just the ESOP by declaring dividends on all common stock. Non–ESOP shareholders could refuse the dividend, technically allowing only the ESOP to receive the dividend. This strategy is dependent on the good graces of the non–ESOP shareholders. Additionally, there may be potentially adverse tax consequences to refusing the dividend. The more certain option is to create a separate class of convertible preferred stock. *Note:* Care should be taken to avoid the creation of IRC Section 306 stock. The sale of IRC Section 306 stock creates ordinary income and is not eligible for the IRC Section 1042 election. A discussion of IRC Section 306 stock is beyond the scope of this book.

Compatibility With the S Corporation Election

Due to tax incentives related to S corporation ESOPs, it is appropriate to consider adopting flexibility with the design of the ESOP to be able to embrace this valuable election in the future. The flexibility is particularly warranted if the company is likely to migrate to a substantial majority stock percentage in the ESOP. With very high percentage ownership ESOPs (up to 100 percent), the tax savings with the S election are substantial. A couple planning considerations are important:

- The S corporation may only have a maximum of 100 shareholders. The ESOP counts as a single shareholder.
- The S corporation is allowed to only have a single class of stock. (A single class of stock with voting shares and nonvoting shares does not violate the single class of stock requirement.) For example, if a separate class of dividend-paying stock (preferred stock) was created for the ESOP in a C corporation, it is important to ensure a convertible provision so the class may be eliminated under certain predictable circumstances. In this manner, as the separate class of stock for the ESOP is eliminated, all that remains is typically common stock. The company will then be free to make the S corporation election.

Senior Management Compensation and Incentives

The senior management of the company, for this discussion, is typically divided into two camps. First, *senior management* may be defined as the active selling shareholder(s). Second, *senior management* may be defined as the successor management team. Compensation issues for each defined group are briefly considered. For analysis, we are assuming the ESOP is being installed as an exit vehicle for a retiring shareholder:

- *Senior management—selling shareholder(s).* This group of managers is typically selling stock to the ESOP and often has an interest in reducing discretionary compensation for the purposes of increasing the stock value. Such discretionary compensation is often added back to the income of the company for valuation purposes. The practical effect of the adjustment is to increase the value of the stock being sold by the shareholder to the ESOP.

- If discretionary shareholder compensation is adjusted for valuation purposes, the shareholder must understand that such an adjustment represents a concession that is being made. The ESOP is purchasing stock based on an availability of financial resources and cash flow. It is clearly improper for the shareholder to continue taking the higher discretionary amount after the ESOP is installed.

- The ESOP fiduciary may want the compensation of the shareholder to be subject to an employment agreement to remove the possibility of improper compensation to the shareholder. A recent court case (*Delta Star, Inc., et al. v. Andrew W. Patton, et al.*, United States District Court for the Western District of Pennsylvania, Civil Action No. 96-2183) concentrated on the excessive compensation that the most senior officer of an ESOP company, also serving as the ESOP trustee and a member of the board of directors, unilaterally declared over several years.

• *Senior management—successor team.* Compensation issues for this group are often different than for the selling shareholders. This team often cannot set its own compensation. They are often interested in strong incentives that help them personally.

- Successor members of senior management may not fully embrace the ESOP because they wanted the business. In many cases, such desires are misplaced because such managers have limited financial resources and would have to acquire an equity interest with after-tax dollars.

- Additionally, the benefits of participating in a qualified plan, such as an ESOP, are perceived by senior managers as being disproportionately low in relation to their contributions to the company.

- Incentives for senior managers to overcome such objections are compatible with an ESOP, but they must be very carefully considered and implemented. The overall compensation package of senior management must be considered, including cash compensation, participation in the ESOP, and other incentives. The more common incentives are as follows:

  ○ *Deferred compensation.* Such plans as stock appreciation rights (SARs) and phantom stock are forms of deferred compensation. Although the plans may be linked to company financial performance and have certain attributes similar to equity investments, ultimately, the proceeds will be taxed as ordinary income. It is important to note that no stock is actually received by the managers.

  ○ *Stock option plans.* These may encompass incentive stock options or nonqualified stock option plans. Such plans typically provide the manager with the right to acquire stock under a predetermined set of circumstances. It may result in shares of stock actually being issued.

  ○ *Stock bonus plan.* The manager may acquire stock in the company by having a bonus declared that is used to purchase stock. The stock is purchased, in essence, because the transaction is reported on the manager's tax return. Shares of stock are issued, in this case, as the manager pays for them with the bonus.

Whatever forms the incentives take, if the company has an ESOP, fiduciary concerns are to be addressed. The incentives must be viewed in light of the full range of obligations of the managers. Care must be taken if the managers receiving the incentives are also ESOP fiduciaries or board members. There may be conflicts of interest that could potentially impose substantial personal liabilities on the managers if the agreements are not reasonable.

Special S Corporation Considerations

As part of the EGTRRA, provisions are aimed at eliminating certain abusive S corporation ESOP practices. The intent of the EGTRRA anti-abuse provisions of the legislation is to preserve the tax deferral nature of ESOPs only in S corporations providing broad-based plan participation.

Certain complex standards must be completed to determine if certain employees are disqualified persons and if nonallocation contribution rules are in effect. Although such provisions are beyond the scope of this discussion, it is noted that the anti-abuse testing considers synthetic equity as part of the computations:

- *Synthetic equity.* The anti-abuse legislation identifies synthetic equity in an attempt to give this class of compensation an equivalent number of shares of stock on which the synthetic equity is based. Synthetic equity includes, but is not limited to, the following forms of compensation:
  - Stock options
  - Warrants
  - Restricted stock
  - Deferred issuance stock right
  - Other similar rights or interests
- Creative compensation strategies are compatible with the installation of an ESOP in an S corporation, but the anti-abuse legislation must warrant a close examination of any compensation program to ensure compliance with federal legislation. Failure to address these issues may result in significant penalties to both the company and the affected individual.

Prior to implementing any incentive programs for senior managers, consult with an experienced attorney who is knowledgeable about ESOPs and fiduciary obligations. The extra caution at the time of consideration may prevent an unintended consequence later.

ESOP Trustee and Transaction Considerations

It has been previously stated that virtually anyone may serve as an ESOP trustee. Clearly, although this is technically the case, serving in the capacity of an ESOP trustee during the time of a transaction between the plan and a selling shareholder requires additional diligence.

Historically, when ESOPs were first created, only C corporations could sponsor a plan. Correspondingly, most ESOPs installed in closely held companies constituted minority position blocks of stock. Typically, the ESOP acquired at least 30 percent of the outstanding stock so that the selling shareholder qualified for the IRC Section 1042 tax deferral. Early ESOP transactions in C corporations typically were not very complicated. It was a common practice, but not necessarily recommended, for the selling shareholder to serve as the ESOP trustee under such circumstances.

Two events have affected ESOP transactions recently that are tied together, and both relate to S corporations. During 1996 and 1997, Congress passed legislation enabling S corporations to sponsor ESOPs. The Small Business Job Protection Act of 1996 and the Taxpayer Relief Act of 1997 enabled S corporations to have an ESOP. One of the pronounced drawbacks of the legislation, however, is the relatively small percentage of qualifying payroll that may be used for plan contributions. The EGTRRA expanded contribution limits for S corporation ESOPs significantly. Payroll contribution limits were increased to 25 percent of qualifying payroll, and employee self-directed contributions to 401(k) plans generally do not count against the ESOP's 25 percent limit. The legislative summary is very brief and not intended to be comprehensive. The point is, S corporation ESOPs have recently received considerable incentives through Congressional actions. The result of the legislation is that ESOP transactions are generally becoming more complex.

Recent trends in ESOP transactions often include several of the following issues:

- Shareholders will often consider selling a controlling interest in the subject S corporation to the ESOP. The tax savings for an S corporation that is either a high-percentage ESOP owned or 100 percent ESOP owned is significant. Issues that may arise under such circumstances include applying an appropriate premium for a controlling interest in the business and determining if the ESOP is gaining control both in appearance and fact.

- With an S corporation, it is often easier for a selling shareholder to provide seller financing if there is no consideration of the IRC Section 1042 tax deferral. If the shareholder is providing a portion or all of the debt financing, there is an issue, for example, of determining if the terms of the debt are at least arm's length.

- Often, the plan sponsor is an operating company that leases its facilities from the controlling shareholder. Prior to the ESOP acquiring the stock, it is often appropriate to have in place a long-term lease that protects the company in such matters as having a reasonable lease rate after the transaction and having the ability to stay in the facility into the future.

- Key employees may receive employment contracts or other agreements with financial incentives to stay with the company after the ESOP is installed. Common financial incentives may include deferred compensation, phantom stock, or SARs. Such agreements have to be negotiated and executed. Clearly, it is desirable to ensure that such agreements are reasonable and fair to both the recipients and the company.

The preceding examples are intended to illustrate that ESOP transactions may be accompanied by a host of issues that are all related to the deal. Increasingly, because the issues are becoming more complex, many shareholders decide to engage the services of an independent trustee.

Benefits of an Independent Fiduciary

An outside or independent fiduciary offers many advantages in ESOP transactions. In this analysis, the term *fiduciary* designates the party that is representing the interests of the ESOP participants. The fiduciary may be an independent trust company, or it may be a party assuming the fiduciary role for the benefit of the ESOP. The use of the term *fiduciary* is broader than just using the term *trustee* in this section because some entities and individuals offer independent fiduciary services and capabilities without being the trustee of the ESOP. The fiduciary must have the opportunity to review all significant terms of the proposed ESOP transactions and will negotiate the terms on behalf of the ESOP. Clearly, if an independent fiduciary is being considered, the fiduciary should ideally have significant experience negotiating transactions:

- An independent fiduciary will negotiate on behalf of the ESOP. This negotiating process is not intended to destroy an ESOP deal; rather, it helps ensure the ESOP is getting the best possible consideration for the price being paid for the stock.
- Experienced transaction fiduciaries often bring to the table a host of practical insights that may help both the ESOP and the selling shareholder. The following nonexclusive items typically comprise areas of investigation and examination by the independent fiduciary:
  - Familiarity with the transaction documents, including such items as the ESOP (the plan documents), stock purchase agreement, deferred compensation agreements, employment contracts, applicable board and shareholder resolutions, and so on
  - Familiarity with financing structures, such as bank, debt, seller financing and subdebt
  - Familiarity with the valuation process
  - Familiarity with negotiations generally regarding the transaction process
- An independent fiduciary typically communicates the ESOP transaction to the employees. Having an outside spokesperson explaining the stock sale often enhances the credibility of the transaction. Employees are often not knowledgeable about ESOPs, and they may be skeptical about the program at first. Engaging an experienced fiduciary typically helps minimize initial skepticism.
- The fiduciary is assuming a great deal of potential liability. Knowing the possible exposure through experience and study helps the fiduciary prepare for the transaction in a manner that most selling shareholders could never hope to attain. An independent fiduciary may ask for a fairness opinion from an experienced financial adviser. Fairness opinions are considered shortly.
- There will be a cost to engaging an independent fiduciary for the transaction, but the cost is typically a small percentage or amount in relation to the possible liability exposure if the transaction is subsequently challenged for any reason.
- The independent fiduciary may serve for just the stock transaction or may be engaged on an ongoing basis.

ESOP Fairness Opinion

The ESOP fairness opinion commonly refers to an additional written opinion provided by an independent third party typically to the ESOP fiduciary when a significant transaction involving the ESOP occurs. Such significant events as a merger, a sale of the business, a substantial sale of stock to the ESOP, restructuring the business, or a recapitalization are examples of transactions that may warrant the issuing of a fairness opinion.

The fairness opinion is typically intended to state that the applicable transaction is fair to the ESOP from a financial point of view. The fairness opinion is another form of reassurance to the ESOP fiduciary that when the overall terms and conditions of the transaction are evaluated by an independent source, the ESOP is being treated equitably from a financial viewpoint. The fairness opinion looks at a host of issues, in addition to the value of the stock, for the purposes of an ESOP. In this sense, the fairness opinion is a macro analysis of the transaction from an economic standpoint:

- The fairness opinion is typically not provided when the transaction is very standard, such as the ESOP purchasing a minority position block of stock from a shareholder. In such a situation, the terms of the transaction are not complicated.
- The case for the fairness opinion is much stronger when the transaction is more complex and involves, for example, the valuation of multiple classes of stock; the allocation of control premium among stock classes; the consideration of management agreements, including noncompetition agreements and employment contracts; stock options; disagreement among shareholders questioning if they are all being treated equitably; different offers being considered; and other matters.

The fairness opinion is not required by statute regarding ESOP applications. The request for the fairness opinion typically originates with an ESOP fiduciary, a financial institution extending a loan, legal counsel, or some other interested party.

Fairness From Only a Financial Viewpoint

It is essential to understand that the fairness opinion determines whether the transaction is fair to the ESOP from only a financial point of view. The fairness opinion generally is limited to addressing the financial terms of the transaction and providing a degree of reassurance that the overall terms are fair to the ESOP from a financial viewpoint.

The fairness opinion is often linked to the stock appraiser's opinion regarding the value of the company's common stock at the transaction date. The ESOP cannot pay more than fair market value for any stock it purchases.

Common Components of the Fairness Opinion

Typically the fairness opinion contains a number of sections. Those sections discuss the following items (not intended to be an all-inclusive list):

- *Description of the major provisions of the proposed transaction.* The description of the transaction is often in sufficient detail to provide only an overview of the significant aspects of the transaction. Many transactions contain a considerable amount of legal detail in the applicable documents. Although such detail is essential to the consummation of the transaction, it is often not material to an understanding of the fairness of the transaction from a financial viewpoint.
- *A listing of the data, legal documents, financial statements, projections, and other factors relied upon in determining the fairness opinion.* Generally, this section indicates the significant factors that have been considered in reaching the fairness opinion. At a minimum, it is common to see a list of the documents that have been directly and carefully considered or examined.
- *Limiting conditions regarding the scope of work.* Limiting conditions that apply are listed. If a dispute arises centering on the fairness opinion, the statement of limiting conditions that are part of the report may be crucial in restricting potential liability.
- *The fairness opinion from a financial viewpoint.* It is important to note that the opinion is typically restricted to an analysis of only financial matters. The fairness opinion is often a letter addressed to the requesting party.

Rights of ESOP Participants

This section is intended to provide a brief overview of only the most significant participant rights. Generally, the plan members are participants in a qualified defined contribution plan. The actual stock of the employer is owned by the ESOT. Plan participants are not shareholders in the company. The plan fiduciary, in most ordinary instances, votes the shares of the ESOP in accordance with the discretion or direction from the board of directors. Note that the ESOP participants never vote the shares; rather, they may direct the trustee on the vote in certain circumstances.

Right to Demand Employer Securities

An ESOP participant who is entitled to a distribution may demand that the distribution be in the form of employer securities, per IRC Section 409(h)(1). This ability to obtain a distribution is generally referred to as the put option. If the participant does not demand securities, the employer may make the distribution in cash.

From a practical standpoint, closely held companies routinely amend articles of incorporation and bylaws to restrict stock ownership to employees or a qualified trust under IRC Section 401(a). This restriction is permissible as long as the employer will redeem ESOP participants' stock with cash. S corporations do not have to distribute stock.

ESOP Participant Voting Rights

The issue of voting rights regarding stock of the employer in a qualified retirement plan is complex. Only the stock of a closely held company is being considered. There is some direction from both the IRC and ERISA. Generally, the ESOP participants have limited opportunities to direct the trustee to vote the stock allocated in their respective account, per IRC Section 409(1). This is an overview of only a few common voting-related issues. Due to the potential complexity of the topic, if any significant question arises regarding voting rights, the advice of experienced ERISA council is recommended.

- Closely held companies generally have to provide plan participants with voting rights on a limited number of significant issues, such as
  - merger.
  - consolidation.
  - sale of substantially all the employer's assets.
  - recapitalization.
  - reclassification.
  - dissolution.
  - corporate liquidation.

  Absent these major events, the ESOP trustee is ordinarily responsible for voting all the stock held by the ESOP.

- In those significant instances when the voting right is passed through to the ESOP participants, they only direct the trustee to vote the stock allocated to their individual accounts.
- The voting rights of ESOP participants may become very complex, given the specific circumstances or an event that triggers the pass-through vote. An example of a complexity involves unallocated shares held by the ESOP for the benefit of the participants eventually. The ESOP trustee typically votes the unallocated shares, but there are instances when the participants may direct the trustee to vote unallocated shares in some proportionate manner to the stock already allocated to the participants' accounts.
  - ESOP trustees typically vote as directed in pass-through voting situations, but they are not required to do so. The ESOP trustee is to vote according to the responsibilities established by ERISA. For example, the ESOP trustee should only consider the impact an event has on just the stock value for qualified plan purposes. Matters pertaining to maintaining employment or preserving jobs are not to be considered. The fact is that such behavioral issues may have an impact on the vote of the trustee.
- If a situation appears to qualify for a pass-through vote, it is essential to retain the expertise of an experienced ESOP attorney. The failure to properly discharge voting rights could subject a fiduciary to severe penalties.
- If a situation involves issues that represent a conflict of interest for the trustee involved in the process, consideration should be given to engaging an independent fiduciary to review the matter.
- As a practical matter, companies may provide much broader voting rights to plan participants. Expanded voting rights are often a sign of good faith on the part of management to encourage an ownership culture in the company.

Written Materials

The employer must provide plan participants with a range of material that relates to the ESOP in general and the account balance of the individual:

- *General ESOP materials.* The company must make available the following items of information to the plan participants:
  - Summary plan description
  - Summary annual report (annual Form 5500 or Form 5500 C/R for plans with fewer than 100 participants that is filed every 3 years)
  - A report on any material modifications to the plan
- *ESOP participant account balances.* Certain details regarding the specific account for an ESOP participant must be provided:
  - The number of shares in the participant's account
  - The value per share of those shares and the extended amount
  - The value and asset allocation of other account assets
  - The percentage vested
- The following documents are made available for inspection to plan participants, but they do not have to be distributed:
  - The ESOP
  - The ESOT
  - Annual reports to the government
  - Letter of determination and the application
  - Any contracts under which the ESOP was established to currently operate

The plan participant does not have a right to be provided with the ESOP valuation report. This point has been the object of litigation in the past, with courts split on the issue. Currently, the prevailing thought is that the valuation report does not have to be provided to plan participants.

Dispute Settlement

If there is a legal dispute among such parties as the plan participants, the ESOP, the plan sponsor, or the ESOP fiduciary, ERISA provides for access to the federal courts. The ERISA statutes also recognize the relative imbalance in power between the plan sponsor and the ESOP fiduciary on one side and the plan participant on the other. To help level the field, ERISA statutes provide for the granting of reasonable legal fees to a plaintiff.

Federal courts do have a general history of granting reasonable attorney's fees to plaintiffs in ESOP disputes when the issues have merit. The plaintiffs in most ESOP court cases are plan participants who often have few, if any, financial resources. The ESOP's claim procedures normally must be in compliance before litigation may be commenced.

Diversification Requirements

Plan participants that have met certain qualifications are given the right to have their account balances diversified, per IRC Section 401(a)(28)(B). Although the ESOP is intended to be primarily invested in the stock of the plan sponsor, diversification requirements exist as select participants approach retirement age.

The major requirements for diversification are not listed here, but the point is emphasized that such requirements will impose a liquidity obligation on the company. The applicable account balances will have to be diversified with cash.

Generally, ESOP participants at least 55 years of age and with at least 10 years of plan participation may request their account balance be diversified within the limits of applicable statutes. During the first 5 years of the eligibility period, participants may request to have 25 percent of their account balance in employer securities diversified. During the sixth and final year of the eligibility, period participants may request to have 50 percent of their account balance in employer securities diversified.

This diversification obligation requires some form of repurchase liability analysis to address key issues on a timely basis.

Stock Repurchase Obligation

The ESOP sponsor must make a market for the stock as employees who are participants in the plan become eligible for distributions or diversification requirements. Generally, the company has the obligation to redeem the shares, and in some cases, the ESOP may have the option to purchase the stock of plan participants exercising their put rights. This requirement to make a market for the stock is commonly referred to as the repurchase obligation or repurchase liability.

- The repurchase obligation requires the employer to provide a market for the stock allocated to the plan participants' accounts. Correspondingly, liquidity is provided to the plan participants for what may otherwise be a typically illiquid investment.
- Federal statutes provide plan participants with the option of either accepting cash for their ESOP stock, or they may request the actual stock, per IRC Section 409(h)(1) and subject to the following exception:
  - As a practical matter, most closely held companies amend their articles of incorporation or bylaws to place a mandatory call on the stock of a departing plan participant. This is done to prevent the possibility of having actual inadvertent shareholders owning stock who are no longer active with the employer. Such shareholders, if permitted to exist, have significantly different rights as shareholders than as members of a tax-qualified plan whose stock is owned by a trust.

ESOP companies must continually be aware of the repurchase obligation because the total value of the employer's stock in the plan represents a financial commitment in the future that will have to be eventually funded.

Practical Insights

When the percentage of stock in the ESOP is a nominal amount, the repurchase obligation is not typically a significant financial issue for the company. In this instance, the repurchase obligation is easily met by ongoing operations. Many ESOPs are installed to take advantage of the IRC Section 1042 rollover, and there is often a minimum of 30 percent of the outstanding stock in the plan. This percentage is often a significant amount, expressed as a dollar value. The repurchase obligation may not be as easily met from ongoing operations without some advanced planning.

As the percentage of stock in the ESOP increases, the repurchase obligation takes on a heightened priority. With recent tax law changes permitting S corporations to have ESOPs, there are significant incentives for a company to be at or near 100 percent employee owned. As the percentage of stock in the ESOP increases to a significant percentage (for discussion purposes, the *significant percentage* is defined as being in excess of 50 percent, typically a control position), the need for a more thorough analysis of the repurchase obligation becomes necessary.

In this instance, the failure to adequately anticipate the stock repurchase obligation requirements could have a negative impact on the company. Without planning, a number of things could be adversely affected, including the working capital of the company, the ability to provide funds for growth opportunities, the net worth of the company, and other relevant areas.

Repurchase Studies

Because the repurchase obligation for most ESOP companies is a significant financial commitment, management typically will consider initiating some form of repurchase study. The study may be either internally generated or externally generated from a professional service provider:

- *Internally generated repurchase obligation study.* As the name implies, the company undertakes the analysis of the commitment. The analysis may range from preparing a spreadsheet to purchasing special repurchase obligation software from outside service providers.

   Companies with relatively few employees may be well-served with a spreadsheet analysis. It is recommended, at a minimum, that the study be discussed with knowledgeable professionals who can comment on the quality of the analysis. The administration firm is often a good source for comments.

   As the analysis becomes more complex, companies have the option of purchasing specialized software that makes repurchase computations under varying assumptions. A number of costs are associated with such software, including the initial acquisition price and also the time required to master the program and load the relevant data. Once the learning curve is mastered, and the data are entered, the company is typically able to model a range of scenarios (sensitivity analysis). The software providers are typically wonderful resources on interpreting the data and working through the assumptions.

- *Externally generated repurchase obligation study.* An outside professional service provider may complete the repurchase obligation study. This option is more common when the number of employees in the company is significant (often hundreds), or some special circumstances merit a more exacting analysis. A major stock transaction may be a good reason for the study. This option is typically more expensive than purchasing the software, and there is often no opportunity for sensitivity analysis over a wide range of scenarios. The study should be prepared by professionals who understand the refinements and subtleties of such an analysis.

- *Independent (outside) trustees may formally request a periodic repurchase study.* The request typically depends on the size of the ESOP repurchase obligation and the complexity of the issues in the specific case.
- *Common factors to consider.* The repurchase study should be long term in its horizon. Other common variables include employee turnover, the average age of employees (as an indication of future retirements), changes in workforce size, employee terminations, redemption provisions in the plan documents, vesting schedules, release of unallocated shares as debt is repaid, redeeming stock to the ESOP or company, future valuation growth rates (or declines), and other appropriate factors.

Regardless of the source for the repurchase study, ESOP companies are encouraged to give some formalized consideration to the future commitment.

Funding the Repurchase Obligation

Acknowledging the future commitment and attempting to quantify the financial obligation is half the issue; having a plan to fund the obligation is the other half of the equation. Financial resources will have to be provided eventually. The common sources are listed subsequently:

- *Provide funding entirely from current operations.* This pay-as-you-go approach is not typically recommended because companies often miss the financial impact of economic downturns and recessions. This approach could have disastrous effects if the company experiences a sharp decline in cash flow at the time when employees are being terminated and demanding plan payouts. If the ESOP obligation is modest, this strategy is reasonable because the percentage of stock in the ESOP is small.
- *Prefund the obligation.* The prefunding may be accomplished by either making contributions directly to the plan or setting resources aside within the company.

   Contributions directly to the ESOP are tax deductible within allowable payroll limits. Contributions may also be made under appropriate circumstances by using dividends (C corporations) or distributions (S corporations). This strategy builds liquidity within the ESOP and helps perpetuate the plan as stock is redeemed. Unfortunately, cash contributed to the ESOP is no longer available for general company requirements.

   The company could set aside resources and not contribute the funds to the ESOP (sinking fund), so that liquidity is available to redeem stock. The stock could be redeemed into the company treasury, thereby reducing the number of outstanding shares. This will have the effect of reducing the percentage of stock owned by the ESOP (unless the ESOP is already the 100 percent shareholder). Correspondingly, the company could make a contribution to the ESOP in an amount sufficient to redeem the stock. This strategy allows the company to use the resources until they are required for stock redemptions.

- *Provide insurance.* Typically, insurance is a strategy in which a number of larger individual account balances are building. This option is less common, and the company should consult with an insurance authority to analyze the insurance risk.
- *Releverage the ESOP.* The ESOP can be directed to borrow money from a financial institution to redeem stock, like many initial transactions. Working closely with a bank is advisable to ensure it is comfortable lending money for stock-related obligations. The bank may not always be willing to fund this type of transaction, particularly if the company is financially struggling.
- *Sell the company.* This option is not common. Selling the business to meet repurchase obligations is often an indication that the ESOP valuation may be flawed. The valuation is to consider the ability of the company to meet all its financial obligations, including repurchase commitments. Aside from financial considerations, selling the business may be an option when there is no longer a succession management team.
- *Initial Public Offering (IPO).* This is also not a very common situation because there are not many IPO candidates with ESOPs. Prior to the technology sector implosion, many IPO candidates had equity programs for their associates. Such equity programs were more often stock options as opposed to ESOPs.

Election: Redeeming the ESOP Stock Back to the ESOP

The company has the option of directing the trustee to repurchase the eligible stock of participants who have received distributions back into the ESOP. This election has the practical effect of leaving the shares in the ESOP to be allocated to the other plan participants.

- *Cycling ESOP stock.* If the amount of stock in the ESOP is a set number of shares, the issue of cycling the stock through the plan so newer employees may participate occurs. Typically, when an ESOP is installed, a fixed number of shares of stock are sold to the ESOP. The shares of stock are typically released to the plan participants' accounts over time as contributions to the ESOP are completed (for example, in leveraged ESOPs, the repayment of debt releases stock from collateral). Once all the purchased stock is released, there is typically no additional available stock until distributions are made, or stock is forfeited.

  Newer employees who join the company many years after the ESOP transaction have limited opportunities to participate in the ESOP. Often, their only opportunity to have stock allocated to their account is only by a stock redemption into the plan or forfeitures.

  ESOP companies often adopt a plan to purchase eligible stock back to the plan with current cash contributions, so everyone participates. Because the availability of eligible stock is uncertain from year to year, it is possible for the company to adopt a program to cycle a pool of available shares so that stock becomes available each year.

This strategy ensures that a constant flow of shares is coming into the plan while the total number of shares is held somewhat constant.

- *Tax-deductible redemption*. If the stock is purchased by the ESOP, the company will make a cash contribution to the plan to purchase the stock. The cash contribution will be tax deductible within payroll limits.

Election: Redeeming the ESOP Stock to the Company Treasury

The company may also make the election to redeem eligible stock of participants who have received distributions. This action has the practical effect of removing the stock from the ESOP and also removing the stock from the status of outstanding shares. The shares of stock redeemed are not counted as outstanding shares. Such shares are sometimes referred to as treasury stock. Correspondingly, the percentage of stock owned by the ESOP will decrease, and the percentage of stock owned by other shareholders will increase.

- *Three-year rule*. If the selling shareholder(s) elected to receive an IRC Section 1042 rollover (only for a C corporation), the ESOP must hold the stock for at least three years following the transaction date. Stock distribution to participants is an exception. Failure of the ESOP to hold the stock for that period of time will subject the company to significant financial penalties.
- *Stock redeemed with after-tax dollars*. If the stock is redeemed by the company, the purchase will occur with after-tax dollars.

ESOP Termination

An ESOP may be terminated for a number of reasons, but the most common reason is that the employer has been acquired, and the new owner does not want to continue the ESOP. Other common reasons include converting the ESOP into another qualified plan, the company becomes bankrupt, or the company suffers financial reverses.

Typically, when an ESOP is terminated, procedures to be followed are often found in the plan documents. The ESOP may be terminated at any time by the board of directors. There are many protections for plan participants in the event of a termination. For example, when an ESOP is completely terminated, all employee accounts are immediately fully vested.

In most cases, the procedures for terminating the ESOP are found within the plan document. Certain timing complications may arise if the company has been sold, and the provisions of the sale contain a number of contingency clauses. Such matters must be satisfactorily resolved before the final distributions to the plan participants will be complete. Most ESOP terminations are clearly defined situations in which the stock in the company will be redeemed for cash, and the participants will have a number of options regarding where the account balances will be reinvested.

Plan Termination With Outstanding ESOP Debt

The issue of termination may become complex if the ESOP is still leveraged at the time of termination. One common issue is the ESOP-related debt and who is obligated to repay the debt. Determining the order of liquidation may have a significant impact on the proceeds ultimately received by plan participants. In most cases, the ESOP-related debt is the obligation of the ESOP, not the company.

- When the company is sold, and the ESOP is terminated because the buyer does not wish to continue the plan, it is common for the proceeds allocated to the ESOP to first repay ESOP-related debt. Once the debt is repaid, the remaining funds are typically distributed to the participants.
- If the ESOP is being terminated without the company being sold, and there is still ESOP-related debt, the transaction typically merits a close review. It is often appropriate to ask why the ESOP is being terminated before the debt is repaid. Ostensibly, the initial ESOP transaction was consummated with the intention of having the ESOP own the stock free of the debt. The motivation for the ESOP termination may come under question if the termination value of the stock is depressed primarily by the same unpaid debt that was used in the original purchase.

If an ESOP is being terminated, it is always advisable to retain experienced legal counsel, as well as an independent fiduciary, to make sure all applicable regulations are in full compliance.

- Assuming the ESOP is leveraged at the time of termination, one common issue is determining who is obligated to repay the ESOP-related debt. Sometimes, it is not clear if the ESOP-related debt is a general obligation of the employer or a specific obligation of the ESOP. The following example indicates the importance of this distinction. The example is also simplified for ease of presentation:

Example 8-1   Termination of an ESOP

- ABC Company has a fair market value of $5 million before debt.
- ESOP-related debt is $1 million.
- Total shares outstanding: 100,000.
- ESOP shares outstanding: 40,000 (40% of total).
- Investors' shares outstanding: 60,000 (60% of total).

ABC Company is sold for the fair market value of $5 million, and the ESOP debt will be subtracted from the sale proceeds. The balance of the proceeds ($4 million) will be distributed to the shareholders based on the stock owned. There are two scenarios of payout: the ESOP debt is considered as a general corporate obligation, and the ESOP-related debt is considered an ESOP obligation.

(continued)

	Scenario 1 Debt to Company	Scenario 2 Debt to ESOP
Sale proceeds	$5,000,000	$5,000,000
Less: ESOP-related debt	1,000,000	
Net proceeds to shareholders	$4,000,000	
Allocation of proceeds:		
Proceeds to investors (60%)	$2,400,000	
Proceeds to ESOP (40%)	1,600,000	
Total distribution	$4,000,000	
Allocation of proceeds:		
Proceeds to investors (60%)		$3,000,000
Proceeds to ESOP (40%)		2,000,000
Less: ESOP-related debt		(1,000,000)
Net proceeds to ESOP		1,000,000
Total distribution		$4,000,000
Distribution to ESOP	$1,600,000	$1,000,000
Price per share to ESOP	$ 40.00	$ 25.00

This example clearly establishes the importance of determining who is obligated to repay the ESOP-related debt. If the debt is an obligation of the employer, then the other investors participate in the repayment of the debt prior to any shareholder distributions.

Generally, the ESOP documents should discuss the issue of who is obligated to repay ESOP-related debt in the case of the plan being terminated while the ESOP is leveraged. If this issue is not addressed, the plan documents should be amended to make this point clear. Often, the loan structure may determine this point.

Disadvantages of ESOPs

Although there are many positive aspects to ESOPs, they are not universally understood. Often, the negative aspects relating to ESOPs are traced to poorly understood or miscommunicated issues. An ESOP may not be the best succession alternative for any number of reasons. The more frequent objections to ESOPs follow, with a limited analysis of the issues.

Complex Regulatory Environment

Many business owners object to the high degree of rules and regulations surrounding a proposed ESOP transaction. Owners of closely held companies are often entrepreneurial and have succeeded by determination and persistence in the face of a myriad of rules and regulations that, to them, have often held them back. After a career of avoiding entangling rules and constraints whenever possible, the ESOP is an option that comes with many perceived restrictive rules:

- *Flexibility and tax incentives.* ESOPs are extraordinarily flexible in their ability to meet the goals of selling shareholders, but such flexibility comes with a cost. Tax rules, ERISA rules, reporting rules, and countless other rules encumber the freedom that many business owners covet. Those rules are often in place to protect the interests of the ESOP participants.
- The negative impression of the rules must be balanced with the strong attributes of tax incentives to encourage ESOPs. Typically, a balanced education process for the business owner will place the regulatory environment in perspective. Overall, the benefits of the ESOP generally outweigh the negative stigma of regulations.

Fiduciary Responsibilities

This is truly a fair concern for business owners. Typically, prior to the introduction of the ESOP, business owners have limited constraints on how the business is managed. If the degree of control by the business owner within the organization is near absolute (with 100 percent ownership of the stock as an example), the reality of the fiduciary responsibilities is often a significant issue. Fiduciary responsibilities are imposed by the federal government with oversight agencies (the IRS and the Department of Labor) that have far-reaching compliance powers:

- *Reducing fiduciary exposure.* The fiduciary responsibilities may be substantially reduced by using an outside trustee. On larger installations, the outside trustee will substantially limit potential liability. This option may be too expensive for many smaller companies.
- *Engage experienced ESOP advisers as plan consultants.* Such advisers will be a good resource of insights on fiduciary responsibilities. It is emphasized, however, that whoever is the trustee, that trustee may not eliminate the fiduciary responsibilities.
- *Limiting fiduciary financial exposure.* Fiduciary insurance and an indemnification agreement from the company are examples of items that may be employed to provide a degree of peace of mind to the ESOP fiduciary.

A fiduciary may initiate a number of actions to limit liability, but ultimately, fiduciary obligations are the responsibility of the individual. The individual considering assuming ESOP fiduciary obligations should be knowledgeable about the potential liability.

Initial Cost and Ongoing Expenses

Business owners may object to the fees required to install an ESOP. The one-time legal fee for the plan documents, the first-year valuation expense, and other consulting costs may seem to be very high to the business owner. Once installed, the ESOP will have a number of ongoing expenses, such as the annual stock valuation and the cost of the plan administration. These costs may be a significant consideration for smaller companies.

- *Managing the costs.* The ESOP-related costs will not be eliminated, but they may be managed. Experienced ESOP service professionals will provide either an estimate or a range of fees prior to commencing work. Ask for proposals from such service providers.

- *Negotiate with experienced professionals.* They have the best idea of the costs of providing the requested service. Failure to provide an estimate of cost may be an indication that the client is about to pay for a professional learning curve.
- *Transaction fees are part of the ESOP installation.* Professionals have the duty to educate clients on the nature of the work to be provided and the range of fees to be invoiced.

Business owners objecting to the fees are often naive about the costs associated with other transition options. The fees commonly affiliated with other options, such as selling the business through a broker, may be a multiple of the ESOP charge.

Repurchase Obligation

The plan sponsor (company) will continually be making a market for the stock. The stock may be purchased many times over during a longer period of time as employees leave the business, and the stock is purchased back into the plan.

Some business owners only want the ESOP to purchase their stock, forgetting that employees (represented by the ESOP) will want to have their equity stake in the plan redeemed at some time in the future. Business owners who fail to understand this point require an education on transaction mechanics:

- *Understanding the stock valuation.* The long-term repurchase obligation is a direct function of the stock value. The value of the stock must take into consideration the long-term ability of the company to meet its repurchase obligations. This must be communicated to the selling shareholder(s). If the owner is still concerned about the ability of the company to service the repurchase obligation, then the underlying assumptions of the valuation may need to be re-examined.
- *Complete a stock repurchase obligation study.* The study typically illustrates the ability of the company to meet all its ESOP-related obligations under a range of operating conditions.

There are a host of opportunities to address this concern. One of the best strategies is to communicate the issue of the repurchase obligation to the employees. Remind the employees that the company must remain profitable if ESOP account balances are to be converted into cash one day in the future for everyone.

Employees Fail to Understand and Appreciate the ESOP

Shareholders have typically learned about the essence of ownership over time as the company evolved through the rites of growth and success. Shareholders who have been active with the business know first-hand about long hours, personally guaranteeing company debt, meeting payrolls, and countless other obligations associated with managing the business. Often, many associates of the company are unfamiliar with the technical aspects of owning a business because they are only employees. Ownership attributes and best practices may be learned by most people. The challenge is to persist in the educational process.

Some employees are simply short-term oriented and will never understand or appreciate the opportunity to have a stake in the business. By applicable statutes, these employees participate in any qualified benefit plan, but they typically will not be employed long enough to build any significant account balance.

- *Employee communications.* Employees often need to learn about the obligations and reward of ownership. Many have been loyal employees but have not experienced the special obligations of being an owner. It is important to have an ongoing program of communications for the employees regarding the ESOP.
- *Employee acceptance or buy-in.* The power of employee ownership does not depend on 100 percent of the employees embracing the ESOP. Only a sufficient number of employees have to buy in to the program to make a difference, and that number is often much smaller than shareholders imagine. A limited number of dedicated and focused employees who understand the ESOP is often all that is required to have a significant impact on the financial performance of the company.

Successful ESOP companies have ongoing educational and communication programs to continually remind the employees of the benefits and obligations of owning a piece of the company.

Summary

Most of the objections to ESOPs are not founded on fact. If the business owner is serious about providing a plan of succession for the company, the ESOP is an attractive option that merits serious consideration.

There are many successful ESOP installations throughout the nation in every conceivable industry. Interested business owners should contact one of the major ESOP associations and request a list of existing ESOP companies that would be willing to serve as a referral. Another excellent source of information is ESOP referrals from professional service providers. Existing ESOP companies will typically gladly share their insights regarding employee ownership and the ESOP. Just ask.

Chapter 9

Financial Considerations

This chapter examines the many facets of financial matters as they relate to the installation of an employee stock ownership plan (ESOP). We assume that an ESOP feasibility study has been completed or is in process (either informal or formal), and questions regarding how the transaction will be financed are being raised.

We will examine the many sources of financing an ESOP transaction. Depending on the facts and circumstances, business owners may enjoy a wide range of options, including self-funding strategies and the use of outside financial institutions. The array of options is very broad.

Financing Overview for ESOPs

There are many sources of funding for an ESOP. For the purposes of this book, we have conveniently classified the sources as either internal or external. Internal sources are understood to include the employer. External sources include a range of possibilities, including financial institutions or, perhaps, shareholders of the employer (seller financing). It is common for the ESOP to borrow money from either an internal or external source to purchase employer securities.

ESOP Loan Exemption

Typically, qualified employee benefit plans are prohibited from borrowing money from a party in interest or to have a loan guaranteed by a party in interest to purchase the stock of the employer. This is a prohibited transaction. This prohibition would make it virtually impossible for an ESOP to acquire employer securities. A special exemption for ESOPs exists that enables them to borrow funding to acquire employer stock, per Employee Retirement Income Security Act of 1974 (ERISA) Section 408(b)(3) and Internal Revenue Code (IRC) Section 4975(d)(3).

ERISA Conditions for the ESOP Loan Exemption

- The loan exemption requires the ESOP to satisfy the statutory ESOP definition of ERISA Section 407(d)(6) and IRC Sections 409 and 4975(e)(7).
- The interest rate must be reasonable.
- The loan must be for the primary benefit of ESOP participants.
- The only loan collateral permitted is employer securities purchased with the loan proceeds, contributions to pay the loan, and income on such property.

Over time, the understanding of the ESOP loan exemption has been expanded to include a number of other operating aspects. The major provisions are summarized subsequently:

- The loan must be used for purposes of acquiring employer securities under equitable and prudent financing terms. The terms of the loan must be as favorable as those that would be determined by arm's-length negotiations between independent parties.
- The ESOP is only permitted to pledge as collateral the stock that was purchased with the loan proceeds, contributions to pay the loan, and income on such property. Additionally, as the loan is repaid, the shares pledged by the ESOP must be released on a pro rata basis. The release of shares from the pledge may be based on either principal only or principal and interest payments. The lender must not have any recourse against any ESOP assets, other than the stock of the employer in the plan that has not been released and other pledged assets. Liquid investments that happen to be in the ESOP, other than income on pledged assets and contributions to repay the loan, cannot be pledged for the loan.
- The ESOP loan must be for a fixed period and must satisfy certain requirements in the case of a default. Generally, the lender, who is a party in interest, is prevented from accelerating the loan repayment schedule in the case of default.

The regulations are clear in the requirement that the terms of an ESOP note be at least as competitive as the terms that would be arrived at by arm's-length negotiations. We will soon see that shareholder or seller financing is often employed with leveraged ESOP transactions. These regulations provide a strong background of elements that need to be considered when structuring ESOP transactions.

Financing an ESOP—Internal Sources

With an ESOP transaction, the plan sponsor (employer) is going to ultimately provide the cash flow to make the event succeed. We will consider a number of financial sources, the first one being an internal source. *Internal source* is generally understood, for our purposes, to mean the employer or shareholders.

The employer is typically a candidate for ESOP financing when a number of circumstances exist either together or in part. The following nonexclusive reasons are common elements when internal sources are used exclusively for the ESOP transaction.

Financially Successful Employer (Plan Sponsor)

Generally, the financially successful closely held company is a strong candidate for an ESOP because financing options are optimized. The controlling shareholder(s) wants to avoid any use of outside debt, when practicable. Some owners are very averse to having virtually any debt in the company. If the company is sufficiently profitable in relation to the proposed ESOP transaction, it may be possible to fund the ESOP without additional outside debt.

Prefunding the ESOP

One popular strategy is for the plan sponsor to make contributions to the ESOP for a period of time, thereby building a significant cash balance in the ESOP, so the transaction can occur without the use of third-party financing. Recent increases in the contribution limits to qualified plans under the Economic Growth and Tax Relief Reconciliation Act of 2001 (EGTRRA) make the prefunding option more attractive. In most instances, the ESOP contribution limit is 25 percent of qualifying payroll, a significant increase over the pre-EGTRRA limit generally set at 15 percent of qualifying payroll.

There are some practical limits on the length of time a plan sponsor may make contributions to the ESOP before stock is sold to the plan. The ESOP is intended to be primarily invested in the stock of the plan sponsor, and only having cash is counter to the spirit of the ESOP. There is some question regarding how long the company may prefund an ESOP before stock is sold to the plan. It is best to ask a knowledgeable professional about the amount of time prefunding may last.

The company receives a full tax deduction for the cash it contributes to the ESOP in the year the contribution is made within contribution limits.

Example 9-1   Contribution Timing

Timing may be an important consideration when the company is enjoying a profitable year. Prior to the end of a profitable fiscal year, the company may sign the appropriate legal papers and create the ESOP. If the ESOP is legally created by the last day of the fiscal year, the company may make an actual contribution or accrue the ESOP contribution. If the company has a fiscal year-end of December 31, the ESOP could be legally created prior to the last day of the fiscal year.

Stock Contributions to the ESOP

A plan sponsor may create an ESOP and fund the plan with stock issued from its balance of authorized but as yet unissued shares. The employer could also contribute stock held in its treasury to the ESOP.

The advantage of this strategy is that the company gains a tax deduction for the fair market value of the stock contributed to the ESOP. The company receives a tax deduction for a noncash transaction. The basic effect is that cash is conserved, and the contribution becomes a form of capital formation. The following example illustrates the journal entries for this capital formation strategy:

Example 9-2   Stock Contribution to an ESOP

The fair market value of a share of stock for ESOP purposes is $100 per share. There are 100,000 shares authorized but only 20,000 shares issued to a sole shareholder (80,000 shares are unissued). The company contributes 2,000 shares to the ESOP for a deductible contribution of $200,000 (2,000 x $100 = $200,000). The journal entry will be recorded as follows:

Debit	ESOP contribution expense	$200,000
Credit	Capital stock	$200,000

Note: For the current year, the debit to ESOP contribution expense will reduce profitability for the year, with a corresponding reduction in retained earnings. The real gain in the equity of the company is the tax savings by making the contribution to the ESOP without a corresponding cash expense.

Considering this transaction, the stock account of the corporation will look like the summary in the following schedule:

	Before Contribution		After Contribution	
Shareholder	20,000	(100%)	20,000	(91%)
ESOP	0	(0%)	2,000	(9%)
Total shares	20,000	(100%)	22,000	(100%)

The primary disadvantage of this strategy is that there is dilution to the existing shareholders as new stock is issued to the ESOP. Under the appropriate circumstances, this is a viable strategy that primarily benefits the company and ESOP participants.

The existing shareholders may agree to the dilution because they want to encourage employee ownership in fact, and providing stock to the ESOP accomplishes the goal. Giving the employees a direct stake in the company in this manner may provide an incentive for the employees to work at making the company more financially successful. In the longer outlook, the shareholder may have a much more valuable company by sharing some equity today with the employees. This may be a prelude to directly selling stock to the ESOP in the future when the company is more valuable.

Inside Loan From the Company to the ESOP

The company typically has significant internal liquidity already, and it will use the liquidity to fund the ESOP. The money already in the company will be either contributed or loaned to the ESOP for the purpose of purchasing employer stock.

If internal funds are used for the ESOP transaction, the reporting falls within Statement of Position 93-6, *Employers' Accounting for Employee Stock Ownership Plans*. This is typically referred to as an employer loan. Typically, the entry will indicate the reduction in on-hand cash (because the cash is being paid to the selling shareholder) and the recognition of a reduction in equity. The following example illustrates this point:

Example 9-3   Inside Company Loans to the ESOP

Assume the company is providing $1 million cash to fund the initial ESOP transaction. The ESOP will take four years to repay the cash advance to the ESOP. The recording of the initial transaction will typically be as follows:

Credit	Cash	$1,000,000
Debit	Unallocated ESOP stock	$1,000,000

This entry will record a reduction in company equity because the debit to unallocated ESOP stock is a contra-equity account reported on the company's balance sheet. Each year, 25 percent of the unallocated stock amount will be released from the collateral account as the company contributes the appropriate amount to the ESOP.

Debit	ESOP expense	$250,000
Credit	Unallocated ESOP Stock	$250,000

In some cases, a C corporation may have a substantial retained earnings balance and significant on-hand cash. The ESOP, in combination with an IRC Section 1042 rollover, is an attractive option for shareholders to remove cash from the company without the double taxation that declaring a dividend would create.

Financing an ESOP—Seller Financing

Somewhat related to internal financing, the selling shareholder(s) want to avoid third-party debt and still wishes to finance the ESOP. We will consider this external financing for discussion purposes. In other instances, the company may not be able to borrow sufficient funds to complete an ESOP transaction (typically, the situation is a C corporation wishing to complete a 30 percent stock transaction to qualify for an IRC Section 1042 rollover). The selling shareholder may decide to provide the financing directly by making the loan to the ESOP.

S Corporation Application

If the ESOP is being installed in an S corporation, the sale of the stock is relatively straightforward from a tax planning standpoint. The selling shareholder will be subject to possible capital gain taxes on the sale of his or her S corporation stock to the ESOP. Unlike a

C corporation, the S corporation–selling shareholder will not be able to elect the IRC Section 1042 tax deferral. Correspondingly, there will not be any restrictions on the selling S corporation shareholder, either.

The selling S corporation shareholder may wish to provide some or all selling financing for the transaction. If this is the case, the shareholder sells stock to the ESOP and may simply take a note back from the ESOP. The transaction has many opportunities for tax planning, including possible installment sale treatment on the sale.

C Corporation Application

This analysis is related to the C corporation and structuring an IRC Section 1042 rollover:

- *Qualify for IRC Section 1042 rollover.* The selling C corporation shareholder wants to qualify for the IRC Section 1042 rollover. The shareholder can extend credit to the ESOP to purchase the 30 percent block of stock in this typical case, and the proceeds will come back to the shareholder over time, subject to debt repayment. The debt repayment is typically determined by contributions limited by qualifying payroll. It often takes several years to repay the ESOP debt.
- *Reinvestment time for qualified replacement property (QRP) is a problem.* The problem for the selling shareholder is the time permitted to invest the proceeds in QRP. The full proceeds must be reinvested within 12 months following the date of the transaction. If the debt is repaid during a period that exceeds the 12-month period of time, and other funds are not available to purchase QRP, those proceeds will be subject to taxes.
- *Installment sale often impractical.* An installment sale may be considered, but the disadvantage of an installment sale is that taxes will only be deferred until the installment proceeds are collected. There is no long-term deferral of the gain such that the IRC Section 1042 election would provide because the ESOP installment note will be amortized in a reasonably short time, typically from four to seven years.

Leveraged QRP Solution

An option for the shareholder to consider is the use of leveraged QRP. The shareholder can purchase high-quality securities for the QRP, as previously discussed. These securities may be leveraged, and those proceeds may be loaned to the ESOP to buy the shareholder's stock.

- Major financial institutions can offer programs enabling the shareholder to borrow a very high percentage of funds against the value of the QRP. In practical terms, the financial institution is providing a margin account to the shareholder. In some cases, the percentage of funds that may be borrowed against the QRP may be as high as 90 percent.
- Traditional brokerage firms may have more severe restrictions expressed as a percentage of funds that can be advanced against the QRP. Stocks that are QRP are typically a lower percentage advance rate than the advance rate for high-quality

bonds. Banks are not necessarily bound by the same percentages as brokerage firms and may agree to advance a higher percentage. The bank may be able to structure the note with additional collateral provided by the shareholder. In this case, the shareholder may provide the financing for the ESOP by providing only a small amount of cash.

Floating Rate Note

One popular vehicle for accomplishing this type of transaction is a floating rate note (FRN). This is similar in concept to the ESOP note described earlier in this book. In this case, the FRN is used to provide financing for the ESOP, whereas the ESOP note permits great flexibility in the QRP investment portfolio.

The FRN should be the highest quality financial instrument, typically AAA rated. The intent is to hold this note as QRP for a longer period of time. Common terms for such FRNs are 30–60 years. Because the FRNs are high quality, the investor may often obtain a cash advance of as much as 90 percent of the face value. The FRN may be purchased with a modest payment.

The seller finance option is obviously not for all proposed transactions, but there are a number of applications and circumstances when seller financing may be a logical option:

- The company cannot obtain the loan from a bank. It may be an appropriate option when the company cannot obtain a sufficiently large loan to allow the ESOP to purchase enough stock for the intended shareholder goals.
- Often, a successful service company with a small asset collateral base is such an example. The selling shareholder may have to personally guarantee all or most of the note anyway.
- The seller may agree to finance the ESOP because the company is subject to balance sheet credit tests. The seller may agree to subordinate the note to the interests of a primary creditor. The common application is a construction company subject to bonding requirements.
- Seller financing may also be used if the company requires flexible financing due to a high degree of seasonal sales. Traditional financial sources may not offer the flexibility required for such seasonal businesses.
- In addition to the personal guarantee, a financial institution may require that the selling shareholder pledge a certain amount of QRP as collateral on the ESOP note. When such demanding conditions are placed on traditional financing, the shareholder may conclude that providing the financing and earning the interest is a viable option.
- A potential financial benefit of seller financing is interest income. The shareholder providing the financing may charge the ESOP a reasonable rate of interest. If the shareholder can negotiate a more favorable rate with the lender, then the shareholder may actually earn the spread between the interest rate typically charged by the financial institution and the interest rate charged to the ESOP. In such cases, it is best to employ experienced financial advisers to structure the transaction so it is fair to the ESOP from a financial perspective.

Financing an ESOP—Third-Party Financing (Bank Debt)

The intent of this section is to illustrate a number of considerations that are common to ESOP loans from a financial institution. This is not intended to be a comprehensive section on securing bank debt for a company because that is beyond the scope of this book.

Historical Note—Repeal of ESOP Loan Interest Exclusion

Banks used to enjoy a financial incentive to make ESOP loans under certain circumstances. If the ESOP loan circumstances were met, 50 percent of the interest received could be excluded from the gross income of the lender.

The Small Business Job Protection Act of 1996 repealed this incentive under IRC Section 133.

Overview of General Banking Concerns

Senior lenders, typically commercial banks, are an economically attractive source of funds. The reason for the financial attraction is that senior lenders only advance funds when perceived risks to the loan are minimized. The following attributes are essential ingredients to attaining senior-level debt:

- *Stability and predictability of cash flow.* Attractive loan customers have a proven history of financial performance. The core business is typically well-established, and the cash flow required to service the debt has a high degree of predictability.
- *Strength of management.* The bank is interested in seeing a team with a record of financial success managing the company. The bank also looks for continuity in the management team. If the senior management of the company has been together for a period of time, the likelihood of the company meeting its obligations is greatly enhanced.
- *Security of principal.* Most banks begin by assessing the underlying base of assets that will collateralize the loan. Obviously, a strong asset base with a significant debt capacity will enhance the likelihood of a favorable loan decision. This is common with successful, stable, and well-established manufacturing companies.

  When the underlying asset base does not exist, as in many successful service companies, the bank will have to consider other types of loan protection, such as personal guarantees and, perhaps, the pledge of additional collateral on the loan.

Banks with ESOP lending experience insist on any extension of credit being a sound business decision. There are some attractive aspects to an ESOP loan that may favorably tip a credit decision in favor of an ESOP candidate:

- *Properly structured ESOP loans rarely default.* Most business owners do not want to over-leverage the company they have worked so hard to make successful.
- *Business owners often sell stock to the ESOP in stages over a number of years.* This places sharply reduced financial strain on the business in meeting its obligations.

- *The ESOP company enjoys a number of favorable considerations.* The debt principal is deductible for income tax purposes. (All corporate debt principal is repaid with after-tax dollars.) This deductibility of the debt principal enhances cash flow.
- *Employee communication is a critical success factor.* When the ESOP is properly communicated to the employees, those companies typically perform better financially. This is a soft or intangible consideration that is difficult for a bank to weigh in the decision process. The fact still remains that these companies are often strong credit candidates.

Generally, financially challenged, closely held companies are not strong candidates for leveraged ESOPs. Typically, such firms have weak balance sheets and erratic profitability. A senior lender will not typically assess this candidate as a good ESOP prospect. Making employees take wage concessions in order to purchase a financially distressed company is often a prescription for a challenging ESOP with a high probability of an unsuccessful long-term installation.

Common Loan Mechanics

"Mirror" Loan

The bank will often loan the funds to the company directly. Greater loan security is attained by having the company pledge the full assets of the firm as loan collateral. The company will then loan the money to the ESOP. This internal loan, or "mirror" loan, often has identical terms as the loan from the bank on such matters as amortization period and interest. Although having identical terms is common, it is possible to have a different loan amortization schedule for the "mirror" loan. The "mirror" loan is sometimes also referred to as a back-to-back loan.

The application of having a different amortization schedule is to enable the company to retire the bank note in advance of the internal note (the "mirror" loan). If the company enjoys greater success and has the cash to repay the bank note, it may decide to repay the bank note early and reduce the risk to the financial institution. The "mirror" loan will typically be left in place and amortized over its original period.

The "mirror" loan is the vehicle that releases shares of stock from collateral, and there is often merit in releasing those shares over a longer period of time. The application, in this case, is to have the shares of stock released to the ESOP over a prolonged period of time to provide a benefit that rewards commitment to the employer. New employees will be able to participate in the ESOP in this manner.

Gradual Sale of Stock

Due to practical lending limits, ESOPs using outside debt are often structured so that the ESOP acquires stock over time.

- If the shareholder is interested in selling all the stock to the ESOP (say 100 percent), the goal will only be achieved by selling the stock in stages the company can afford. Often, the stock will be sold in multiple transactions.
- As a result of this practical limitation, time is an ally of a potential ESOP installation. The company is literally buying itself. The more time for planning and repaying

acquisition–related obligations, the more flexibility there is to install a program that meets the ability of the company to finance the transactions and the shareholder being paid for the stock.

Loan Collateral

The bank is always interested in having a secure loan. The terms the bank requires will vary based on the circumstances of each proposal. The bank is first interested in having the loan collateralized by the full resources of the company:

- *Personal guarantee.* The bank may ask for additional collateral by having the shareholder personally guarantee the ESOP note. This guarantee is in addition to the collateral base provided by the company and the company guarantee.
- *Pledge of QRP as loan collateral.* The bank may also ask the shareholder to pledge QRP as collateral either in part or total. If QRP is pledged, there is often a mechanism to release QRP from the pledge as the ESOP note principal is repaid.

C Corporation ESOPs

This is a common application for bank debt and ESOPs. The selling shareholder typically wants enough financing for a minimum 30 percent transaction (to qualify for the IRC Section 1042 rollover). Bank-imposed limits on the creditworthiness of the company often dictate how much stock can be sold at one time.

An ESOP-based loan often has the disadvantage of being viewed by a financial institution as nonproductive debt. The debt is being used to purchase the stock of a shareholder, but the funds are not being employed to enhance the competitiveness of the company through such traditional activities as purchasing new equipment; expanding resources, such as inventory and accounts receivable; and so on.

Cash flow considerations are typically paramount to an ESOP loan. The bank wants to make sure that both its loan is secure, and the note will be repaid in a timely manner.

S Corporation ESOPs

Many of the mechanics of the previous section on C corporation ESOPs apply in full here. The one distinguishing feature of C corporation transactions is meeting the IRC Section 1042 rollover requirements. The S corporation ESOP has no such requirements, and the loan will often be structured in a manner to meet the goals of the shareholder(s).

If the overall percentage of stock owned by the ESOP is very high, there are some benefits to the S corporation tax environment.

Example 9-4   One Hundred Percent ESOP

The ESOP owns a commanding percentage of stock in the company, say 100 percent. The bank makes a traditional loan to the company, and the company makes a "mirror" loan to the ESOP. As a 100 percent ESOP company, the company has no federal income tax liability. If the company has strong profitability, the excess cash it can generate may be applied in full (pre-tax dollars) toward reducing the loan from the bank to the company. The "mirror" loan will typically be left in place because this loan repayment is subject to more stringent payroll contribution limits than is the case for some corporations.

Example 9-5   Smaller Percentage ESOP

The ESOP does not own the commanding percentage of stock. In this case, the other share-holders will typically require a distribution from the company to pay income taxes related to their prorated share of income reported on Form K-1. The payment of the distribution must be made in the same percentage to all shareholders, including the ESOP. The distribu-tion to the ESOP will follow the stock ownership, not the payroll of the plan participants. The cash contributed to the ESOP will be allocated to the shares of stock. Unallocated stock will receive a distribution, and that distribution may be used to reduce debt. Allocated stock will receive the same distribution, but that cash will remain in the account balance of the participant.

Summary

Structuring the funding for an ESOP may assume any number of profiles. The range of options includes funding by the employer, seller financing, and third-party financing. From a practical standpoint, ESOP transactions may become complex due to the many factors that enter into structuring a transaction. There are now a significant number of financial institu-tions with ESOP loan experience. These institutions understand the tax incentives of ESOPs and the positive impact such incentives have on the mechanics of repaying the debt. It is often worthwhile for business owners to look for experienced ESOP lenders.

Chapter 10

Litigation and Significant Cases

This chapter provides an overview of how litigation and federal court cases have had a material impact on the development of the regulatory environment for employee stock ownership plans (ESOPs). When ESOPs were first authorized, there was, at best, a vague understanding of the practical applications of the plans. With time, the administration of ESOPs has come into much sharper focus, as well as a refined understanding of fiduciary obligations.

The Employee Retirement Income Security Act of 1974 and ESOPs

The Employee Retirement Income Security Act of 1974 (ERISA) was landmark legislation signed into law with the intent of achieving a number of important national goals. One of the most important of those goals was to provide a foundation for a comprehensive system of retirement plans that were intended to compliment Social Security. The ERISA legislation addressed a number of retirement programs, including pension plans, profit sharing plans, 401(k) savings plans, and ESOPs.

ESOPs were created by the legislation both to provide a long-term retirement benefit and to encourage employee ownership. This special dual role of ESOPs marks them as unique among qualified retirement plans. In the case of ESOPs in closely held companies in which the securities are not actively traded, the stock of the plan sponsor must be valued by an independent professional. This valuation mandate is ongoing as long as the plan sponsor (the company) continues to have an ESOP that owns stock in the plan sponsor.

The Importance of Court Cases

By design, the ERISA legislation is very general in its wording in many instances. In 1974, having a national program in place to encourage retirement saving was deemed to be important. Congress knew that legislation as sweeping as ERISA would eventually have to be interpreted by the courts and appropriate administrative agencies regarding a broad range of implementation issues. The interpretation of the statutes over time becomes essential to an understanding of the application of the ERISA legislation.

As a qualified retirement plan, ESOPs enjoy a host of tax benefits like all other qualified plans, including the compounding of asset values free of all taxes until the assets are withdrawn. To encourage employee ownership as another worthwhile social goal, ESOPs were also granted special tax-oriented incentives.

The strongest tax incentive in 1974 was the ability to repay ESOP-related debt, including principal, with tax-deductible dollars. Since that time, other powerful tax incentives have been legislated to encourage employee ownership.

Due to the special dual nature of ESOPs, they come under the direct administration of both the IRS and the Department of Labor (DOL).

The IRS

The IRS has a direct interest due to the fact that contributions to an ESOP are tax deductible within certain prescribed limits:

- Those contributions serve a wide range of purposes, such as providing cash for plan liquidity, providing cash to repay ESOP-related debt, and contributing stock to increase the capital base of the plan sponsor.
- Determining the fair market value of stock in closely held companies as a basis for ESOP-related transactions has a direct impact on the revenue of the Department of the Treasury. Valuation issues are often the focus of IRS challenges in ESOP litigation. Most commonly, the IRS seeks to determine if the ESOP paid more than the fair market value of the stock of the closely held company.
- If the IRS successfully challenges an ESOP transaction by having it classified as a prohibited transaction, the offending parties are subject to a range of equitable solutions to the ESOP. The courts may impose an equitable solution to restore the ESOP economically. In more serious cases, the courts may impose excise taxes on prohibited transactions:
  - *Initial tax.* An initial excise tax may be imposed on the prohibited transaction in an amount of 5 percent of the disputed amount for each year in the taxable period or part thereof by ERISA Section 4975(a):

- ◦ In general, the taxable period for prohibited transactions begins with the date of the transaction and ends on the mailing date of the notice of deficiency, the date on which the correction of the prohibited transaction is completed, or the date on which the tax imposed by ERISA Section 4975(a) is imposed.
  - ◦ The practical impact of the penalty is that the initial tax of 5 percent per year (or partial year) may be imposed on a taxable period spanning several years.
  - – *Additional tax*. In certain instances, when the initial tax is imposed on a prohibited transaction, and the prohibited transaction is not corrected within the taxable period, an additional excise tax of 100 percent of the amount involved may be imposed by ERISA Section 4975(a).
- Clearly, the potential exposure of both the initial excise tax and the additional excise tax are intended to serve as an onerous deterrent.

The DOL

The DOL has a direct interest because it is the agency established by the ERISA legislation to enforce the provisions of the law and protect the retirement system of the country. One important area of concern for the DOL is the conduct of plan fiduciaries and the discharge of their responsibilities:

- The power of the DOL is substantial, and the agency has a mandate to ensure that the retirement system of the country is being safeguarded.
- When ERISA was enacted, the legislation contained a comprehensive ability to provide its own remedies. It was recognized by Congress that any dispute between plan participants and a plan is typically very one-sided, particularly when the plan is backed by the full resources of the plan sponsor (the company). Congress enhanced the ability of plaintiffs in such disputes.
- To the prevailing party, ERISA provides the right to recover attorneys' fees and other costs incurred in the litigation. This recovery of litigation costs is in addition to any other recovery of resources attained by the prevailing party. In effect, the legislation provides that the full resources of the plan may be committed to pay the legal costs of the attorney suing the plan.
- Pronouncements and legal actions brought by the DOL with regard to ESOPs are closely watched by professionals and other interested parties because of the DOL's authority and the extensive potential penalties.

Significant Court Cases

The following court cases represent a number of important decisions and areas of interest to the ESOP community. The list is not comprehensive, but cases with important rulings are listed. It takes many years for the cases to be fully resolved by the legal system, including appeals. We have attempted to include only those cases in which settlements are known. The court cases discussed generally include the following information:

- Sufficient background information to understand the issues of each case
- The court's decision
- Summary of the important issues decided in each case

Court Case: *Donovan v. Cunningham*

Donovan v. Cunningham, 541 F. Supp. 276 (S.D. Texas 1982), affirmed in part, vacated in part, reversed in part, 716 F.2d 1455 (5th Cir. 1983), is the first to address fiduciary responsibilities regarding an ESOP-based valuation. Valuation professionals understand the concept of fair market value, but an ESOP fiduciary must also be knowledgeable about *adequate consideration*, as defined in ERISA Section 3(18).

In this instance, Secretary of Labor Raymond Donovan brought an action against the ESOP administration committee of Metropolitan Contract Services, Inc. (MCS) for its failure to comply with fiduciary responsibilities in determining the fair market value of the stock and the adequate consideration regarding the ESOP transaction.

Background Information

MCS formed an ESOP and purchased 2 blocks of stock from the sole shareholder, Kenneth Cunningham. The first ESOP transaction was in August 1976 for 14 percent of the outstanding stock of MCS, and the second transaction was in February 1977 for an additional 20 percent block of stock. Mr. Cunningham served as the chairman of the board of directors and the CEO. The board of directors also served as the ESOP administration committee. The ESOP administration committee relied on an independent valuation report dated June 1975 that determined a 100 percent interest in MCS. This valuation report, dated well before the actual ESOP transactions, was used to determine the price per share the ESOP paid for MCS stock.

The secretary of labor commenced an action against Mr. Cunningham and the other members of the ESOP administration committee. The action charged that the members of the ESOP administration committee breached their fiduciary responsibilities in a number of areas. The fiduciaries relied on a single valuation report prepared in June 1975 for 2 ESOP transactions that occurred in August 1976 and February 1977. At the time of the transactions, the valuation report was beyond 1 full year, and in the case of the second transaction, the report was approaching 2 years. During that time, many of management's projections used in the valuation report no longer remained valid. Further, the valuation report established a 100 percent interest in the company (a control position), but the ESOP purchased minority blocks of stock. The ESOP was not intended to gain a controlling interest in the company; however, no adjustment was made for the minority position of the ESOP. Finally, the valuation report was not commenced for the purposes of an ESOP.

Court Decision

The court decided that the members of the ESOP administration committee breached their fiduciary responsibilities. They failed in their duties in a number of areas:

- The valuation report they relied upon was out of date by the time of the actual stock transactions.

- The financial projections used in the valuation report were no longer valid.
- The report was not originally undertaken for the purposes of an ESOP.
- The ESOP purchased a minority position in the company, not a controlling interest.

The court said it is appropriate for ESOP fiduciaries to rely, in part, on the reports of other professionals when discharging their responsibilities, but there is an obligation to understand the content of those reports. In this case, there is an obligation to understand issues such as the underlying financial assumptions in the valuation report, the difference between a minority position and a controlling position, and having the valuation report completed in a timely manner for the purposes of an ESOP.

Summary

The timing is important because ESOPs had only been in existence for a brief period when the case was commenced. ERISA legislation was newly enacted, and many of the administrative aspects of the law were being refined, both in practice and in the courts. This case indicates what can happen when general standards of fiduciary conduct are applied to a specific situation. The valuation professional must be careful and diligent in the role of financial adviser to an ESOP fiduciary. It is not enough to just understand the determination of fair market value; the valuation professional must also know the requirements of a valuation undertaken for the purposes of an ESOP.

Court Case: *Hines v. Schlimgen*

Martin Hines et al. v. Frederick P. Schlimgen, Mark C. Rowley and Rowley & Schlimgen, Inc., U. S. District Court, Western District Court of Wisconsin, Civil Case 85-C-1037-S, October 10, 1986, is a case in which the court determined that the purchase of stock in Rowley & Schlimgen, Inc. (Schlimgen) by the ESOP trustees was flawed in several respects. The result is that the ESOP trustees and company were held liable for the overvaluation of the stock.

A beneficiary of the Schlimgen ESOP brought an action against both the company and the company's ESOP trustees for breaching their fiduciary duties by directing the ESOP to purchase stock for more than its fair market value.

Background Information

In August 1980, Schlimgen purchased 740 newly issued shares of stock, a minority interest, for $125 per share. The price per share was determined on the basis of a valuation report prepared by an individual who subsequently became the controller of the company. The price per share was for a controlling interest.

The central issue in the case is whether the ESOP trustees breached their fiduciary duties by directing the ESOP to pay a price for the stock in excess of fair market value. The value of the stock was determined by an individual who subsequently became the controller of the company. The ESOP trustees did not question the value placed on the company shares by the board of directors.

Court Decision

The court decided that the ESOP trustees breached their fiduciary duties by not acting in the best interests of plan participants. They failed in their duties in several areas.

The ESOP trustees failed to have their own qualified independent appraisal.

The valuation report was flawed in many respects by reference to Revenue Ruling 59-60. The court noted flaws in the report in a number of areas, including

- ignoring a loss year without explaining the impact of the computation in the earnings base.
- not considering employee bonuses as ordinary expenses.
- failure to consider specific company risk factors, such as thin management, diversification requirements, undercapitalization, and lack of computer equipment.
- using an inappropriate earnings multiplier.
- failure to recognize that the ESOP shares were a minority position. The court allowed a minority position discount of 20 percent and noted that the discount could be much higher.

The court determined the fair market value of the stock to be $56 per share. The ESOP trustees and company were liable for the difference in the stock price, the court costs, and attorney's fees. Note that under ERISA, the plaintiffs may recover attorney's fees.

Summary

This case is significant in a number of critical aspects. The valuation report used by the ESOP trustees was inadequate for two primary reasons. First, the report was not prepared by a qualified independent appraiser. Second, the valuation report contained numerous flaws when the requirements of Revenue Ruling 59-60 were examined. The court noted that the ESOP was in a minority position, and a minority position discount should have been applied. Finally, under ERISA statutes, the court has the authority to assess the ESOP trustees and the company with attorney's fees.

Court Case: *Las Vegas Dodge, Inc. v. U.S.*

Las Vegas Dodge, Inc. v. U.S., 85-2 U.S. Tax Case, Paragraph 9546 (D. Nev. 1985), is an early case in which an emphasis on earnings capacity was determined to be a proper methodology in arriving at fair market value for the purposes of an ESOP. The IRS asserted that the price of stock in Las Vegas Dodge, Inc. (Las Vegas Dodge) was overvalued; therefore, the company's tax deduction was overstated.

Background Information

Las Vegas Dodge engaged a qualified independent appraiser to determine the fair market value of the company's stock for the purposes of an ESOP. The appraiser determined that the value of the stock was $61.35 per share. In arriving at the opinion of value, the appraiser emphasized the earnings and dividend capacity of the company. Additionally, the appraiser cited items such as the capable management of the company, the excellent business location, and the past financial success of the company. The ESOP purchased the stock at the preceding price from the 2 controlling shareholders of the company, who were also the managing officers. The IRS claimed the value of the stock to be in the range of only $5.36 to $8.00 per share. This range was substantially based on the book value of the company.

Court Decision

The court found persuasive the valuation approaches used by the independent appraiser for the company that emphasized earnings and dividend capacity. These approaches are preferred when valuing the interests in an operating company in which growth is assumed.

The company exercised good faith in arriving at a determination of fair market value for its stock, and the valuation approaches were reasonable.

Summary

This is an earlier case in which the IRS contended that the fair market value of the company is its book value. The book value is often very low in relation to the earnings potential of the business. In this instance, the book value had little relationship to the value of the company regarding its earnings potential and future economic benefits. Note that in this case, when tax deductions are involved (related to the contributions to the ESOP), the IRS followed a methodology that minimized the tax savings by emphasizing book value, an unrealistically low number. It is likely that under a different valuation purpose, such as gift or estate taxes, the IRS approach may have been to emphasize valuation methodologies producing a much higher figure. Following the guidelines of Revenue Ruling 59-60 and documenting results are essential elements in defending your work against challenge.

Court Case: *Gary L. Eyler v. Commissioner*

Gary L. Eyler v. Commissioner, 69 TCM 1995-123, CCH Decision 50,538M, is a case in which entering into a prohibited transaction for the purposes of an ESOP proved to be a devastating lesson for Gary Eyler. Fiduciary compliance with adequate consideration guidelines requires that the value of the stock for the purposes of an ESOP has a two-part test. First, the price cannot exceed fair market value, and second, fair market value must be determined in good faith. These guidelines were not followed in this case.

Background Information

Mr. Eyler was the majority shareholder, chairman, and CEO of Continental Training Services, Inc. (CTS). CTS operated a series of vocational schools to train truck drivers and operators of industrial equipment. The company enjoyed significant growth, and in 1986, Mr. Eyler decided to pursue an initial public offering (IPO) for the firm. In preparation for the IPO, the company retained both Prudential-Bache Securities (Prudential) and Raffensperger, Hughes & Co. (Raffensperger) as underwriters. The underwriters conducted a due diligence investigation of CTS and determined that an estimated price for the IPO would be between $13 and $16 per share. Once the offering price range had been established by the underwriters, they attempted to determine the level of investor interest by marketing the stock at that price range. The underwriters concluded that the level of interest was minimal at that time and did not encourage the IPO at this point. The decision was made to wait for more preferential market conditions.

Rather than consider lowering the price range for the IPO, Mr. Eyler decided to sell a portion of his stock to an ESOP in 1986. In December 1986, CTS's board of directors adopted the ESOP. The directors named CTS's vice president of human resources as the ESOP trustee and appointed several insiders, including Mr. Eyler, as the ESOP plan committee. Neither the ESOP trustee nor the ESOP plan committee was involved in the decision to sell CTS stock to the ESOP. The board of directors decided to have the ESOP purchase stock from Mr. Eyler. They authorized the ESOP to borrow approximately $10 million for the transaction that was guaranteed by both CTS and Mr. Eyler. Mr. Eyler did not participate in the board's discussion and decision to have the ESOP purchase his stock, although he did serve as the board's chairman and was the controlling shareholder in the company.

The ESOP fiduciaries did not engage an independent appraiser to advise them on the value of the stock for the ESOP transaction. Supporting the ESOP transaction price of $14.50 per share, CTS's board of directors relied on a statement by the company's CFO, who decided the price was fair. The company's CFO was previously employed in a major brokerage firm. The price determined by the board of directors was within the IPO range, but the figure actually used was not determined by an independent appraiser for the purposes of an ESOP.

In 1987, after the purchase of the stock by the ESOP, CTS acquired a public trucking company. CTS experienced financial difficulties following the acquisition and filed for bankruptcy in 1989.

The IRS determined that Mr. Eyler engaged in a prohibited transaction when he sold his stock to the ESOP for more than fair market value. Mr. Eyler responded that the transaction was not prohibited because the ESOP purchased the stock for adequate consideration (fair market value determined in good faith), and the board of directors acted in good faith in determining the share price.

Court Decision

The court decided that Mr. Eyler did engage in a prohibited transaction because the ESOP paid more than adequate consideration for his stock. The ESOP failed to obtain the services of an independent appraiser to determine the specific fair market value of the stock at the date of the stock transaction. Mr. Eyler and CTS relied on a range of prices determined for a proposed IPO several months prior to the ESOP transaction. The range of prices was not established for the purposes of an ESOP.

- The ESOP fiduciaries did not question the transaction price and substantially failed to conduct any additional due diligence to determine if the price was appropriate in light of known facts. The ESOP fiduciaries should have questioned the price when the IPO was unsuccessful.
- The court rejected Mr. Eyler's argument that the standards of establishing fair market value were met by the ESOP fiduciaries. The price range cited by Mr. Eyler as support for the actual ESOP transaction price of $14.50 was originally developed for an IPO. The court noted that the price range for the IPO assumed the company was going public, and a market for the stock was going to be established. A marketability

discount should have been applied to the range of IPO prices. Under the company ownership structure with an ESOP, the company remains closely held, with no established public market for the stock. The court noted a market-making mandate for the company according to ESOP regulations, but it still noted that a lack of marketability discount is appropriate.

- Additionally, the court determined the range of value developed for the IPO was inappropriate because the financial strength of the company was not considered, including the impact of ESOP-related debt. Under the assumed IPO, the company was to receive additional capital without incurring any debt, and the range of prices reflected this financial position. When the ESOP was installed, the company increased its debt significantly. By accepting the debt, the company was now under the restrictions of the bank loan covenants that place a number of constraints on corporate actions. These loan covenant restrictions were not considered in the IPO range of value.

- The court determined that Mr. Eyler failed in his responsibilities when selling his stock to the ESOP. The ESOP paid more than adequate consideration for his stock, thereby creating a prohibited transaction. More significantly, the court upheld the position of the IRS that a good faith attempt was not made to determine the fair market value of the stock.

- The IRS imposed first tier excise taxes (5 percent annually on the amount of the prohibited transaction) and second tier excise taxes (100 percent of the amount of the prohibited transaction). In total, the excise taxes imposed on Mr. Eyler amounted to $12.5 million, in addition to the $10 million ESOP transaction being voided. The sentence is harsh, but the intent of the legislation is to send a clear message that the fiduciary responsibilities must be taken seriously.

- The court ruled that the ESOP paid more than adequate consideration for the stock. The court noted the many errors that were made when the transaction price was determined. Significantly, the court did not say what the ESOP transaction price should have been. No attempt was made by the court to provide a preferred transaction price; it concluded only that the price used was improper.

Summary

This case is a Tax Court memorandum case that often does not have the same legal impact as a decision from a federal or an appellate court. The decision is still significant for a number of reasons. Mr. Eyler failed to determine fair market value in good faith for the stock he sold to the ESOP. The assessment of stock value was critically flawed on several accounts. The assessment of value was originally developed for an IPO, not an ESOP. The value should have been questioned when the IPO was not successful. The eventual transaction price was developed by an individual who was not a qualified independent adviser to the ESOP. The assessment of value did not consider a lack of marketability discount. Finally, the excise tax penalties imposed by the IRS in this case serve as a clear signal that fiduciary responsibilities in ESOP transactions are to be taken seriously.

Court Case: *William R. Davis v. Torvick, Inc.*

William R. Davis, et al. v. Torvick, Inc. et al., No. C–93–1343 CW, 1966 WL 266127, (N.D. Cal.), U.S. District Court, contains a number of issues of interest to appraisers doing ESOP valuations. First, the accounting firm for Torvick, Inc. (Tovick) completed the valuation that relied on faulty financial projections. Another key issue is the behavior of the trustee of the Torvick profit sharing plan that converted the plan to an ESOP.

Background Information

Torvick was a Mercedes-Benz dealership with a profit sharing and trust plan (profit sharing plan) to which employees made contributions, and the company provided a matching amount, depending on financial conditions. The trustees of the profit sharing plan included Mr. Robert Torvick, Mr. Roy Bracket, and Mr. Blain Torvick. An ESOP was created after the profit sharing plan, and Mr. Robert Torvick was instrumental in convincing employees of the company to authorize the transfer of their profit sharing plan balances into the ESOP. Periodic participant statements were issued by the profit sharing plan indicating the account balances that were to be invested for the benefit of the employees.

The profit sharing plan was represented by the trustees as having significant assets. In fact, most of the assets of the profit sharing plan had been loaned to one of the fiduciaries (Mr. Robert Torvick) and entities controlled by him. The loans were improperly made between the profit sharing plan and a party in interest. The profit sharing plan was substantially unfunded, even though employees made contributions through payroll deductions. The plaintiffs argued that the transfer of assets from the profit sharing plan to the ESOP effectively hid the mismanagement of the profit sharing assets. The ESOP was given inflated stock in the company.

The company's accounting firm, Pisenti & Brinker (CPAs), also prepared the ESOP valuation. The CPAs significantly based the value of the company on an inflated projection of earnings. Further, the valuation report did not mention the loans from the profit sharing plan to either Mr. Robert Torvick or entities controlled by him. The valuation report was used, in part, by Mr. Robert Torvick to convince employees to transfer profit sharing plan assets into the new ESOP. The overall value in the ESOP valuation prepared by the CPAs was approximately $1 million.

The company experienced significant financial problems and declared bankruptcy. The company stock in the ESOP was worthless. The total amount of assets that were supposed to be in the profit sharing plan was approximately $870,000. The actual assets in the profit sharing plan were only approximately $40,000. The difference, over $800,000, was loaned to either Mr. Robert Torvick or entities he controlled or was simply missing.

Court Decision and Out-of-Court Settlement

The CPAs clearly placed themselves in a difficult position by providing professional services to Torvick and completing the ESOP valuation. The independence of the CPAs was clearly compromised with regard to the ESOP valuation. Further, the CPAs based their valuation of the company on faulty financial projections. Prior to the court trial, the CPAs settled with the plaintiffs for an undisclosed amount. Rather than going to trial, the CPAs understood the weakness of their position and settled.

The court found that Mr. Robert Torvick violated ERISA and damaged the ESOP on a number of counts. Loans that Mr. Robert Torvick directed the profit sharing plan to make to both him and entities controlled by him are loans between the plan and a party in interest. The loans are a violation of ERISA. Mr. Robert Torvick misrepresented the true financial picture of the profit sharing plan to company employees when he encouraged them to switch their account balances to the ESOP. In this case, he breached his fiduciary duties by failing to act in the best interests of the ESOP participants. Mr. Robert Torvick was also in violation of ERISA by having the ESOP rely on the CPA's valuation report that contained flawed financial projections.

As a result of breaching the fiduciary duties imposed by ERISA, the court concluded that Mr. Robert Torvick was personally liable for the losses to the ESOP that resulted from those breaches and for other such equitable relief deemed appropriate by the court.

Summary

The case highlights the importance of fiduciary responsibilities. Mr. Robert Torvick was found in violation of ERISA fiduciary duties, and he was personally liable for all plan losses and other equitable relief decided by the court. The settlement of the CPAs is also noteworthy. Clearly, the CPAs were not independent in this case. The CPAs certainly understood this fact and elected to settle with the plaintiffs rather than risk a court-imposed settlement.

Court Case: *Delta Star v. Patton*

Delta Star, Inc., et al. v. Andrew W. Patton, et al., United States District Court for the Western District of Pennsylvania, Civil Action No. 96-2183, is a case is based on valuation and management compensation issues as they relate to the common stock in a closely held company for the purposes of an ESOP. Due to excess compensation paid to the president of Delta Star, Inc. (Delta), the stock value for ESOP purposes was depressed. This is the first case of its kind to focus on the duties of an individual who is serving in multiple capacities for an ESOP company. In this case, an individual who determined his own compensation served in the following capacities: the president of the company, an ESOP trustee, and a member of the board of directors.

Background Information

Delta was created as a corporate spin-off from H. K. Porter Company (Porter) in 1989. Under the provisions of the transaction, the ESOP acquired 98.63 percent of the stock in Delta, and management, consisting of 9 key employees, owned the remaining balance of just 1.37 percent. Mr. Andrew W. Patton, president, was one of the management shareholders with a small equity stake in the company. It is significant, in this instance, that the ESOP had the overwhelming percentage of stock. For all practical purposes, Delta is an entirely employee-owned company.

When Delta was formed, 3 individuals served as the ESOP board of trustees: Mr. Patton and 2 other company officers. The ESOP board of trustees voted the stock in the ESOP, and they elected themselves as the board of directors of Delta. The board of directors then elected the company officers, and Mr. Patton was appointed chairman and president. Mr. Patton was advised to have at least 1 outside board member, but that advice was rejected. In this instance, the ESOP board of trustees effectively controlled 98.63 percent of the company stock for ongoing operational considerations. This ESOP board of trustees had control of the company, and their fiduciary responsibilities in such circumstances are substantial.

At the time of the spin-off, Porter established the base salary of Mr. Patton at approximately $201,000. During the next 5 years (1990–94), Mr. Patton unilaterally increased his base salary to just over $301,000 in annual increments not exceeding $50,000. During this same period, Mr. Patton also declared annual bonuses to himself that ranged from zero to $1,040,000 and averaged approximately $450,000. The bonuses typically represented a multiple of Mr. Patton's base salary and far exceeded industry norms. Other compensation determined by Mr. Patton for himself included multiple country club memberships, several luxury cars, and lawn care for his home. Mr. Patton unilaterally declared the salary increases, perks, and bonuses without consulting either of the other two company directors or the ESOP's board of trustees. Mr. Patton made active attempts to conceal his compensation from other board members. Further, he decided his compensation without any reference to commonly accepted sources, such as industry standards, written compensation plans, compensation consultants, or consideration of the company's financial performance.

The company's board of directors approved the Delta Star Benefit Restoration Plan in 1990 to reward company executives for reductions in ESOP benefits as a result of compensation limits imposed by the code. This Benefit Restoration Plan primarily benefited Mr. Patton. Additionally, the board of directors authorized the Delta Star Supplemental Executive Retirement Plan in 1991 to reward the same group of executives with additional retirement benefits. The two benefit plans were adopted and subsequently modified for the primary benefit of Mr. Patton, who was to receive unusually high proceeds from the benefit plans, largely due to the excess compensation he approved for himself. Indeed, compensation bonuses approved by Mr. Patton for his own account had the impact of significantly increasing the payments in the benefit plans to his advantage. The company did not consult an outside compensation authority prior to adopting the benefit plans.

During the period from 1989–94, the sales of the company fluctuated, rising from approximately $41.6 million in 1989 (the first year as an independent company) to a high of approximately $59.8 million in 1991 and falling to approximately $28 million in 1994. When sales increased from 1989–91, income remained stable, averaging approximately $2.7 million for the 3-year period. When sales declined in 1993 and 1994, the financial performance of the company suffered, and an operating loss was reported in 1994. The depressed financial performance was largely attributed to the excess compensation paid to Mr. Patton. The substandard financial performance of the company directly and negatively impacted the value of its stock for ESOP purposes. Delta stock was the only asset of the ESOP.

Court Decision

The court examined ERISA statutes regarding fiduciary behavior and determined that they applied in this case. Mr. Patton was an ESOP fiduciary due to the fact that he served on the ESOP board of trustees. He breached his fiduciary duties to the ESOP in several respects:

- First, he was prevented from acting with total loyalty to the ESOP participants by his actions as a company officer and director.
- Second, Mr. Patton failed to realize the inherent conflict of interest he had with his fiduciary duties by engaging in unsupervised, self-serving activities that maximized his salary, bonuses, and fringe benefits. The matter of his total compensation package should have been the appropriate responsibility of the other members of the board of directors and the ESOP board of trustees.
- Third, Mr. Patton violated ERISA statutes prohibiting self-dealing. He voted as a member of the ESOP board of trustees to retain himself on the board of directors. As a director, Mr. Patton unjustly continued to enrich himself at the expense of the company and the ESOP. By unilaterally approving his own compensation and benefits package, Mr. Patton was not independent and did not act with complete fairness to the ESOP.

The court ruled that Mr. Patton breached his fiduciary duties by paying himself an unreasonable base salary and unreasonable bonuses and by authorizing unreasonable fringe benefits. Mr. Patton was ordered to repay over $3.3 million to the company. This amount represents payments to Mr. Patton in excess of his base salary at the time of the spin-off from Porter. A portion of the proceeds were allocated to the ESOP account balances of plan participants who left the company when the value of the stock was depressed due to the actions of Mr. Patton.

Summary

This case is significant in a number of critical aspects, even if the facts and actions of the defendant are clearly egregious. It is common practice with many ESOPs in closely held companies to have the same individual(s) serving as both company officer(s) and ESOP fiduciary(ies). The circumstances of this case are excessive, but it is clear that senior managers in an ESOP company should avoid being left in a position to unilaterally approve their own compensation without some form of outside review or support. From a practical standpoint, it is often helpful to have individuals from outside the company on the board of directors. Outside directors may assist in such areas as approving compensation packages for senior management and resolving matters when conflicts of interest arise. Outside compensation consultants may also be an excellent source for data on compensation programs for executives in ESOP companies. If company officers agree to serve as ESOP fiduciaries, they are advised to be mindful of the obligations imposed on them by ERISA.

Chapter 11

Practical Considerations and Employee Stock Ownership Plan Resources

Professionals who are interested in working with clients on possible employee stock ownership plan (ESOP) installations or who wish to learn about this field will gain an understanding from a number of time-honored best practices. ESOPs are not always a logical or even desirable option for certain closely held companies. It is most efficient to quickly qualify the likelihood of a potentially successful ESOP installation. By recognizing a manageable set of variables, ESOP candidates may be quickly screened for suitability. Absent these best practices, the candidate may still be a suitable prospect, but the professional adviser is on notice that the installation will likely be a challenging assignment.

Finally, a number of ESOP-related resources are identified later in this chapter. Only resources that are likely to be readily available are listed. Older ESOP resources may be hopelessly outdated because there have been significant and sweeping changes in ESOP legislation in the past few years.

Qualifying ESOP Candidates

ESOPs are generally a far more viable alternative for the business owner to consider, but there is often a significant amount of misunderstanding about the mechanics of an ESOP.

Misunderstandings about the technical aspects of an ESOP installation are the most common reason for business owners to reject the concept, in our experience. The following observations are offered to assist professionals and owners to quickly determine if a company is a strong candidate for an ESOP.

Qualities of Successful ESOP Candidates

This is a very general heading, and it is emphasized that a successful ESOP installation is a culmination of many complex factors coming together:

- *The candidate is typically a successful and profitable company.* If the candidate is not already profitable, it becomes a serious challenge to determine how the ESOP will be able to purchase any stock.
- *The candidate is well-established and, often, a market leader.* Well-established companies exhibit the predictable cash flow that is essential for an ESOP carrying acquisition debt.
- *The candidate communicates with its employees.* Communication is typically achieved through a number of vehicles, such as quality programs, strategic planning, open door policy, newsletter, bulletin board, and so on. Communications is an integral part of building a company culture of ownership that is the heart of successful ESOP installations.
- *The candidate has qualified management.* The candidate may be in virtually any industry; the difference between successful ESOP installations and unsuccessful attempts is often in the depth of management.
- *ESOPs often succeed when there is a reasonably high incidence of employee education.* Additionally, ESOP success is enhanced when the employees have a significant amount of direct contact with customers or clients.
- *The candidate has an established company culture.* In many cases, well-established companies in smaller communities excel as ESOPs due to a close bond that already exists among associates. Of course, the same holds true for any company with an established culture, regardless of location.
- *Relative size is not a limiting factor.* Companies that employ only 15–20 associates may be excellent ESOP candidates. Very small companies with fewer than 10 employees may not have enough inherent value to warrant the expense of an ESOP. Very small companies that are S corporations may also be subject to ESOP anti-abuse statutes.
- *Time is an ally of an ESOP.* It takes years for the ESOP to pay for the employer stock. The sooner the selling shareholders begin the process of transition planning, the more options they have and the greater the likelihood they will receive an enhanced value for their stock.

Characteristics of Less Successful ESOP Candidates

Generally, we focus on the many reasons why ESOPs succeed, but a number of items commonly define an ESOP in a failed installation, an installation where objectives have been clearly missed, or simply an unsuitable match:

- *The business owner is focused only on the tax benefits of the ESOP.* Such an owner is typically oriented to tax benefits, with no interest or commitment to communicating the

ESOP to employees. Although the tax benefits are often the first serious attention an ESOP receives, a broader commitment to the long-term interests of the company is important.

- *Senior management is autocratic, with little likelihood of changing.* Such an outlook is antithetical to building a company culture of ownership. If the ESOP is to have a reasonable chance of success, it is often the vehicle to provide autocratic senior management (typically the selling shareholder) with a complete exit.

- *Business owner delays transition planning until a crisis arises.* The crisis often is failing health. As mentioned, time is an ally of an ESOP. If there is little time for a smooth transition, it is often impractical for the ESOP to be the exit vehicle. The amount of ESOP-related debt to purchase the entire equity stake of an owner (often a sole shareholder) in a single transaction is not manageable for the company.

- *Type of industry may not be a good candidate.* There are a few industries where an ESOP may not work due to the high value of the company stock in relation to the qualifying payroll. An example of such an industry is natural resources, where the value of the resources is very high in relation to the company payroll. It may not be practical to sell stock to the ESOP because the amortization period could be prolonged beyond reasonable limits.

- *Size of company.* An ESOP may not be practical in very small companies with limited employment. The ESOP anti-abuse legislation is aimed specifically at small S corporations. Candidates with fewer than 10 employees may not be very suitable.

- *Financially challenged company.* Companies that are marginally profitable or losing money are, at best, questionable ESOP candidates. The long-term orientation of the ESOP makes such an investment a questionable endeavor. The facts change somewhat when the ESOP is proposed as one acceptable way to preserve jobs.
  - Saving jobs is a harsh reality that likely means employees will be making compensation concessions to provide the resources the company requires to service acquisition-related debt. Under such circumstances, the company stock must be valued for the purposes of an ESOP, but a significant amount of caution should accompany the valuation analysis. If the company fails for any reason, the price paid for the stock will be questioned, and those questioning the value of the stock will have the benefit of perfect hindsight.

- *Highly cyclical or volatile companies.* Companies in highly cyclical industries should be analyzed over at least one full business cycle, if practical, to assess the relative risk environment. Operating results should be considered over a longer term. If the ESOP is installed, there is the high likelihood that the company will go through additional business cycles in the future. The company must be able to meet ESOP-related obligations over a range of financial results. It is questionable to view the company from a financial perspective based on a few carefully selected years chosen by management.

- *Companies in a start-up mode.* Such companies may wish to share ownership with employees. Although this is a commendable goal, the financial reality is that the business owner may surrender a significant percentage of ownership and receive very little in return financially. Such companies typically have little operating history and, often, modest stock value.

- When the uncertainties of achieving the future prospects are unknown or speculative, caution should be exercised when assessing the value of the stock. Generally, if the company is successful, it is often practical to allow the value of the stock to increase as the company demonstrates financial success.

Practical Insights Summary

ESOPs are a wonderful option for many closely held businesses to consider. The S corporation election expands the range of ESOP applications significantly. However, ESOPs may not be an appropriate match for many candidates for the reasons just listed. Carefully qualifying ESOP candidates will ultimately result in successful installations.

Overview of ESOP-Related Resources

A wide range of resources regarding ESOPs are available to professional advisers. The listing that follows is intended to highlight a number of the currently available and easily located sources.

It is emphasized that two of the best sources of information are the ESOP Association (EA) and the National Center for Employee Ownership (NCEO). For that reason, each is listed separately with an indication of most major publications and resources offered.

The focus of this listing is to identify resources that are helpful in understanding ESOPs. Many articles published in professional journals are not considered because they are often very difficult to locate. If you have a specific request for technical information, you are directed to the EA or the NCEO. Both organizations are virtual wellsprings of information and resources. Their staffs are helpful and friendly; they genuinely want to help you understand ESOPs.

The following resources are not listed in any specific order. The resource headings have been organized to assist in the search for relevant data.

The EA Publications

The ESOP Association
1726 M Street, NW, Suite 501
Washington, D.C. 20036
(201) 293-2971 or toll free (866) 366-3832
www.esopassociation.org

Helpful publications include the following (not an inclusive list; contact the EA):

- *An Introduction to ESOP Valuations*
- Annual Conference CD and Annual Conference Book (conference books have been discontinued in 2011) (a collection of presentations made at the Annual Conference in May)
- *How the ESOP Really Works*

- *Journey to an Ownership Culture: Insights from the ESOP Community*
- *Legislative, Regulatory and Case Law Developments: A Year in Review* (annual update on technical and legal developments)
- *Structuring Leveraged ESOP Transactions*
- *The Definitive Guide to ESOPs* (two-volume set from the Employee Ownership Foundation)
- *The ESOP Association Administration Handbook*
- *The ESOP Report* (monthly publication)
- The EA Membership Directory
- Two-day ESOP conference proceedings book (a collection of presentations made at the traditional two-day conference in Las Vegas each year)
- *Valuing ESOP Shares*, Revised 2005

NCEO Publications

National Center for Employee Ownership
1736 Franklin Street, 8th Floor
Oakland, CA 94612-3445
(510) 208-1300
www.nceo.org

Helpful publications include the following (not an inclusive list; contact the NCEO):

- *ESOPs and Corporate Governance*
- *Employee Ownership Report* (periodical of the NCEO)
- *Leveraged ESOPs and Employee Buyouts*
- *Selling Your Business to an ESOP*
- *The ESOP Reader*
- *Wealth and Income Consequences of Employee Ownership: A Comparative Study from Washington State*

The Ohio Employee Ownership Center

The Ohio Employee Ownership Center (OEOC) was founded in 1987 and is affiliated with Kent State University. The OEOC is a nonprofit organization dedicated to assisting business owners with transaction planning, most typically involving ESOPs. The OEOC will actually help business owners develop succession plans and assist in assembling a team of experienced professionals to meet goals.

The OEOC is one of the few places where you can find information on employee cooperatives (similar to ESOPs but with significantly fewer tax benefits).

Ohio Employee Ownership Center
113 McGivrey Hall
Kent State University
Kent, OH 44242
(330) 672-3028
www.oeockent.org

Other ESOP Resources

- Blasi, Joseph, Richard Freemen, and Douglas Kruse, eds. *Shared Capitalism at Work: Employee Ownership, Profit and Gain Sharing, and Broad-Based Stock Options.* Chicago: University of Chicago Press, 2010.

- Blasi, Joseph, and Douglass Kruse. *The New Owners: the Mass Emergence of Employee Ownership in Public Companies and What It Means to American Business.* New York: HarperCollins, 1991.

- Blonchek, Robert, and Martin O'Neill. *Act Like an Owner: Building an Ownership Culture.* Hoboken, NJ: Wiley, 1999.

- Gates, Jeff. *The Ownership Solution: Toward a Shared Capitalism for the 21st Century.* New York: Basic Books, 1999.

- Hitchner, James. *Financial Valuation: Applications and Models*, 3rd ed. Hoboken, NJ: Wiley, 2011. (See chapter 16 on ESOPs.)

- Howitt, Idelle, and Corey Rosen. *Employee Stock Ownership Answer Book*, 3rd ed. New York: Aspen Publishers, 2011.

- Pratt, Shannon, and Alina Niculita. *Valuing a Business: The Analysis and Appraisal of Closely Held Companies*, 5th ed. Ohio: McGraw Hill, 2008s (See chapters 32–33 on ESOPs.)

- Reilly, Robert, Robert and Schweihs. *The Handbook of Advanced Business Valuation.* Ohio: McGraw Hill, 1999. (See chapters 11–12 on ESOPs.)

- Stack, Jack, and Bo Burlingham. *The Great Game of Business: Unlocking the Power and Profitability of Open-Book Management.* New York: Currency/Doubleday, 1994.

- ———. *A Stake in the Outcome: Building a Culture of Ownership for the Long-Term Success of Your Business.* New York: Crown, 2003.